Past & Present

LAMPASAS COUNTY

OPPOSITE: Photographer Gladden Corbin took this photograph of the historic district in downtown Lampasas from a friend's airplane in the 1960s. Key Avenue (formerly Grand Avenue) crosses from left to right at the top of the image. The Lampasas County Courthouse is visible, surrounded by trees. The curved train track spur leads to the Santa Fe Train Depot, still in use at the time. (The Gladden Corbin family.)

PAST & PRESENT

LAMPASAS COUNTY

Lampasas County Museum Foundation, Inc.

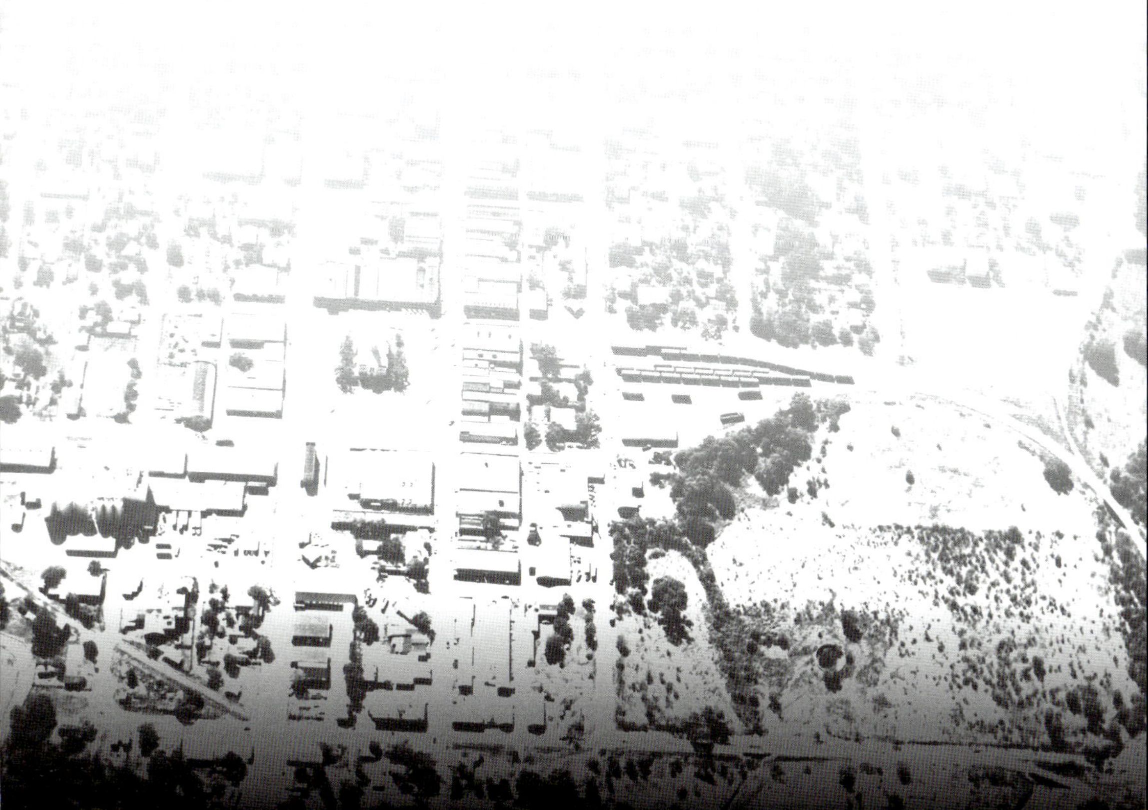

ISBN 978-1-24671-0893-5

Library of Congress Control Number: 2022940765

Published by Arcadia Publishing
Charleston, South Carolina

Printed in the United States of America

For all general information, please contact Arcadia Publishing:
Telephone 843-853-2070
Fax 843-853-0044
E-mail sales@arcadiapublishing.com
For customer service and orders:
Toll-Free 1-888-313-2665

Visit us on the Internet at www.arcadiapublishing.com

On the Front Cover: This c. 1921 view is from the northwest corner of Live Oak and Fourth Streets, looking north. The Hastings Art Studio was one of many photography studios in Lampasas. Later in the 1920s, the *Lampasas Record* occupied the building, and today, the *Lampasas Dispatch Record* is there. After a fire, the large mercantile Stokes Brothers moved to 406 South Live Oak Street, which now houses the Trading Post (E.J.'s Antiques Emporium). (Past, collection of the Lampasas County Museum; present, DP.)

On the Back Cover: The Star Hotel was built in the 1850s at 404 East Second Street by John and Harriet Gracy. A two-story wing was added to the west end in the 1870s along with an attic bunkhouse. In 1926, the hotel was purchased by J.R. Key, who renamed it the Keystone Hotel. Key updated the hotel in 1929, adding indoor plumbing, and again in 1931, adding seven additional bedrooms. (Collection of the Lampasas County Museum.)

CONTENTS

Acknowledgments

The Lampasas County Museum Foundation, Inc., thanks Jane McMillin for writing the introduction to this book and for reviewing the captions. We are grateful to Donnie Price for traveling throughout the county to photograph historic sites as they appear today and to the Lampasas County Historical Commission (LCHC) for sharing with us their historical photographs. We appreciate the Lampasas County Museum Board of Directors for their support of this project. A special thank you to the photographers who came before us, named and anonymous, for recording Lampasas County history. And, finally, a note of thanks to the people of Lampasas County, without whose civic pride this book would not have been possible.

All historical photographs, unless otherwise indicated, are in the collection of the Lampasas County Museum. All contemporary photographs were taken by John Fingerhut (JF), Amy McDaniel (AM), and Donnie Price (DP).

Introduction

This book chronicles change—and sometimes the lack of it—through the juxtaposition of photographs of the past with their contemporary counterparts. Some buildings and historic sites today look nearly identical to the way they appeared in the past, a testament to the resurgence of interest in preserving county history. Others are starkly different: empty lots take the place of limestone buildings; parking lots claim properties that were once local businesses. Empty lots may mean progress, however, as new businesses come to the county and create new economic opportunities for natives and newcomers alike.

The coming of the Gulf, Colorado & Santa Fe Railway had a profound effect in shaping Lampasas County. Post–Civil War railroad construction opened the Texas interior and established commercial arteries as never before. Towns and cities along the rail lines thrived; many if not most of those bypassed died. The legendary mineral springs in and around Lampasas enticed Houston and Galveston railroad investors to remake the small frontier town into a fashionable spa that would rival high-end resorts in the Northeast. This development, including construction of the grand Park Hotel, brought an end to Lampasas's frontier period. Its Wild West character was overlaid with Gilded Age opulence and sophistication that was preserved and perpetuated by prosperous Lampasas families for several generations. Some of their homes survived and have been restored along Third Street in Lampasas, once known as "Silk Stocking Row." Talented entrepreneurs flocked to the town and made it—especially when it was the railroad terminus—a thriving center of commerce and culture whose influence endured for decades, despite downturns in the economy.

The Gulf, Colorado & Santa Fe Railway was also directly responsible for the establishment of the county's other incorporated cities: Lometa and Kempner.

Lometa, the second incorporated city in the county, was established by the railroad in 1885, when it built farther west from Lampasas. The railroad bypassed the earlier established town of Senterfitt. Hoping to capitalize on opportunities afforded by proximity to the rail line, the citizens of Senterfitt moved to the new town of Lometa—buildings and all!

In 1909, when the railroad began building a 100-mile spur to Eden and into the heart of sheep-and goat-raising country, Lometa experienced a boom of its own. The burgeoning wool and mohair industry grew even bigger, as tons of wool and mohair were shipped in and out of Lometa and Lampasas by train. This remained a viable and profitable industry until the 1960s and 1970s, when the use of synthetic fabrics eclipsed it. Thus, Lampasas County lost a major industry, both in terms of the number of wool and mohair producers and in the concentration of prominent Lampasas County buyers. They sold directly to textile mills in the eastern United States and England. As of 2022, Lometa's population stood at 888, and local small businesses include real estate, banking, feed stores, and pipe fabrication.

Near the confluence of Sulphur Creek and the Lampasas River, the Gulf, Colorado & Santa Fe Railway established the town of Kempner, naming it for Harris Kempner, a wealthy Galveston merchant, railroad investor, and philanthropist. The community thrived, with its own school, bank, and businesses, but later fell on hard times. When Fort Hood became a permanent military installation in 1950, Kempner civilians found jobs and greater economic stability. During the 1970s, this part of the county experienced a significant population increase as military families and retirees moved to the town, perhaps for a quieter, more rural way of life. In 1997, Kempner became Lampasas County's third incorporated city. In 2022, the population stood at 1,212.

Small communities throughout Lampasas County, such as Adamsville and Nix, have endured since the county's early days, perhaps because of the proximity of the city of Lampasas, which served as a commercial hub and the seat of county government. In turn, agriculture, for most of the county's history, provided an underpinning for the area economy. Frequent boom-bust cycles during the late 19th and early 20th centuries culminated in the Great Depression of the 1930s, exacting a toll on Lampasas County.

Since rural electrification did not come to parts of Lampasas County until the 1940s, the lifestyle of many farm and ranch families remained much the same as that of their pioneering ancestors. With post–World War II prosperity and the presence of Fort Hood, however, Lampasas County entered a new era of greater affluence and more sustained growth, which continues to this day.

Through the years, Lampasas has lost many landmarks to fire, flood, modernization, and outright demolition. But the influx of new people has focused renewed interest on local history and the preservation of the county's remaining historic structures. Many of these are being repurposed to house such accoutrements of contemporary suburban culture as specialty shops, wine bars, coffee houses, and brew pubs, borne of the 21st century's digital age and lifestyle.

This book emphasizes the everyday life of Lampasas County citizens as each generation met its challenge in rearing the next and, at the same time, responded to whatever history and Mother Nature threw its way.

CHAPTER 1

Places to Live

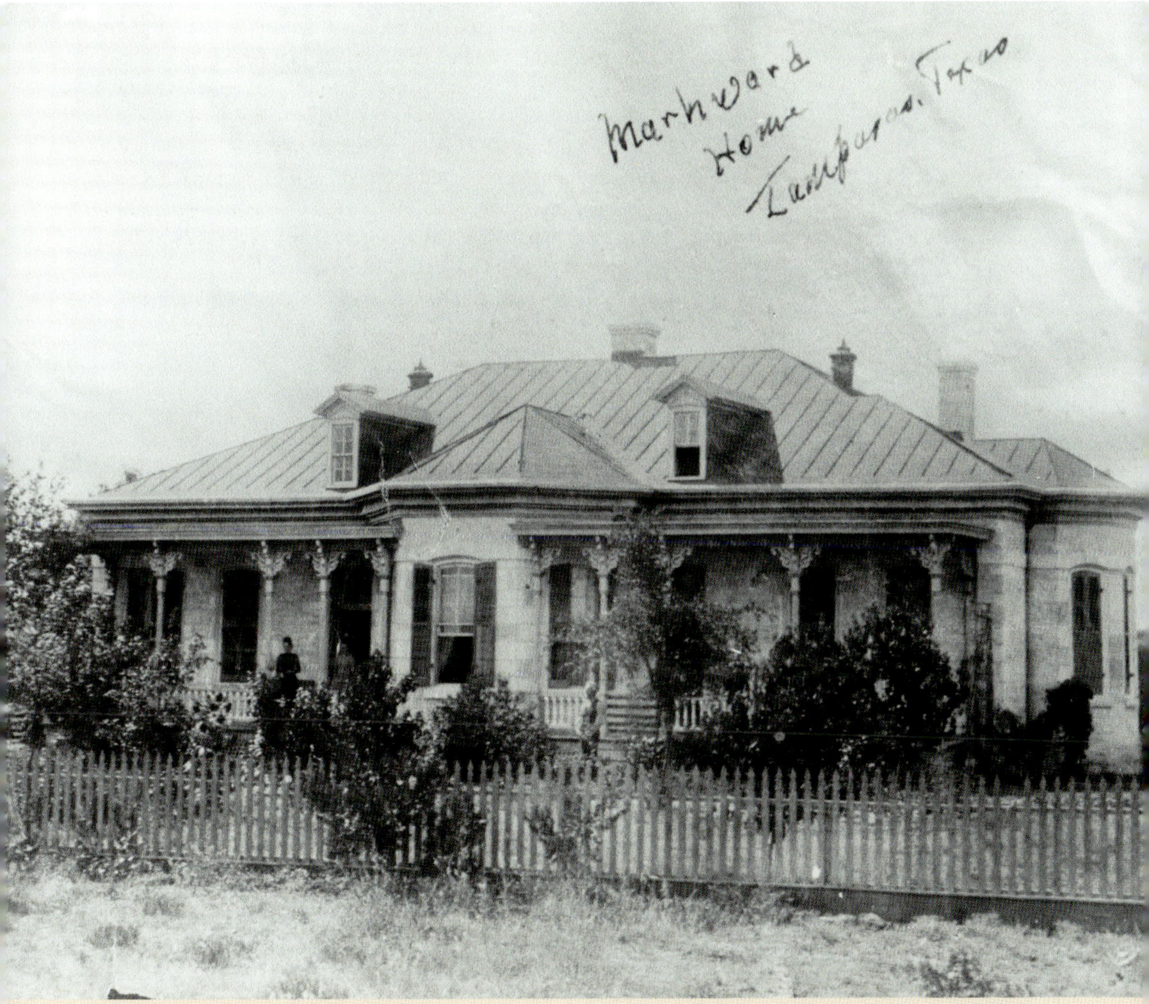

Now known as the Adelphia, an event venue, the Markward home was built in the 1880s by John Markward for his first wife, Adelphia Florence White. They lived in a two-room limestone building while waiting for builder Theo Bauerfeind to complete the larger home. Later, the smaller quarters served as housing for their cook and various guests.

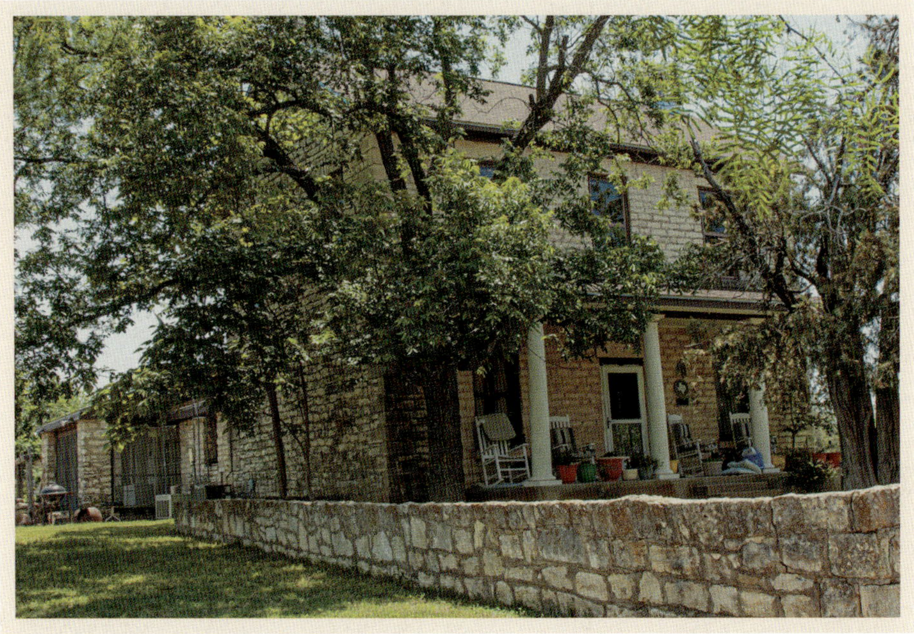

Below, Mary Adkins Walker, a daughter of Dr. Jasper N. Adkins, stands in front of the Adkins House at 1301 Taylor Street on the south side of Sulphur Creek in Lampasas. The original was a wood-frame house, but enough patients paid the doctor in native stone that he soon had enough to build the two-story home seen in this photograph. Completed in 1868, it is thought to be the fourth-oldest house in Lampasas. It has been restored and is privately owned. (Present, DP.)

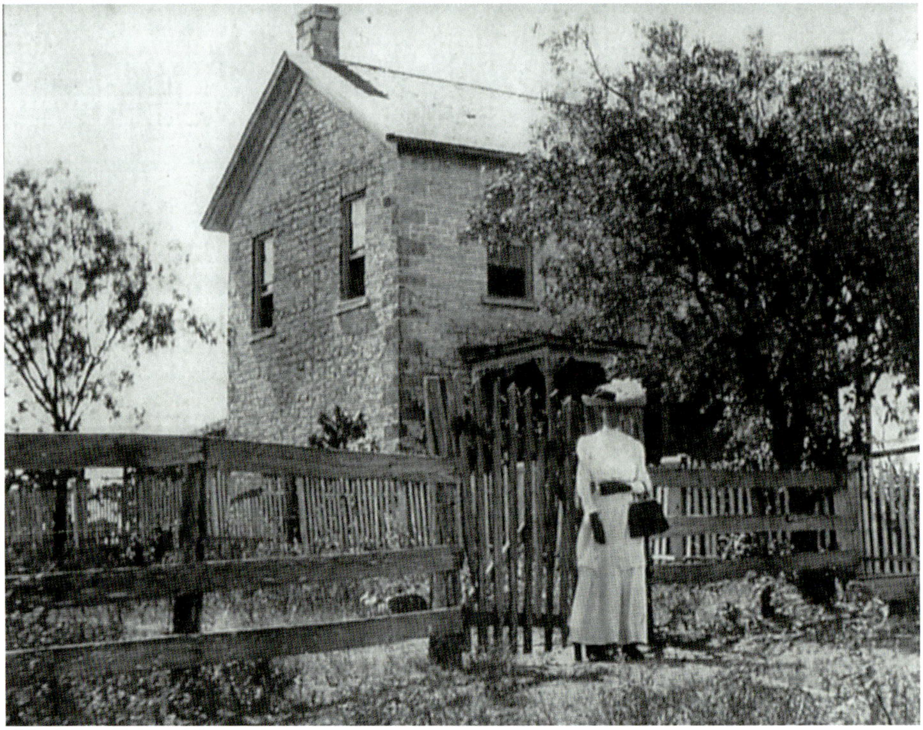

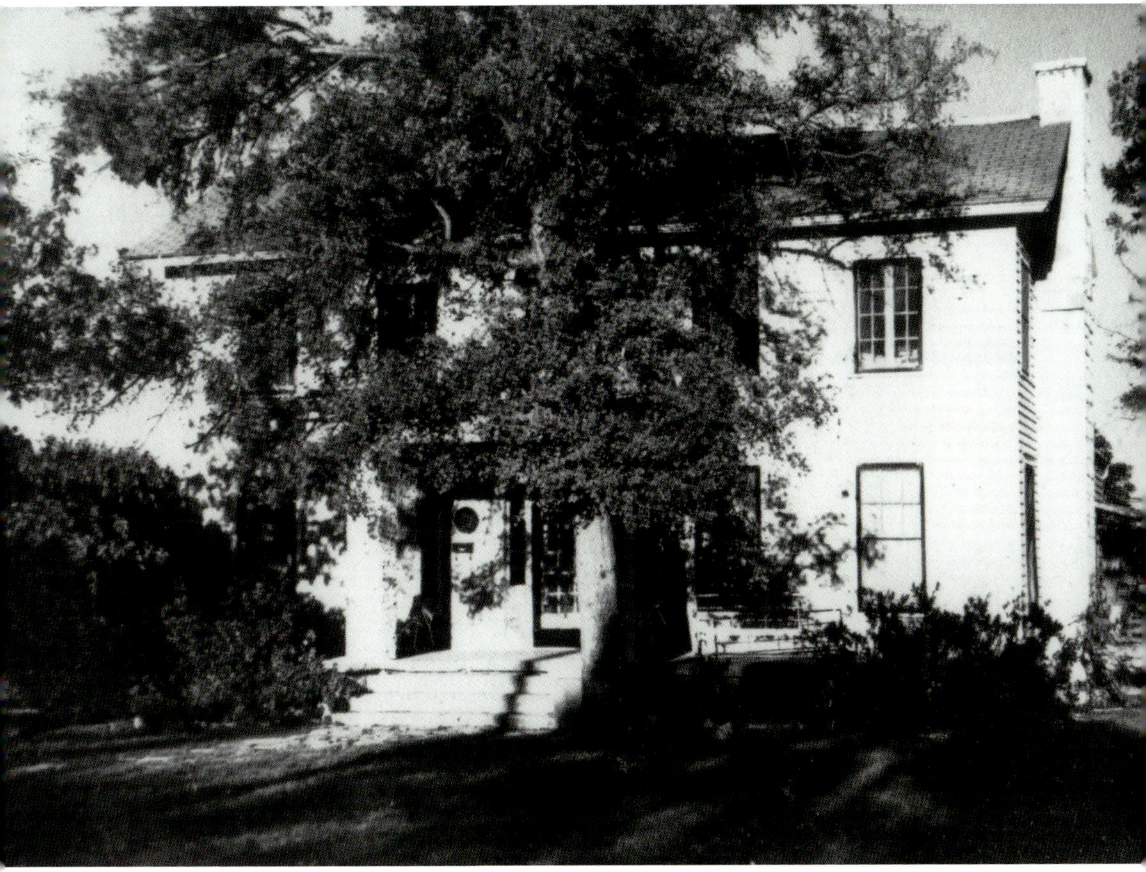

The oldest portion of this two-story home was built in 1872 at 803 South Live Oak Street by the Alexander Jesse Northington family. The family lore is that their horses were stolen by Indians one night while they were in the house. This structure was the only wood-frame house left standing after the flood in 1873. Although it received a historical marker in 1964, the house was torn down in the early 1990s and replaced with a duplex in the early 21st century. (Present, AM.)

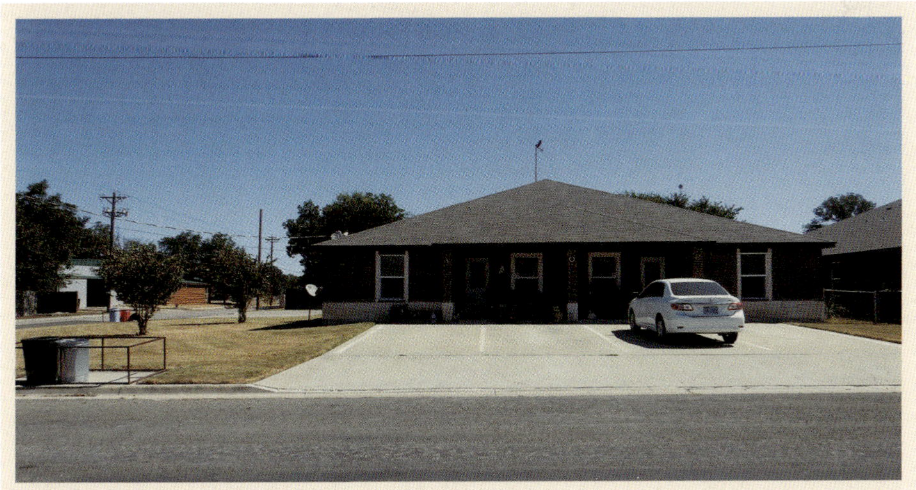

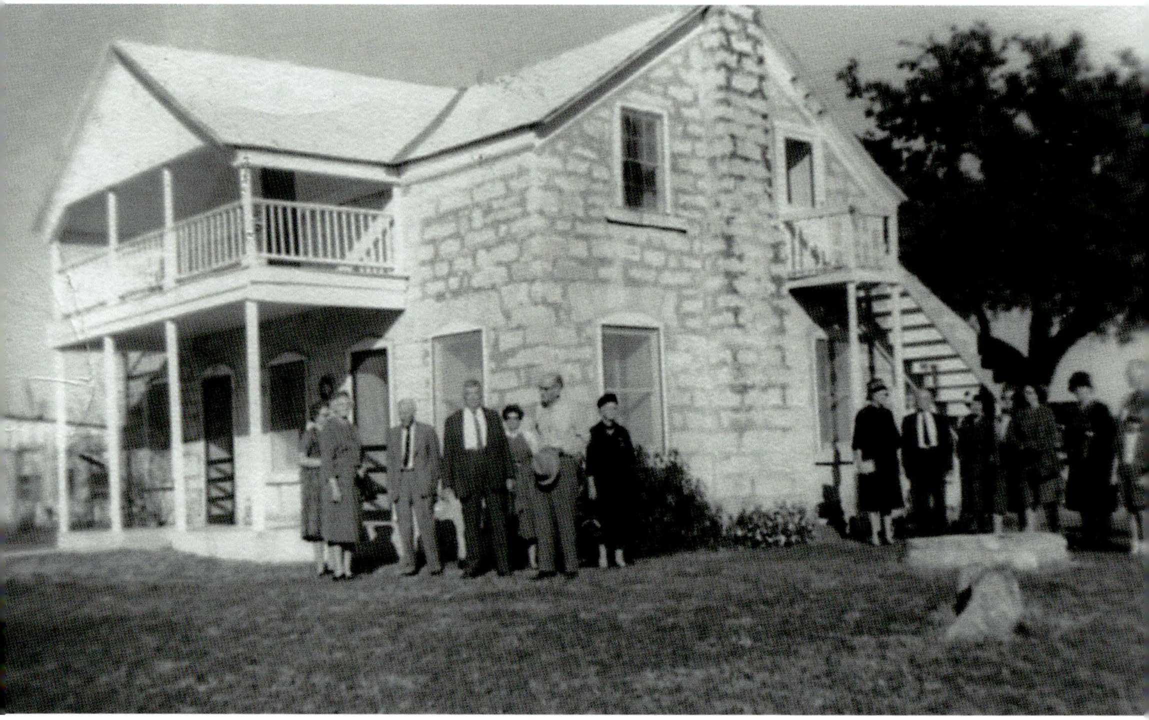

John Patterson was the first to cultivate land in Lampasas County, doing so in the 1850s, not long after the county was established. He completed this two-story home of native stone in Adamsville in 1880 on what is now the east side of Highway 281. The upstairs porch was initially a bedroom, and the kitchen was outside of the home when it was built. The house is a recorded Texas historic landmark and is privately owned. (Present, AM.)

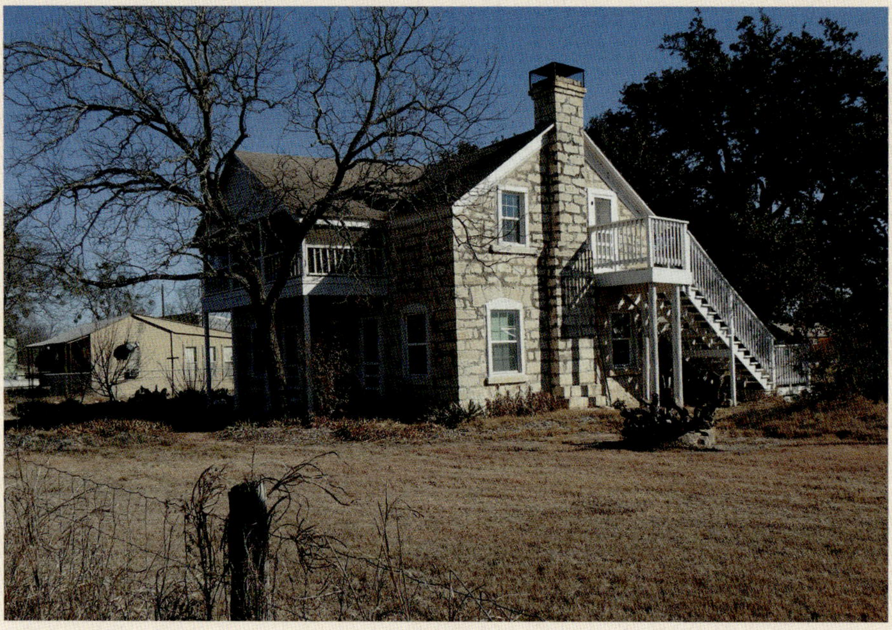

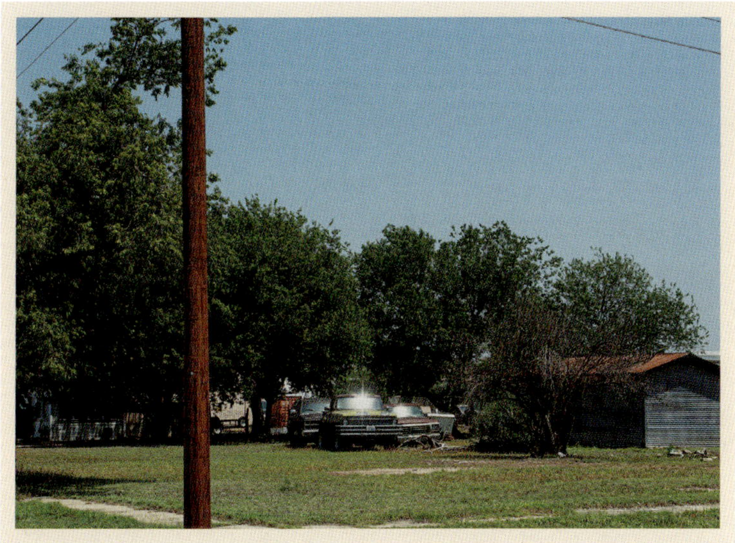

This empty lot at Live Oak and Sixth Streets is where Sam Dickens III, a house painter and decorator, built this c. 1890 home as a wedding present for his wife, Anna Carter. They had two children, Sam Dickens IV and Mary, who was a bookkeeper at Fox and Mills Hardware and later at Lampasas Furniture. She married John Willard Lane, and the house is known as the Mary Lane House. The home was moved to 1311 FM 580 East in the mid-2010s. (Present, DP.)

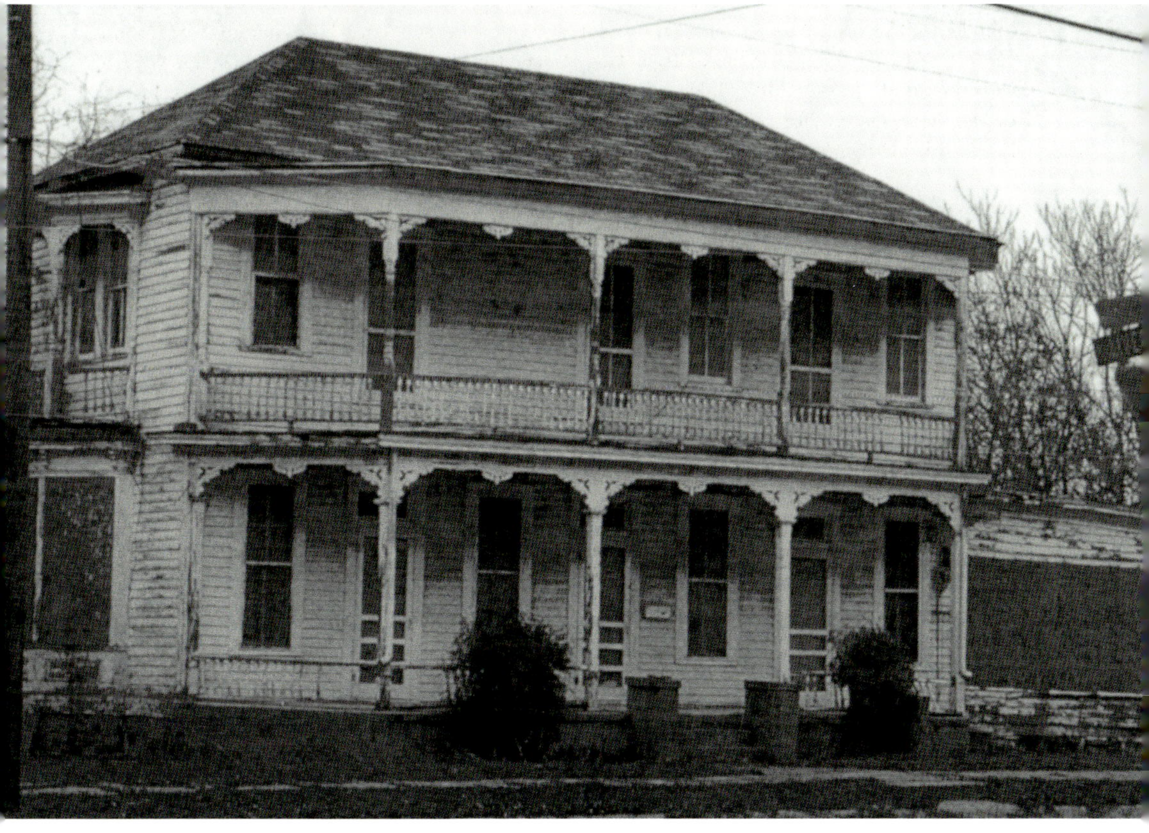

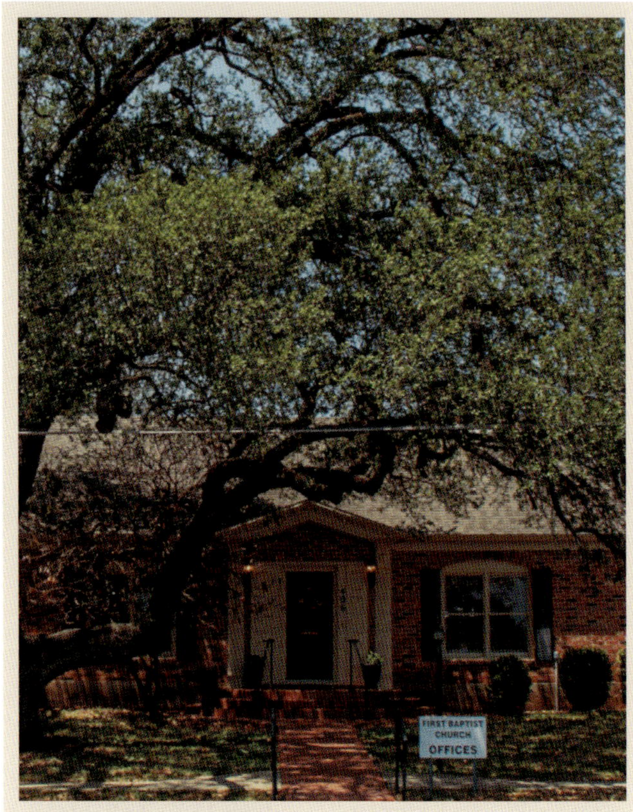

Once located at 406 Walnut Street, the Queen Anne–style W.B. Abney House (below) was built by Judge William Berry Abney in 1895. It was sold in the 1930s after Abney's death and was later torn down to make way for a more modern home. For years, the turret from the 1895 Abney house sat in the backyard. Today, the offices of the First Baptist Church are on the site. (Past, Harold Harton; present, DP.)

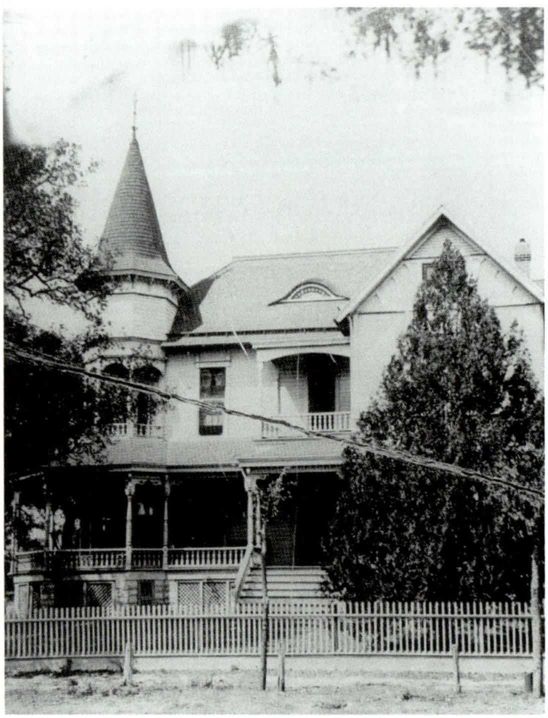

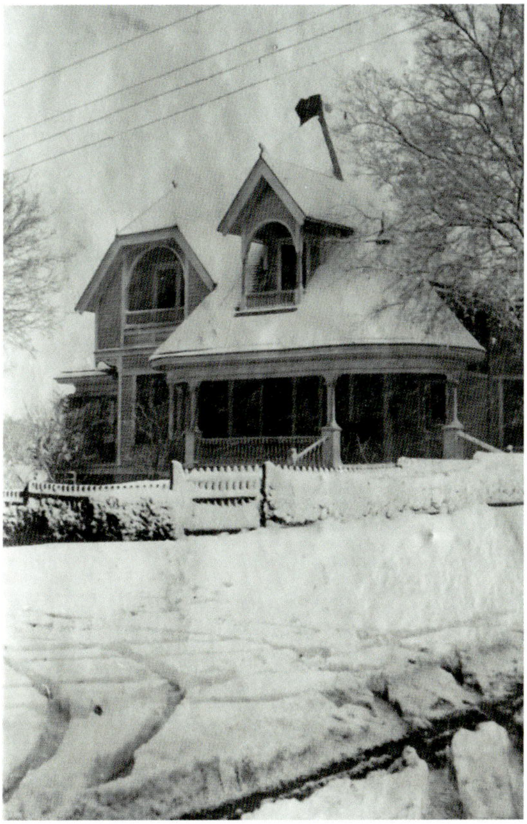

The G.H. Ribble House, shown here covered with snow, was built in 1899 by George Ribble for him and his daughter, Virginia, a well-known local photographer. After George's death in 1902, Virginia married John Hall, and the couple occupied the home. The house features pocket doors, longleaf pine floors, and 10-foot ceilings. The 11-room residence, located at 502 South Broad Street, is being restored in 2022. (Present, AM.)

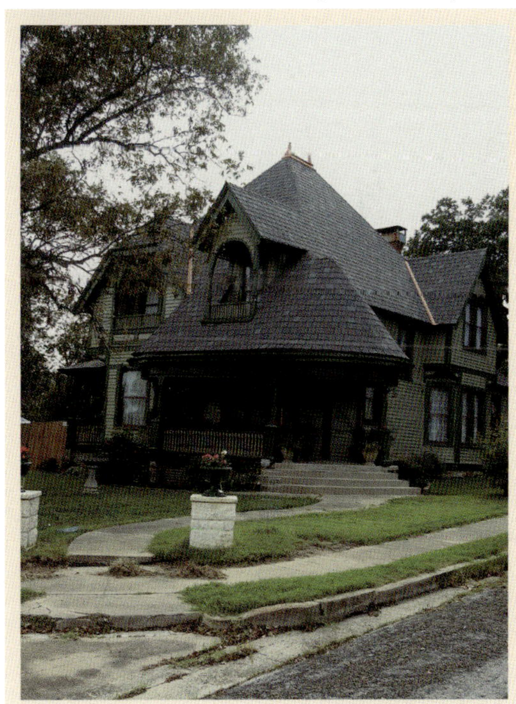

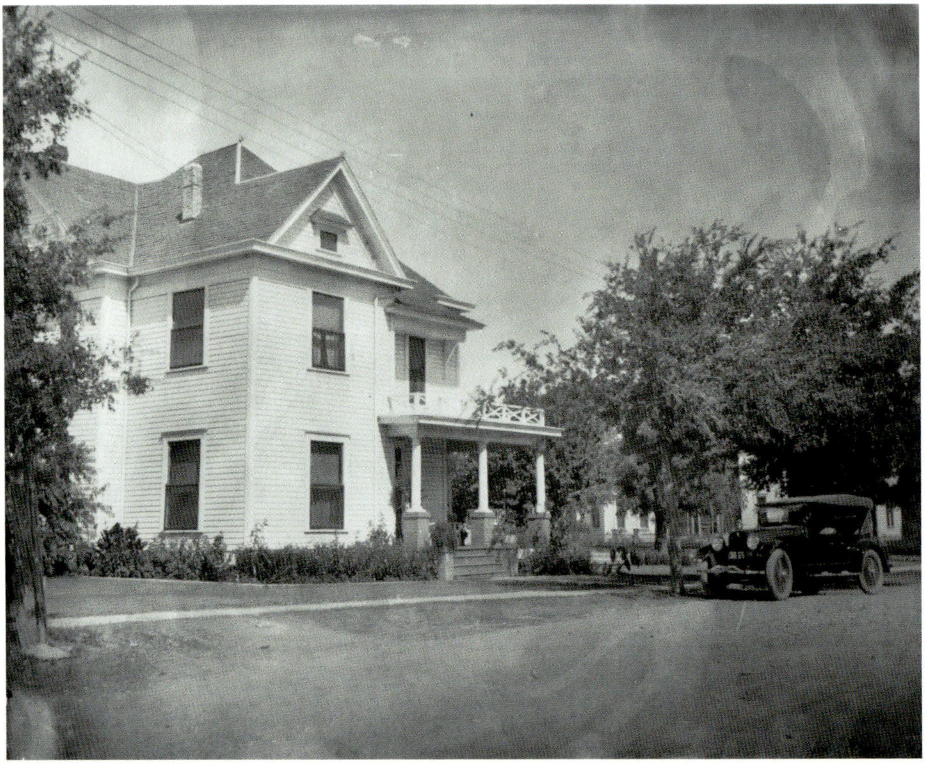

The historic Haby House was built at 108 North Chestnut Street by Emil and Kuhne Wilhelm Haby. Haby arrived in Lampasas in 1906 and operated an ice factory and a soda pop bottling company. He later bought a local electric power plant. Today, the two-story home belongs to the Habys' granddaughter-in-law. Little about the exterior of the house has changed, with the exception of the addition of dark trim around the windows, door, and porch and the significant growth of vegetation. (Present, DP.)

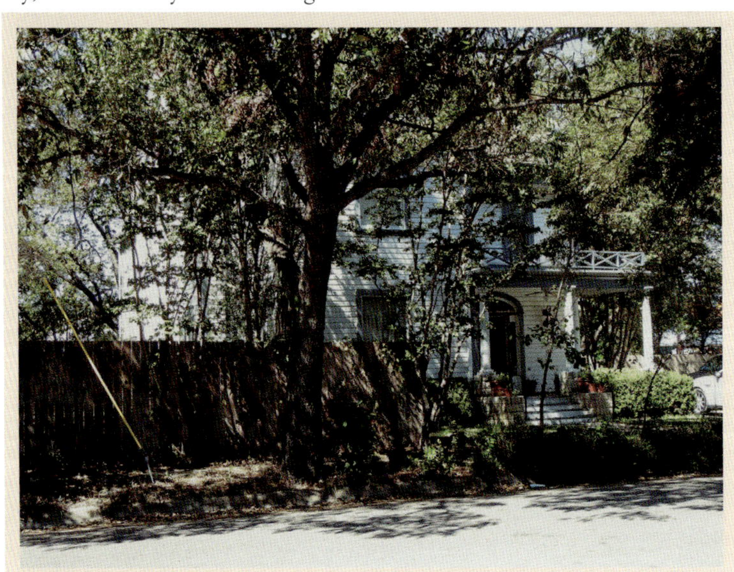

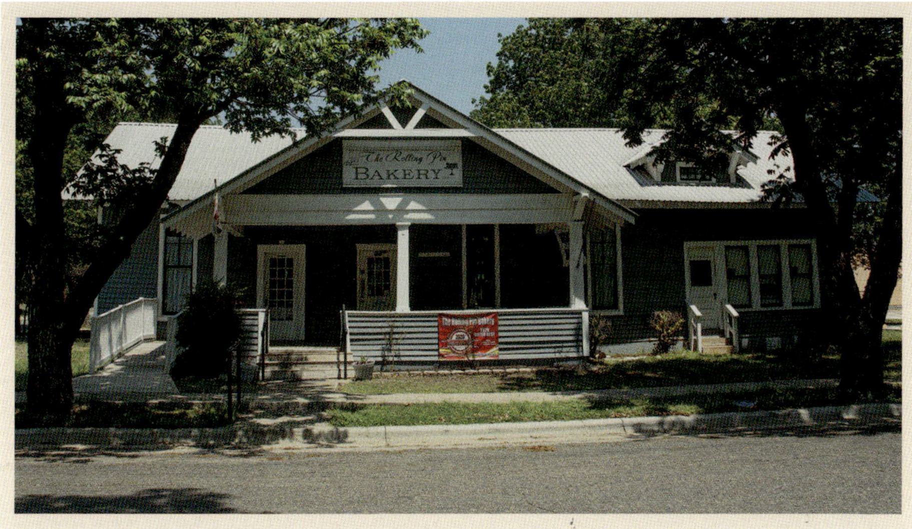

The home of Elvis and Lula Wolf at 107 West Fifth Street was built in the Craftsman bungalow style, featuring exposed roof rafters, simplified decorative beams under the gable, and square columns. Elvis Wolf served as Lampasas County's sheriff and tax collector from 1896 to 1900. Descendants remember that Lula Wolf had a goldfish pond at the house. Today, the building looks much as it did when the Wolfs occupied it. It is now home to the Rolling Pin Bakery. (Past, collection of Anna Wolf Crawford; present, DP.)

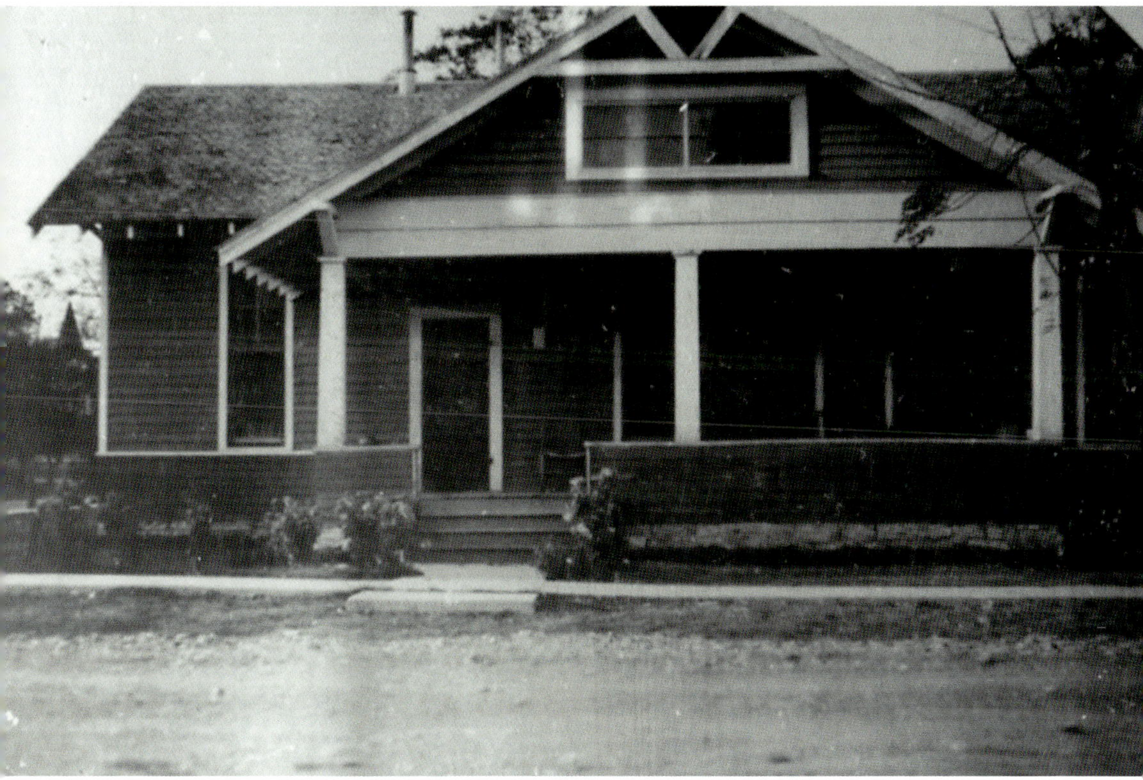

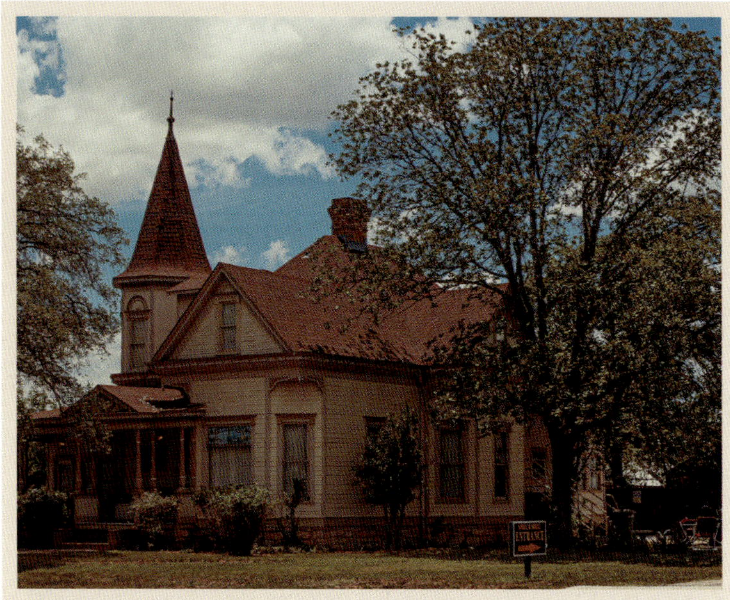

Hosea Bailey built this gracious home (below) at 606 South Grand (now Key) Avenue for his wife, Ellen May, in the early 1900s. In the 1930s, W.C. "Shorty" Gillen purchased the house for his wife, Kate Flippin. The property remained in the Gillen family until Eddie Shell bought it, opening a branch of Shell and Shell Law Offices there in 2018. It is still known as the Gillen House. (Past, Gladden Corbin; present, DP.)

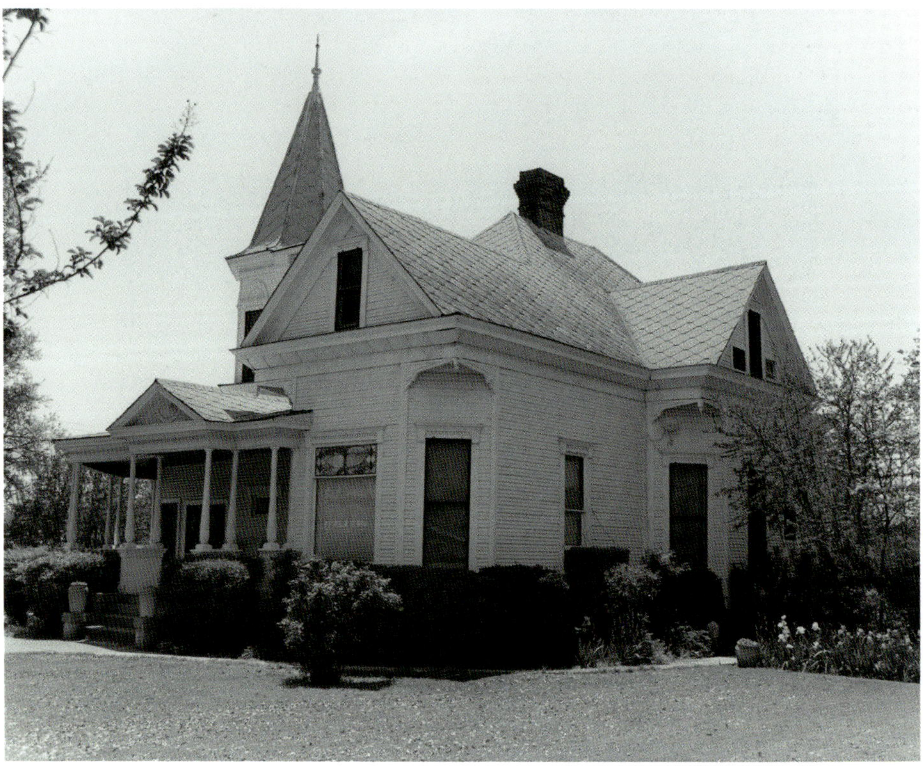

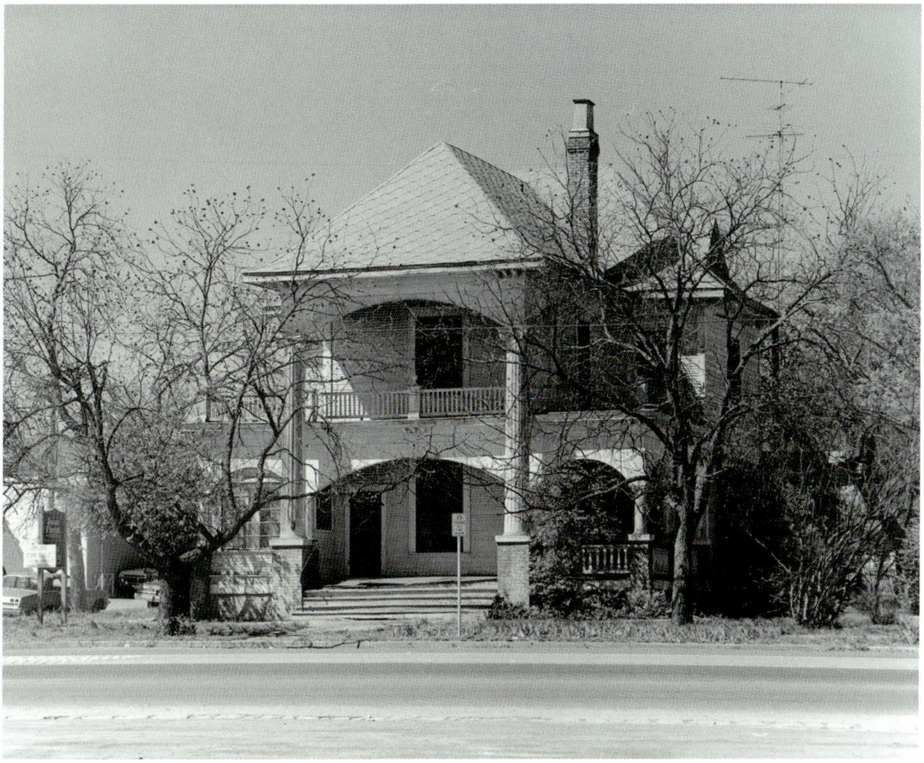

In 1925, a lumber company built this home at 210 South Key Avenue, then Grand Avenue. After the death in 1933 of Harry Easters Sr., his widow, Mary Louise Rainwater Easters, purchased the home and rented out rooms. Later, the home was sold and moved to Spicewood. Today, Hodges & Sargent Pharmacy stands at this location. Pharmacists Daniel Hodges and Jim Sargent built it in 1988. A glimpse of the Cauthen House is visible above the pharmacy sign. (Present, DP.)

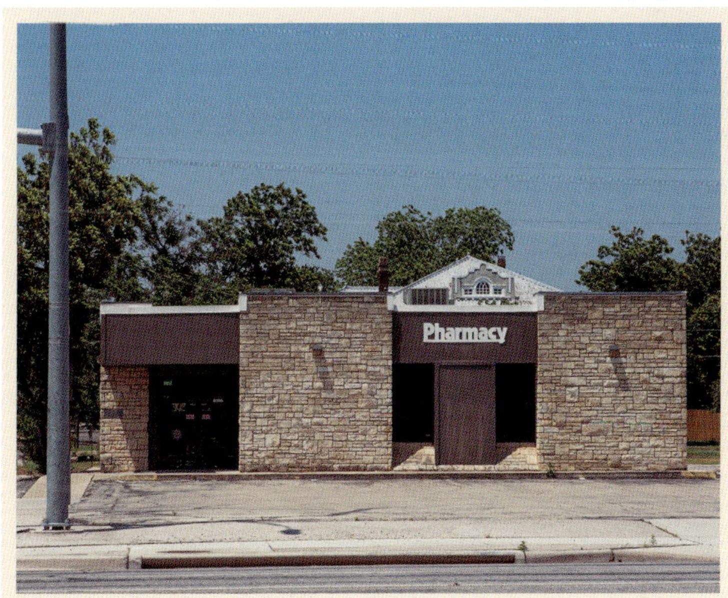

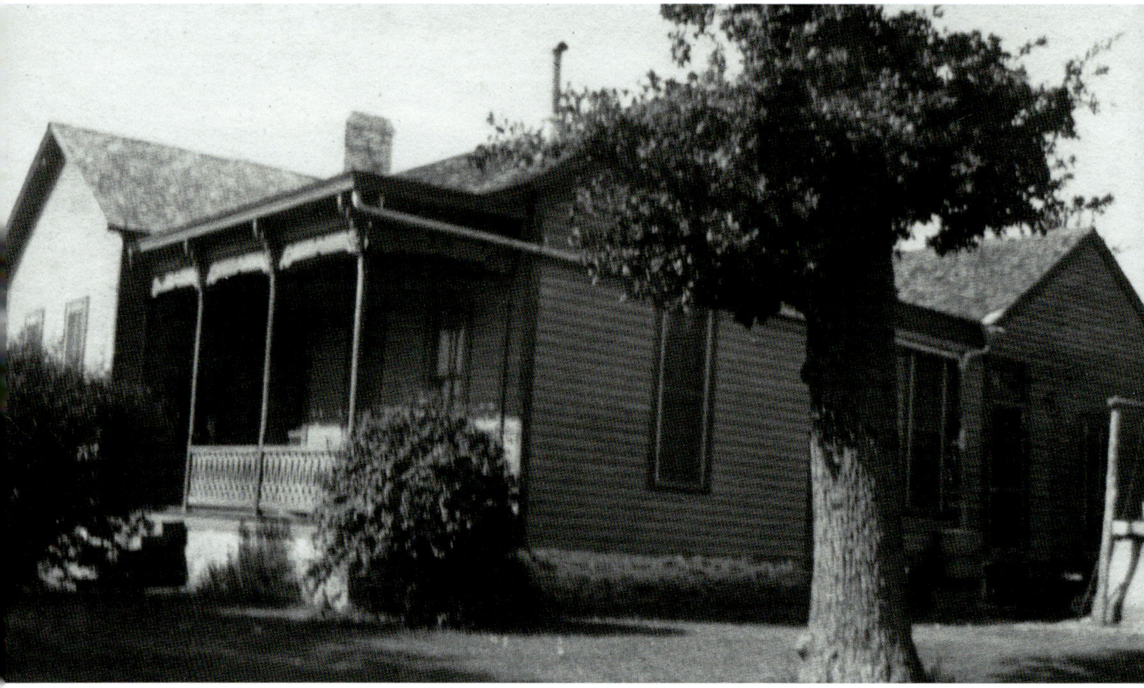

Bessie Eula Page was a teacher and principal for 42 years in the Lampasas school district. She was one of two daughters born to Erencis Marion Noyes and James William Page. The Noyes and Page families were benefactors of the Lampasas County Museum. Bessie Page's 1976 death certificate lists this house at 402 North Key Avenue, where Burger King is today, as her residence. (Present, DP.)

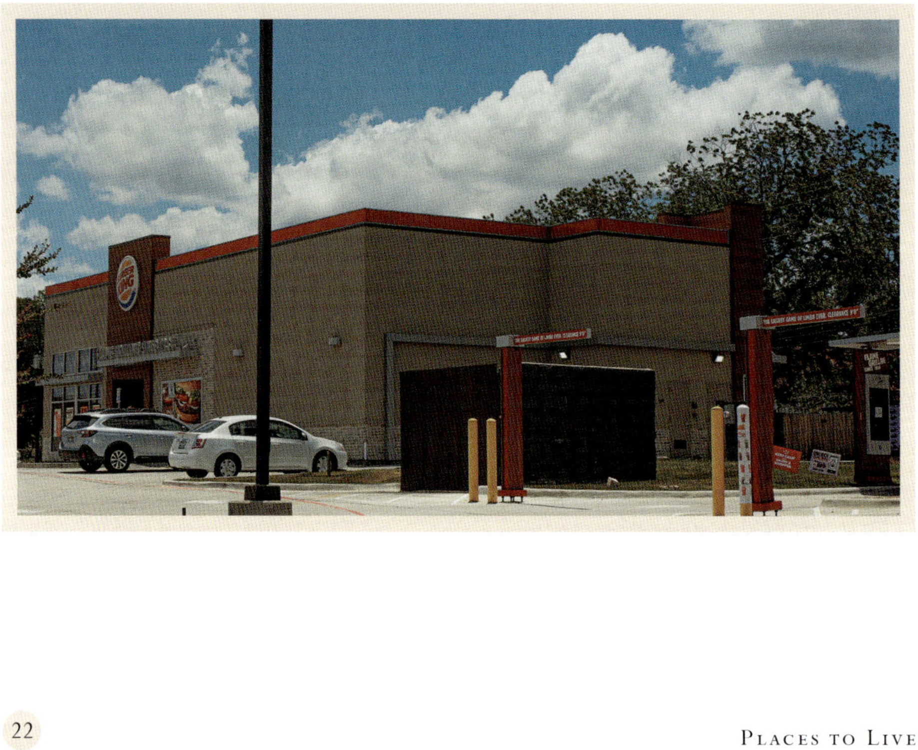

CHAPTER 2

PLACES TO EAT

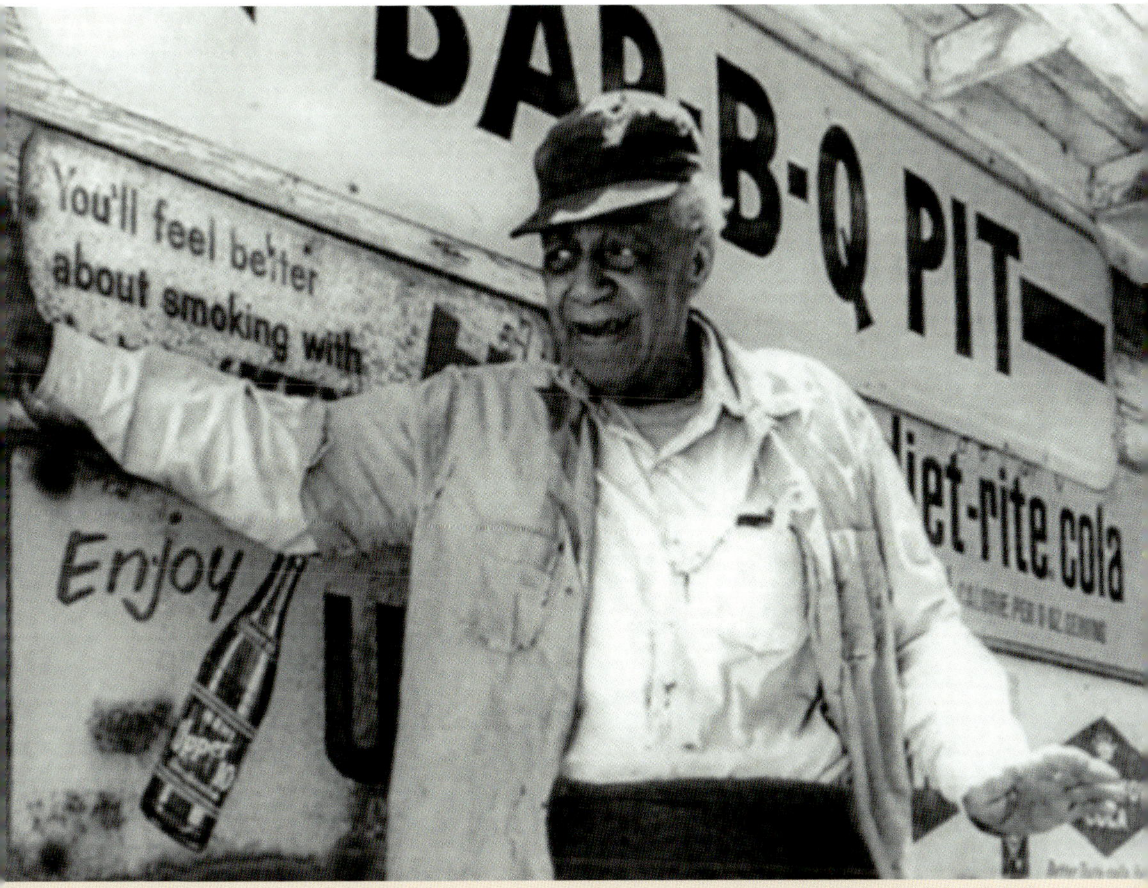

Herbert Pickett Sr., pictured here, was the proprietor of Pickett's Barbecue Pit, once found at 902 East Third Street. Pickett's famous barbecue sauce recipe is in the Lampasas County Museum's cookbook, *Close to Home: Local Recipes, Old and New* (2018).

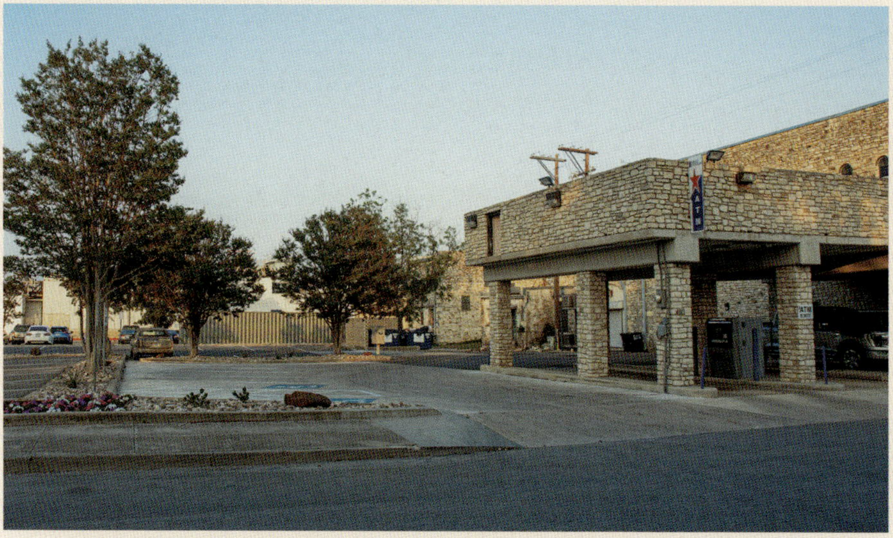

The Bluebonnet Café and Hotel (below) stood on Live Oak Street between Second and Third Streets in Lampasas, where the First Texas Bank parking lot is today. W.S. (Walter Sylvester) Hetherly and his wife, Vanja Wiley Hetherly, purchased the lot in 1916. There they built the hotel and café, which featured a popular chili. After W.S.'s death, his heirs sold the property to the First National Bank, which became the First Texas Bank in 1992. (Present, DP.)

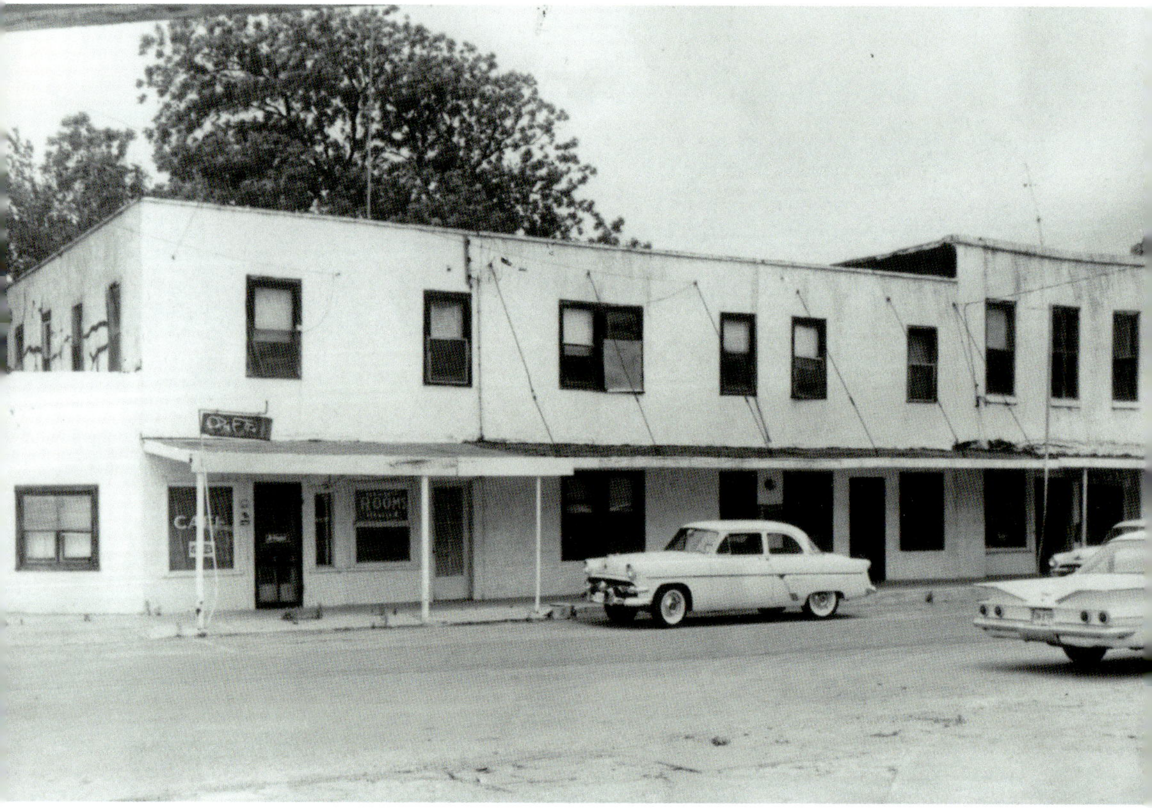

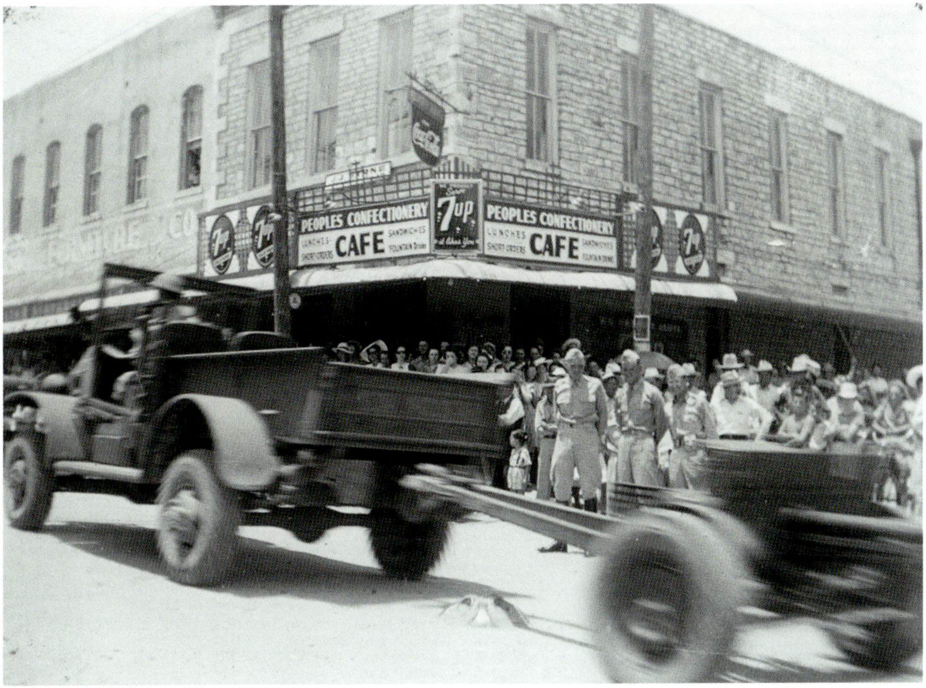

The Peoples Confectionery, shown here in the early 1940s, was on the northwest corner of Live Oak and Third Streets. In 1936, the proprietor announced he would serve "about ten varieties of sandwiches, hamburgers, and fried chicken." The Lampasas Furniture Store, owned and operated by the Briggs family, was next door. Today, the building is home to My Girls Café, a clothing and gift shop, a wine bar, and several antiques dealers. (Present, DP.)

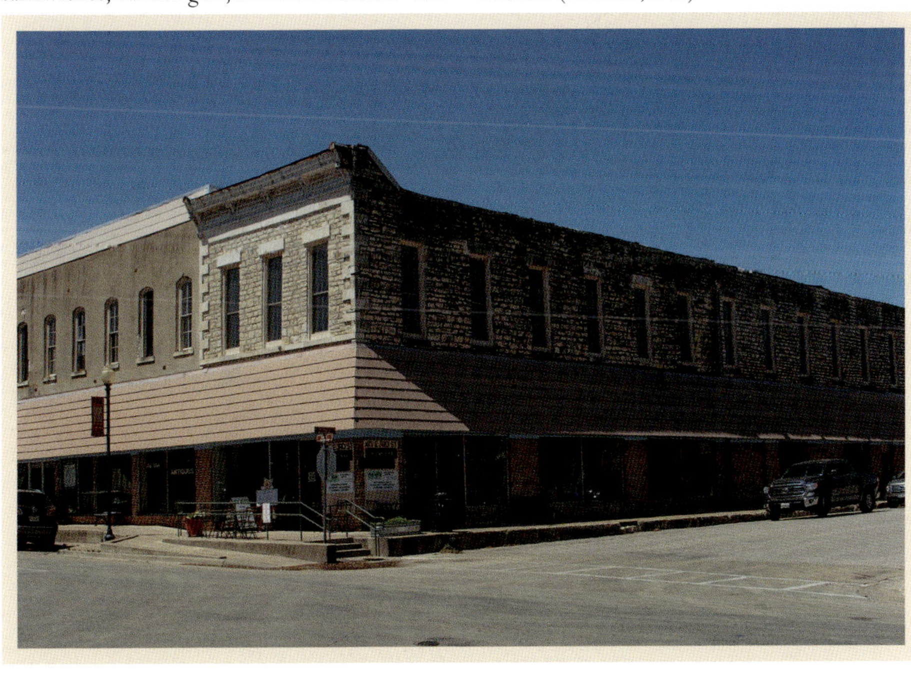

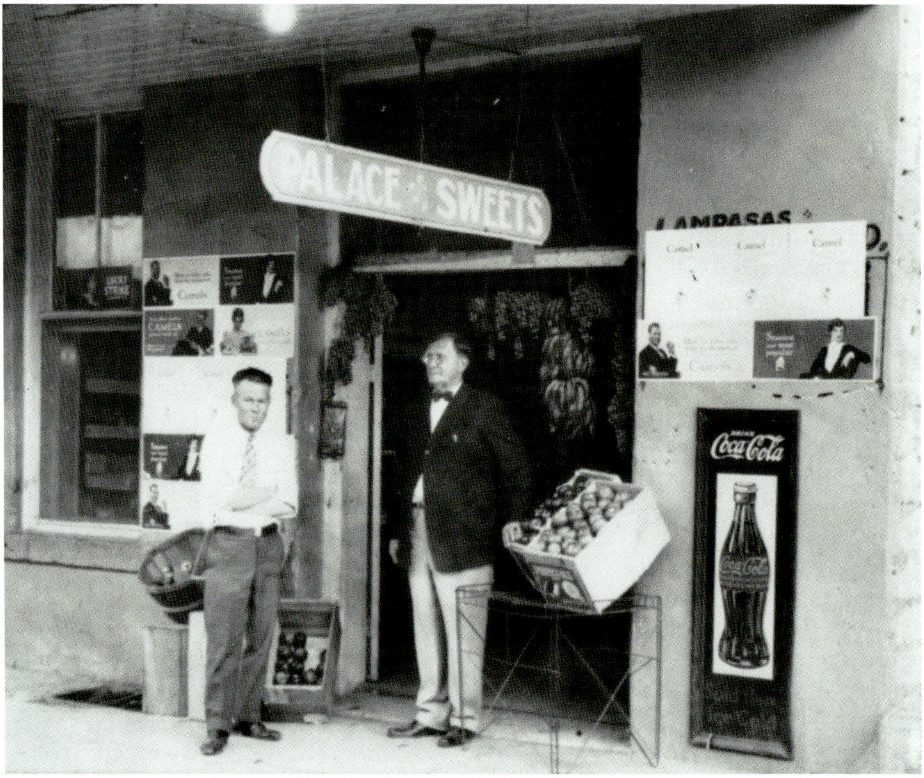

A fire in 1931 destroyed the Palace of Sweets along with other businesses on the Third Street block. Joseph Henry Hicks owned the confectionery since the late 1920s, carrying candies and fruits as well as cigarettes and Coca-Cola. Although Hicks had $1,500 worth of insurance, he did not reopen. Later that year, Laura Elder, the wife of Kellis Elder, opened Laura's Beauty Shop in that location. Today, Merk and Tilleys (a wordplay on "mercantile") offers clothing and gifts for sale. (Past, collection of LCHC; present, DP.)

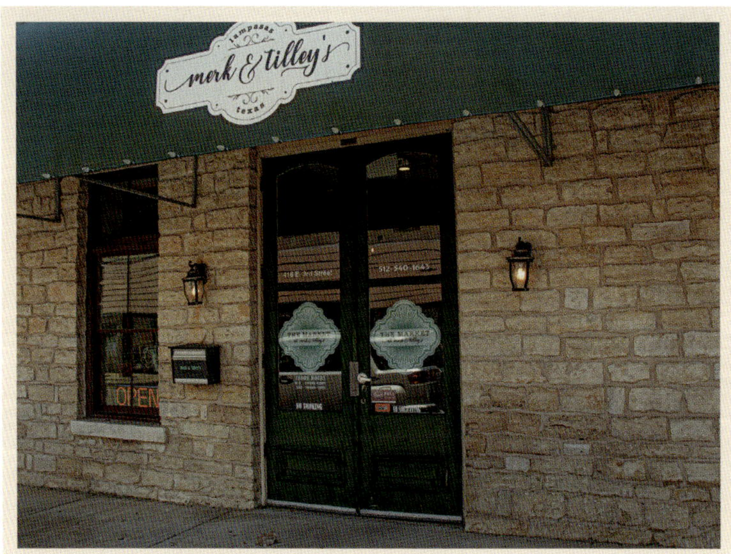

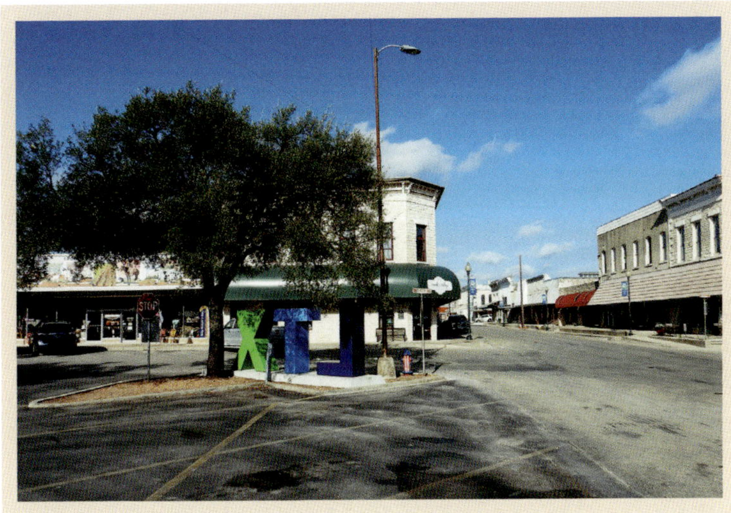

Established in the early 20th century, the Lampasas Candy Kitchen (below) at 404 South Live Oak Street was a favorite spot to enjoy ice cream, candies, and other treats. Fireworks were also sold there, and it was rumored that alcohol could be purchased from the back door during Prohibition. Frank Cox owned it from 1911 to 1967. Mackey's Drugstore, like many others, had a soda fountain serving Coca-Cola. Today, these two storefronts are incorporated into Merk and Tilley's. In the 1870s, this was the site of two saloon gunfights. (Present, JF.)

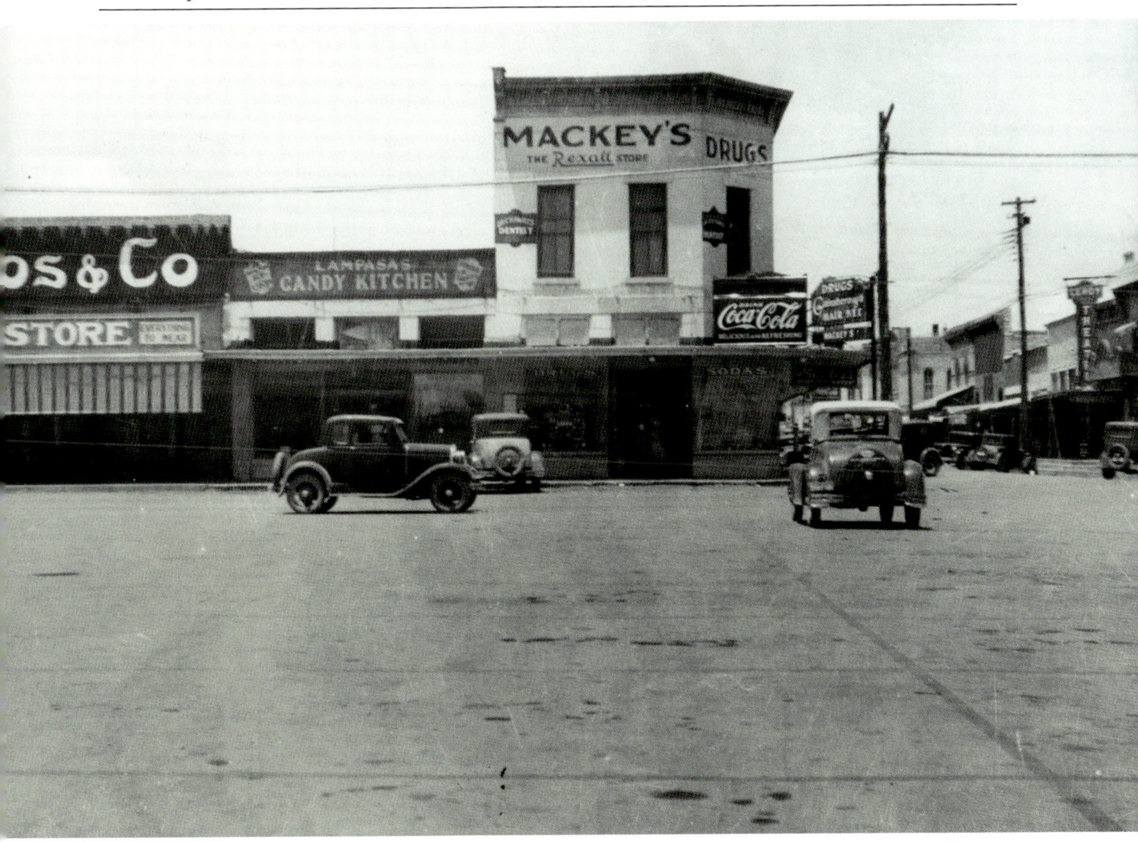

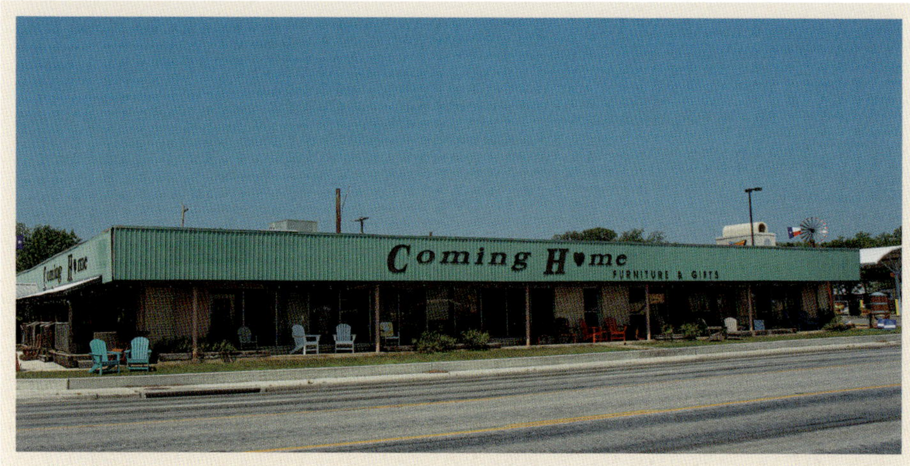

John Bowden opened Bowden's Drive-In Restaurant (below) at 710 South Key Avenue in 1965. The cow that sat atop the restaurant is now on the roof of M&M Butcher Block on Highway 580 East. In 1973, Bowden closed the restaurant and built the Family Furniture Store on the same site. Now called Coming Home Furniture and Gifts, the store is celebrating its 50th anniversary in November 2023. It is run by John's son, Eddie Bowden. (Past, collection of Eddie Bowden; present, DP.)

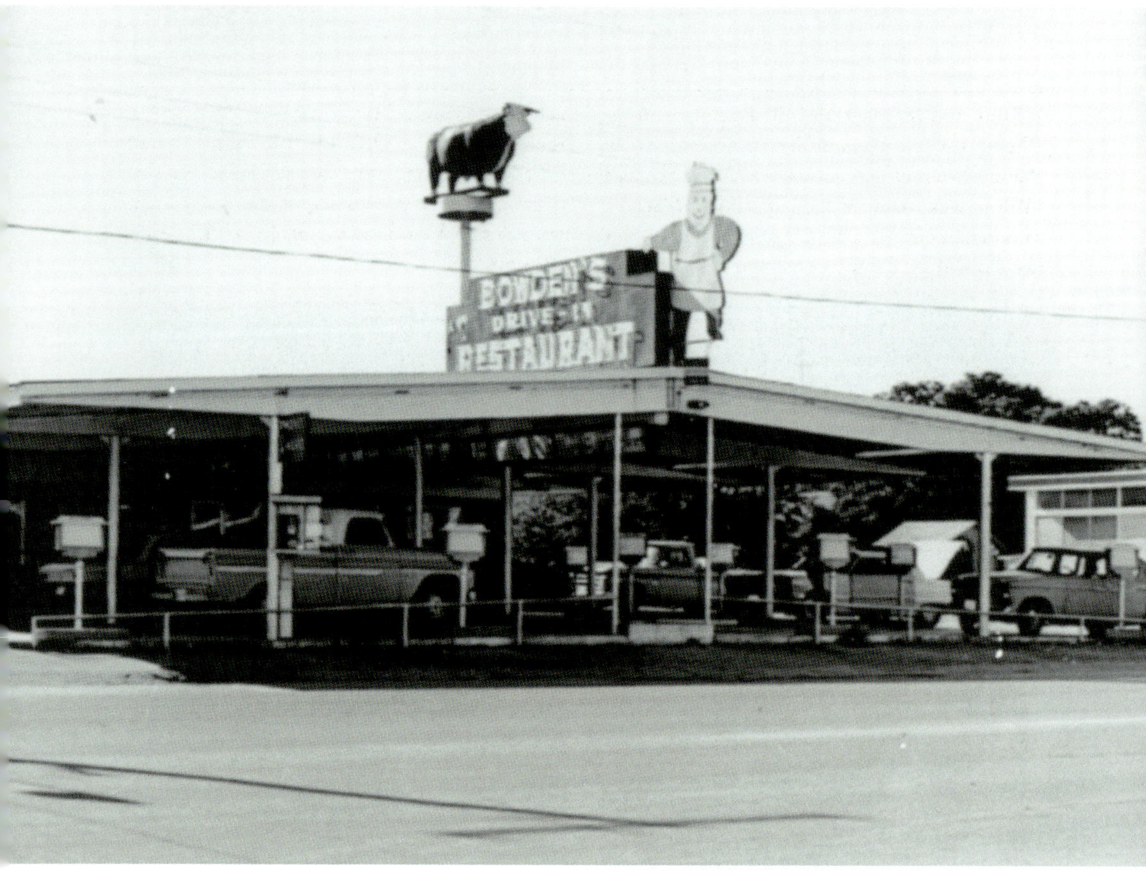

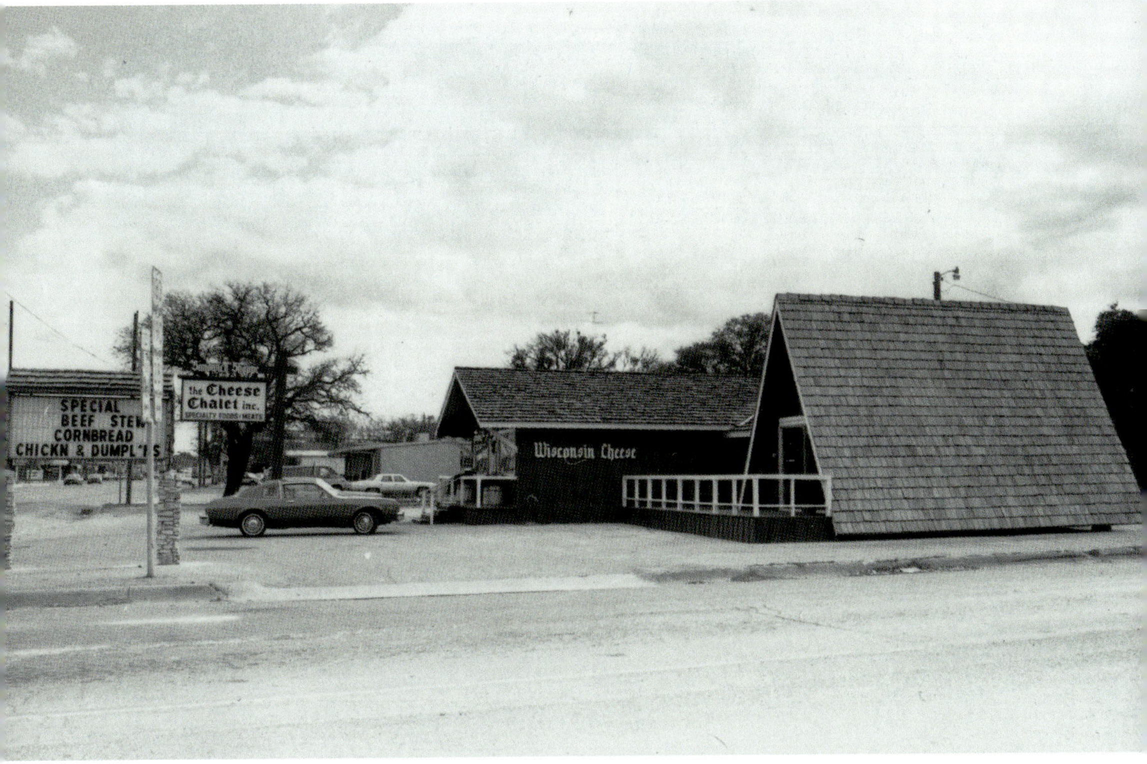

Walter and Mary Dumas Tramp started the Cheese Chalet, pictured here in the 1970s on the southwest corner of North and Key Avenues. Walter was from Wisconsin and so featured Wisconsin cheese. The Cheese Chalet offered homemade meals in its café and sold a variety of treats as well. Strawberry Millionaire Pie was a favorite. In 1987, the café moved to 523 East Third Street on the square. Today, the Key Avenue site advertises one of the many local wineries that have sprung up in recent years. (Present, DP.)

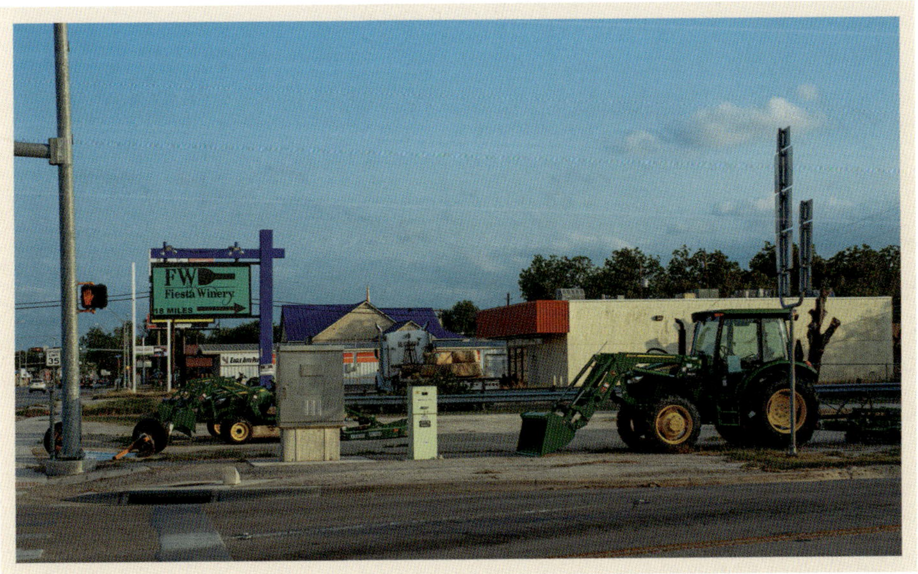

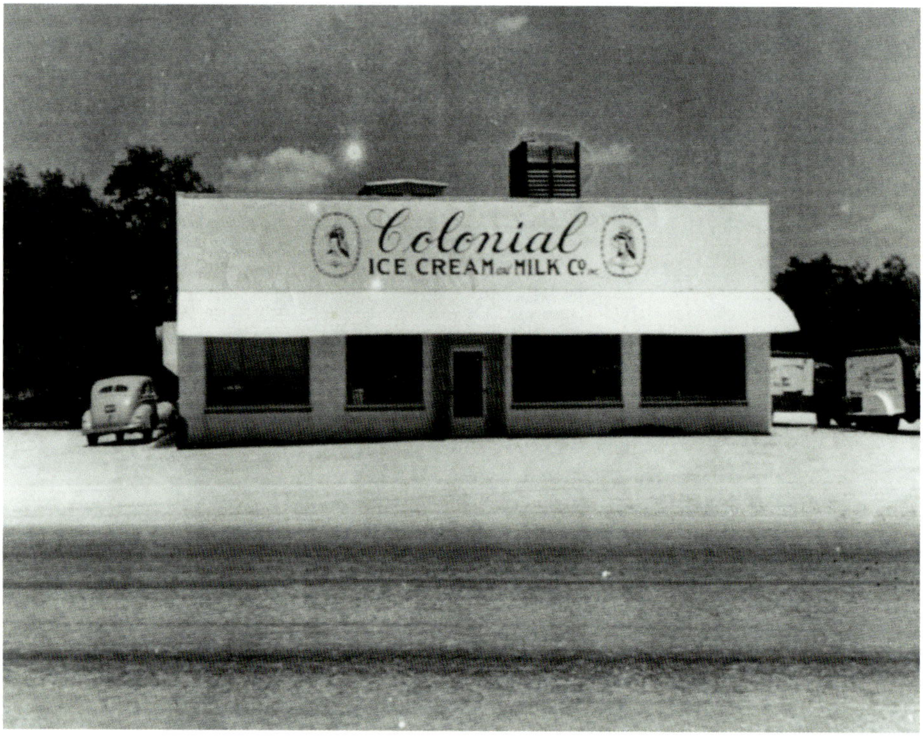

The Colonial Ice Cream and Milk Company was founded in Texas in 1946. Maurice Stanley Hoover opened a store at 911 South Key Avenue in Lampasas that year and continued operations until it was destroyed in the flood of 1957. Trucks picked up raw milk for pasteurization and delivered bottled milk to Lampasas residents, restaurants, and grocery stores. An insulated ice-cream truck took ice cream to local stores. A small café served ice cream. A bank parking lot occupies the site today. (Present, JF.)

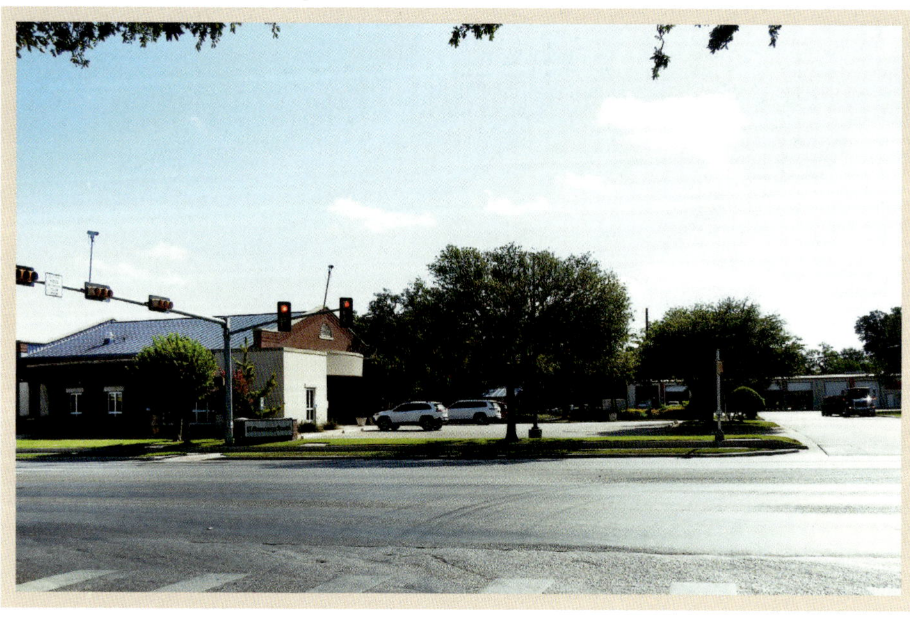

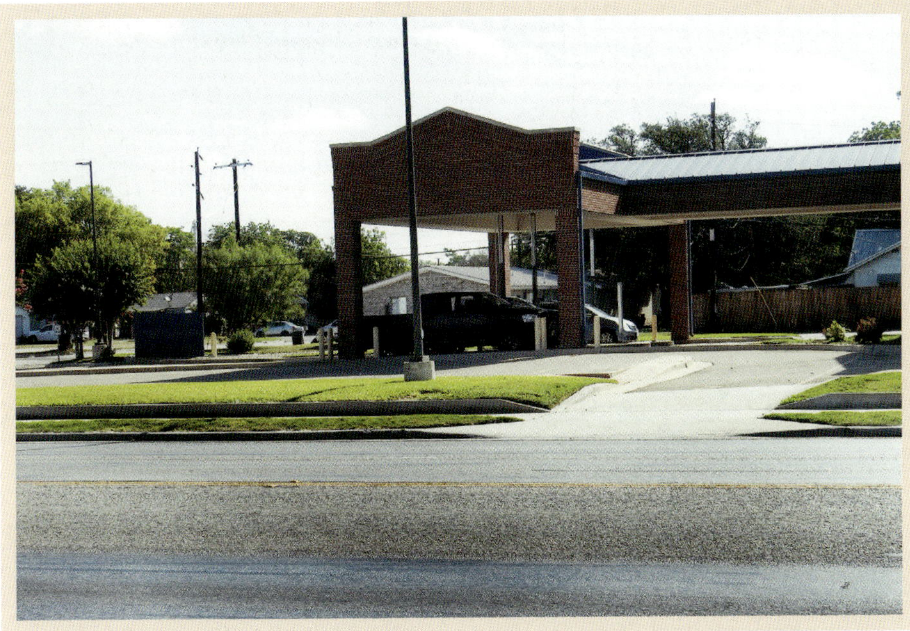

Jofe's Café (below) at 905 South Key Avenue, where a bank stands today, took its name from the surnames of owners Buck Jones and Maurice Field. Delbert and Stella Martin leased Jofe's in 1947. In 1948, the Brownwood *Collegian* reported that two college instructors' clubs met for dinner in the café's clubroom and that most ordered seafood, having heard that "fish is good brain food." In 1952, the Martins opened their own restaurant one block north. (Present, JF.)

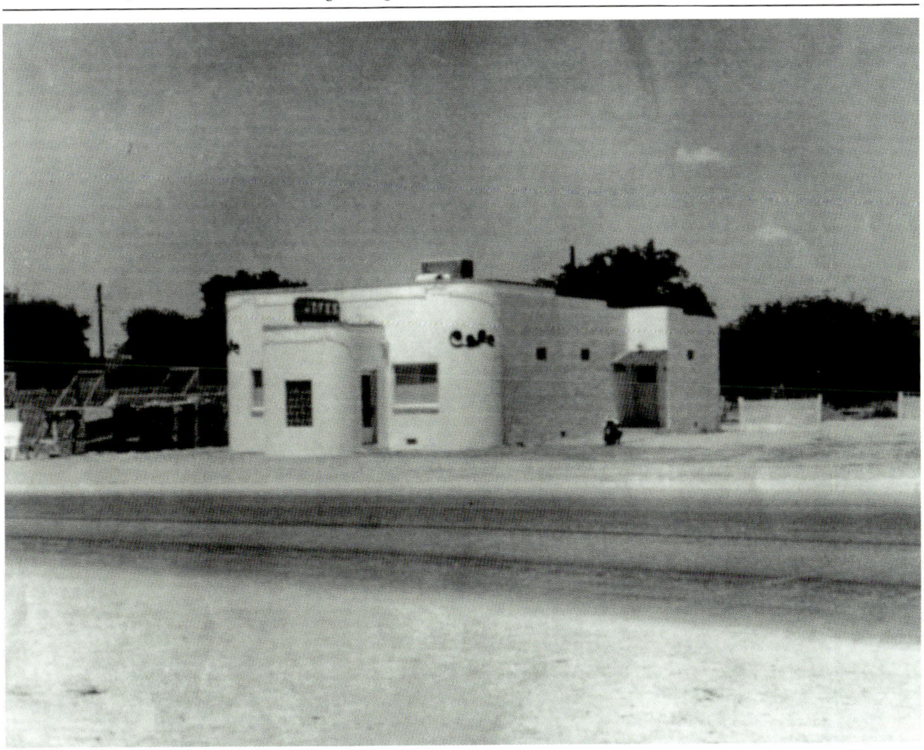

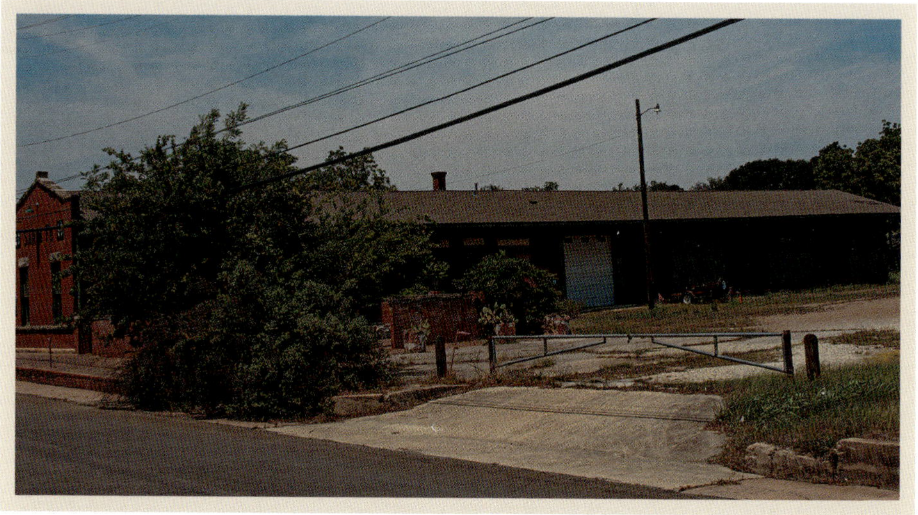

An advertisement in a 1904 Lampasas *Daily Leader* extolled the "world famous Santa Fe Eating House," while also promoting "one way colonist" railway tickets to California. In 1914, Charles Wachendorfer took over the Eating House, which provided supper for crew and passengers from the nearby Santa Fe Depot on Second Street. The early photograph below shows the hustle and bustle of the main passenger train station in town. Today, the building has been restored and is privately owned. (Present, DP.)

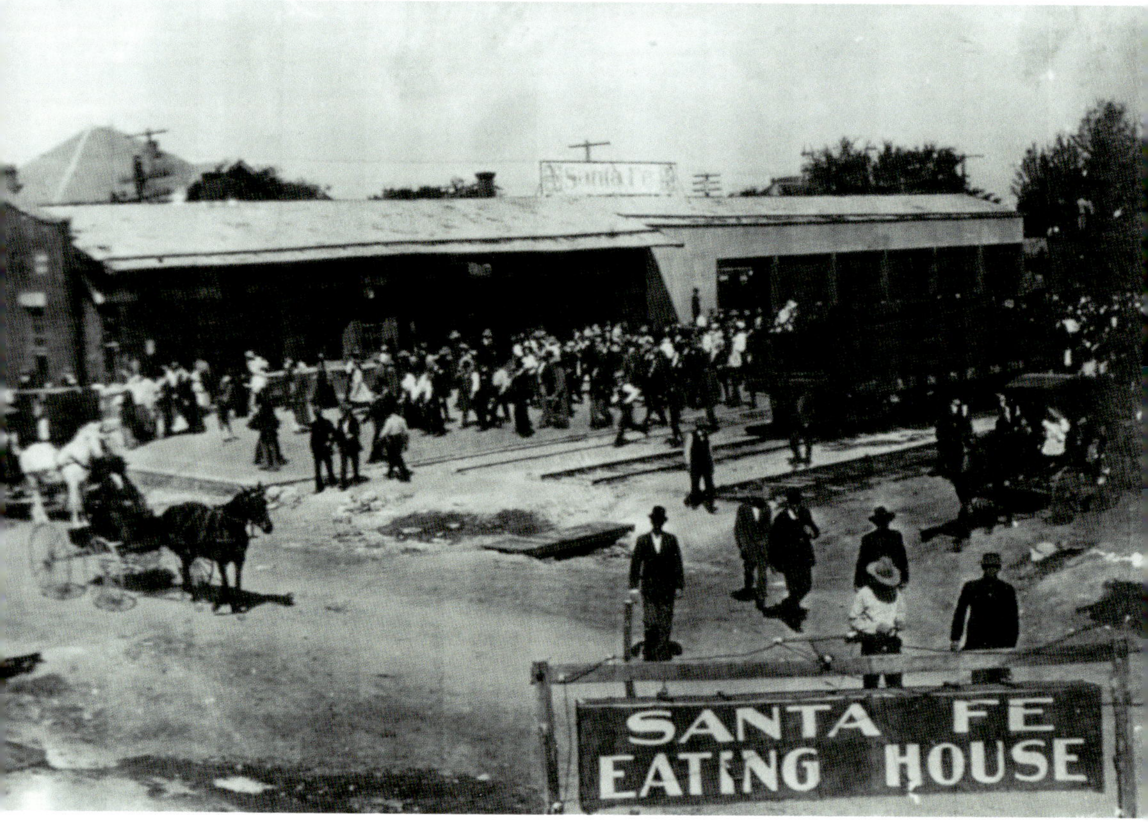

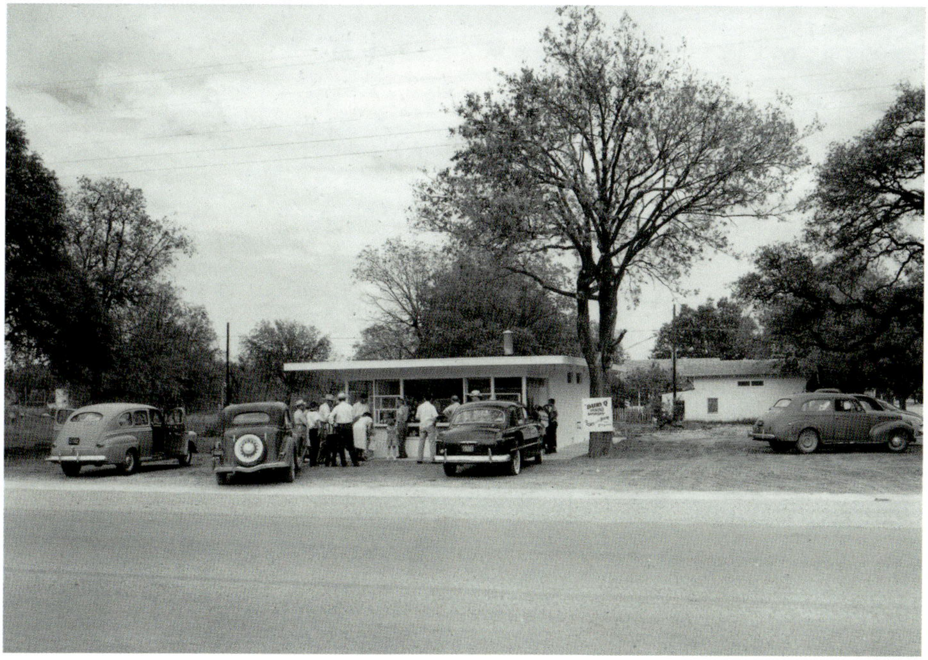

The Dairy Cue, or "Dairy Q," as the sign reads here, celebrated its grand opening on Key Avenue in 1950. Elvis Presley visited the eatery often in 1958 when he was stationed at Fort Hood. Established by J.B. Storm and his wife, Robbie IraDell (neé Upton), the drive-in changed its name to Storm's in the early 1970s. The current sign is a replica of an earlier sign and was presented to the Storms' son, Robbis, on his retirement from the business. (Present, AM.)

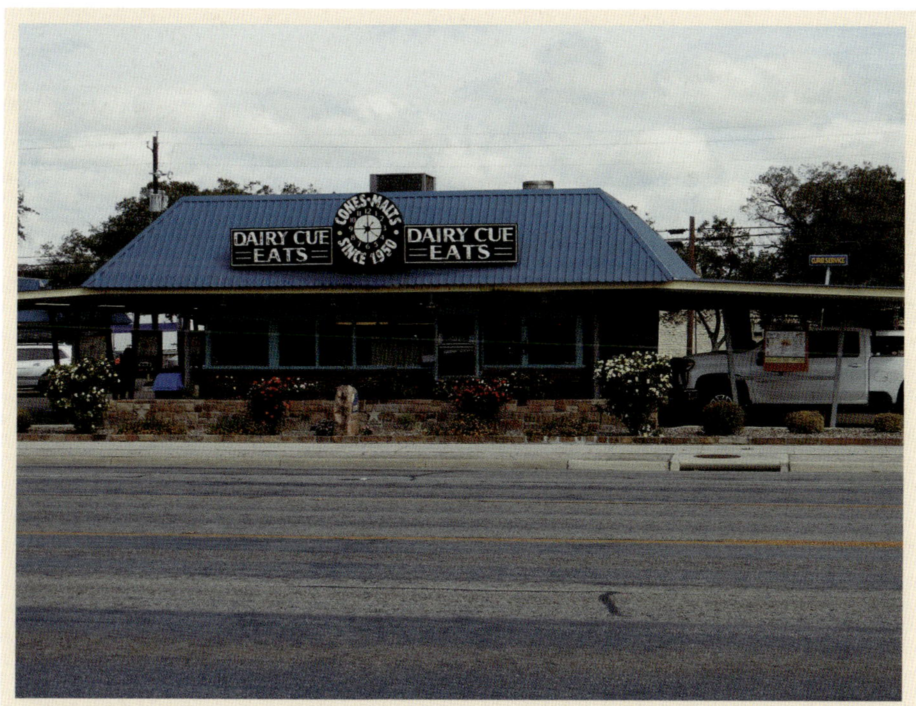

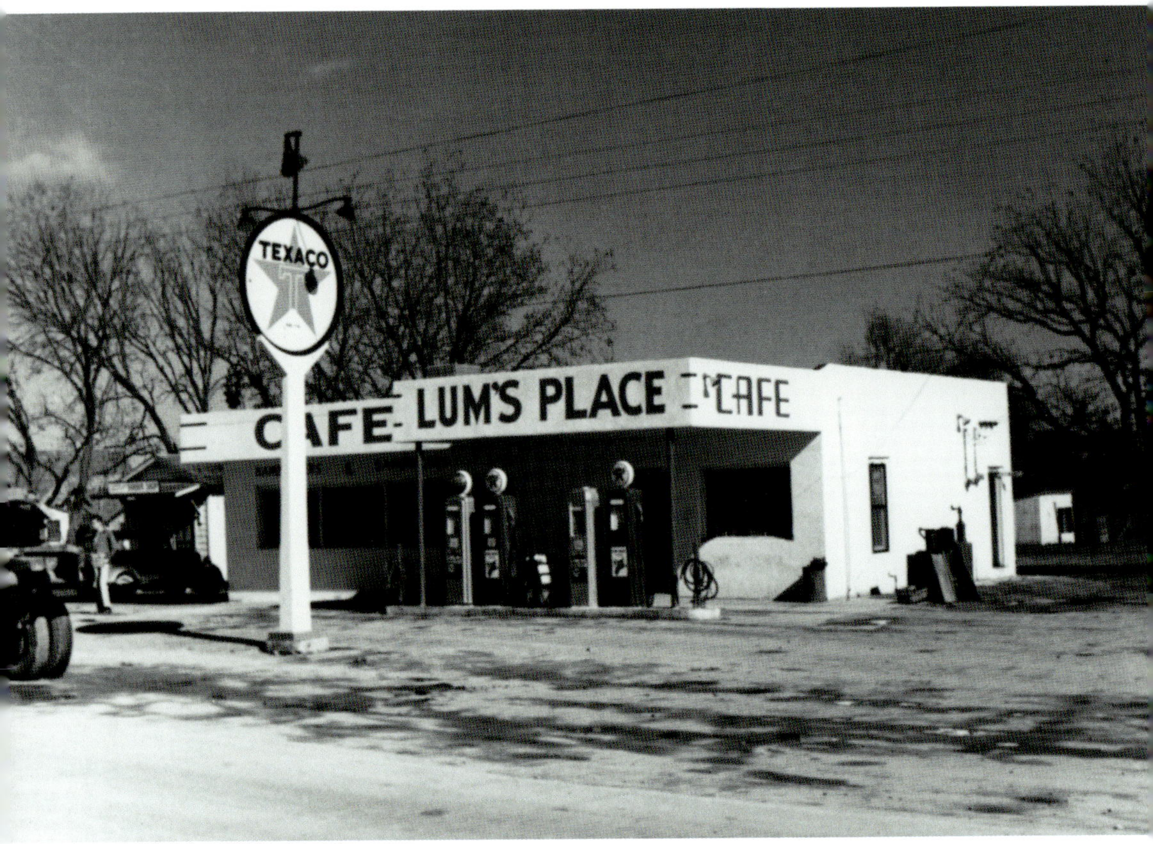

Lum Scott built Lum's Place where Benny Boyd's car dealership is today at 603 North Key Avenue. Lum's served hamburgers, chicken-fried steak, and fried chicken and was popular with local teenagers in the 1950s. Each booth had a small jukebox; one Lampasan remembers it costing a dime to play a song. The Scotts lived in a large house behind the café. The Texaco station in front was run by Andrew Jackson Straley Jr. (Past, Virgil Wooten; present, JF.)

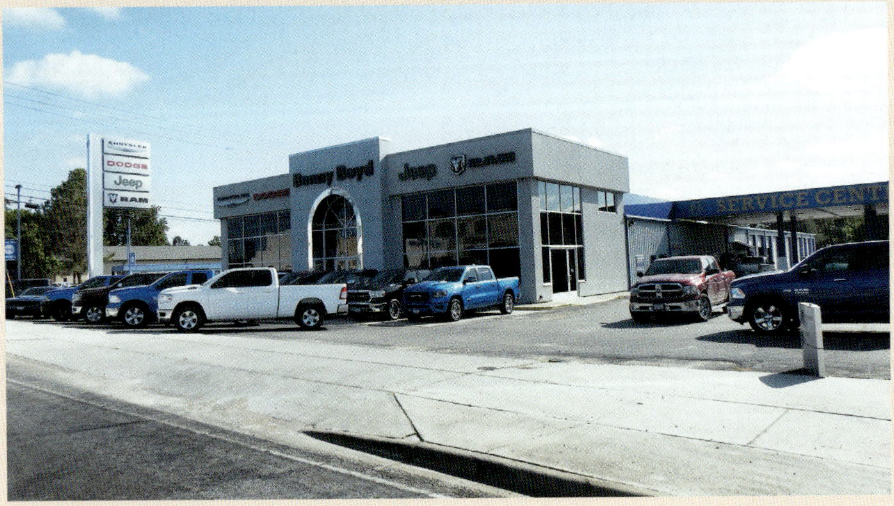

CHAPTER 3

Places to Shop

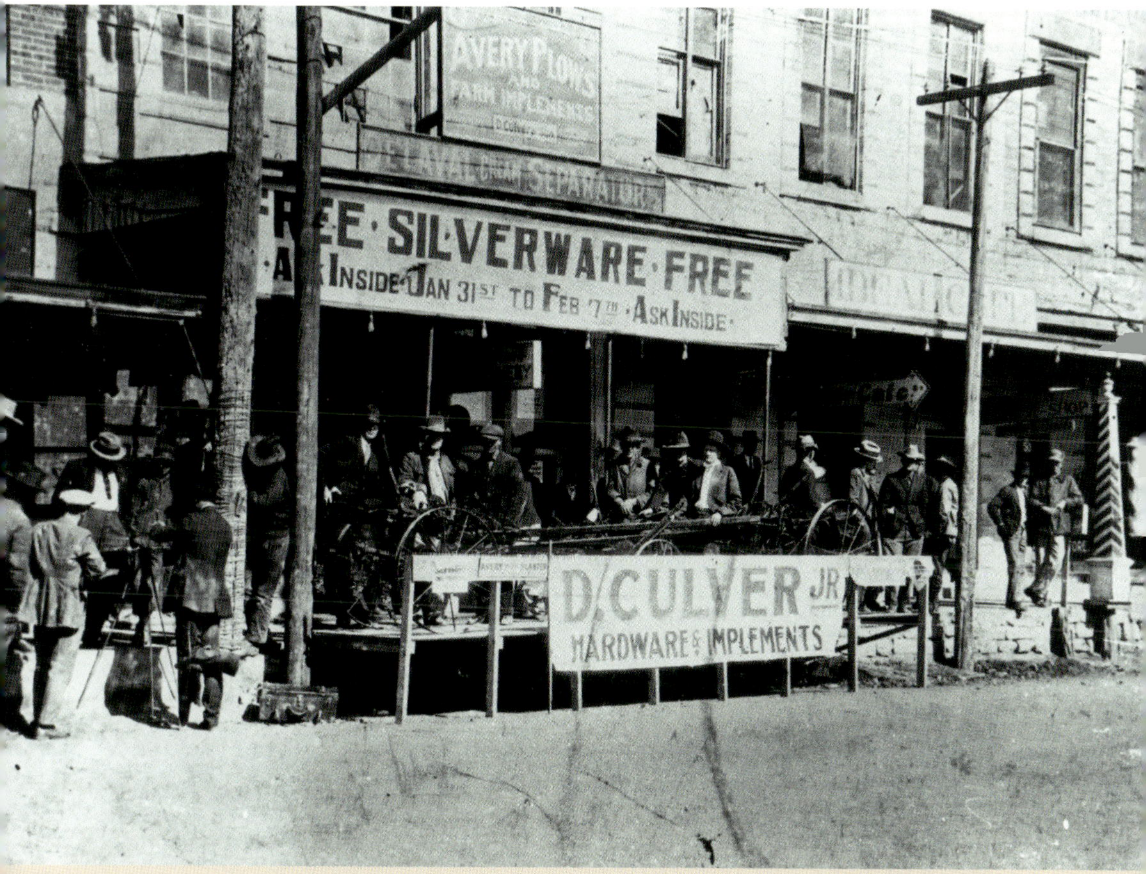

East Third Street was and is one of the main shopping streets in Lampasas. In this view, Daniel Culver's hardware store, at 515 East Third Street, offered free silverware the first week of February to entice customers. DeLaval cream separators and Avery plows and farm implements were necessities in the surrounding ranching and farming communities.

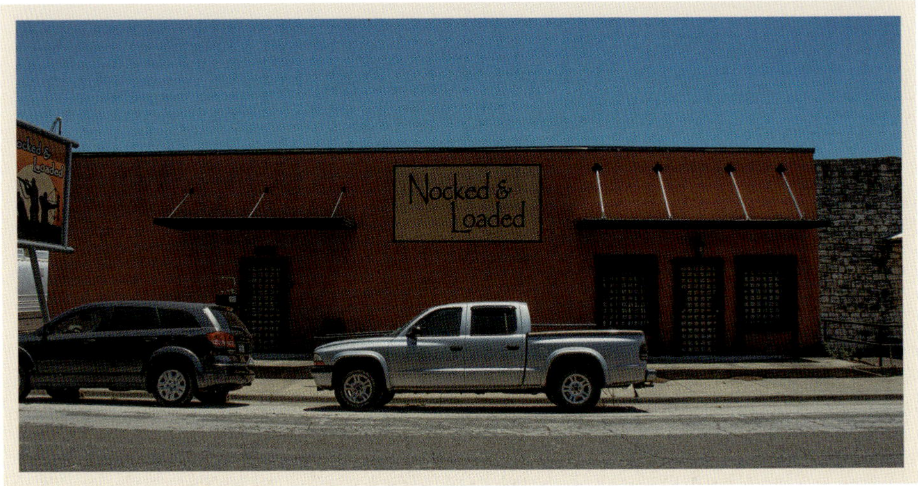

Leonard Harlien owned this business at 304 East Second Street between Western Avenue and Main Street in the late 1940s and 1950s (below). Due to the rubber shortage during World War II, he recapped tires. When rubber became more available, he added new tire sales to the business. He also provided road service, and many of his customers were truckers because he had the equipment to help them quickly. Most recently, the building housed Nocked and Loaded, a hunters' supply store. (Past, Kay Gray Fox; present, DP.)

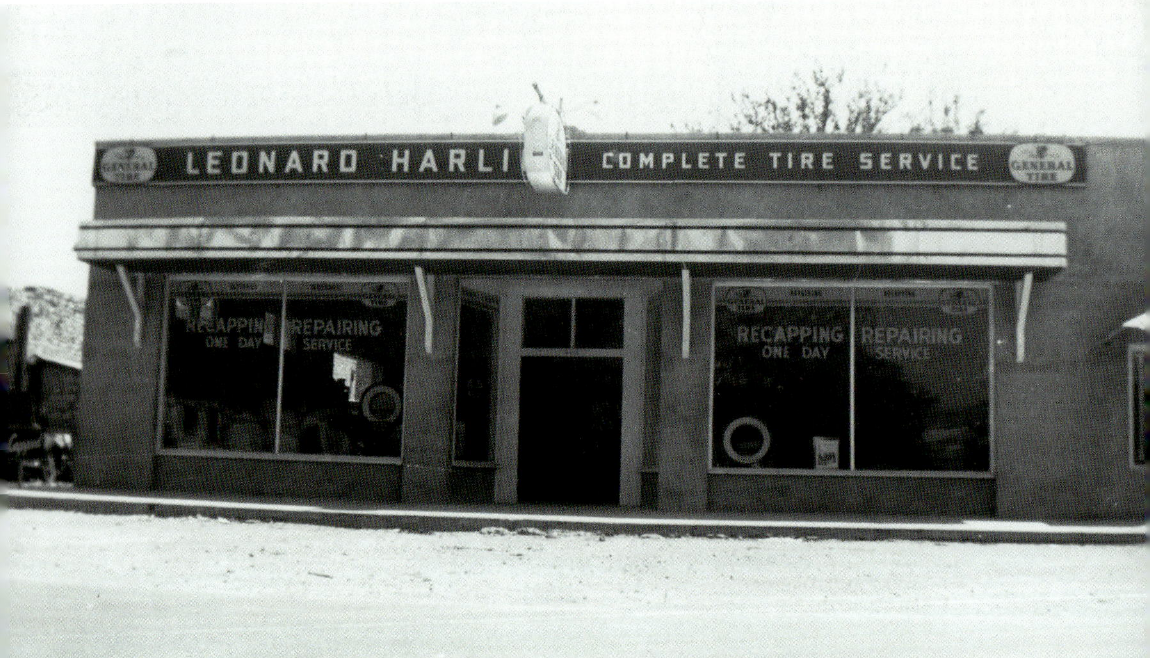

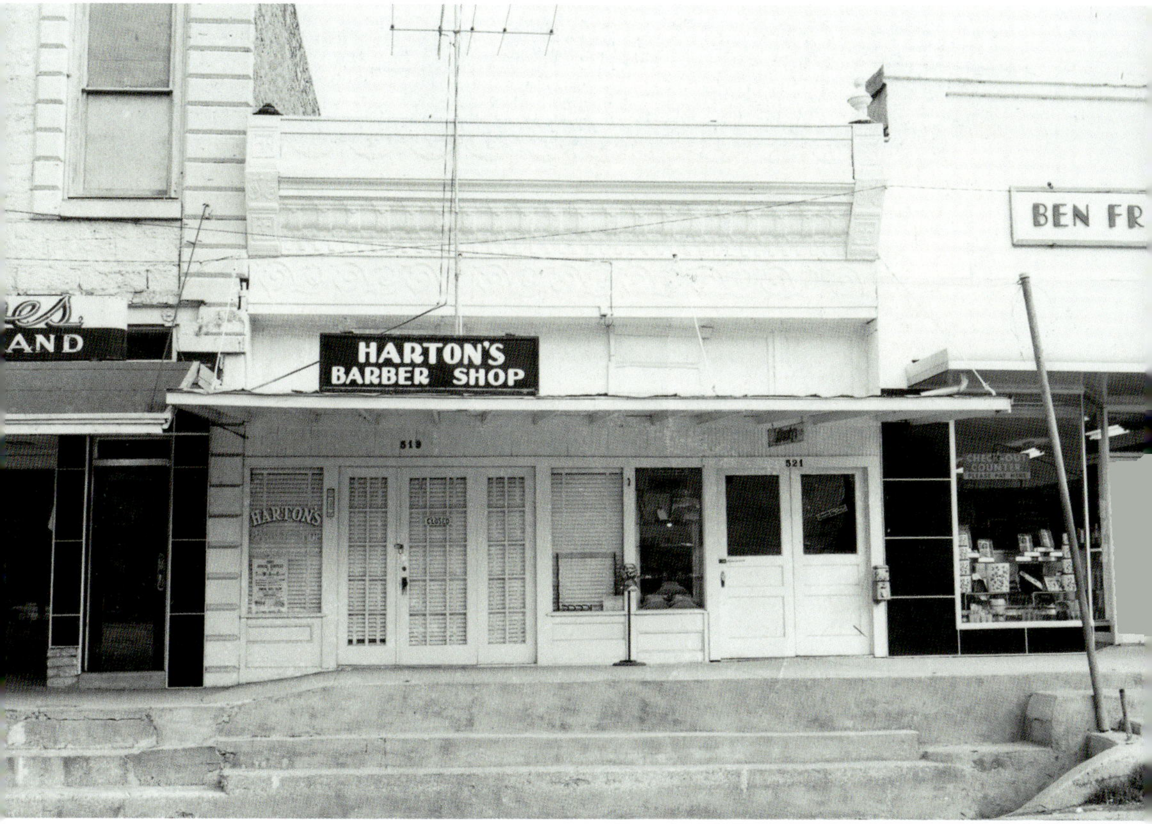

In the mid-1950s, 519 East Third Street was the home of Harold Harton's Barber Shop, where men could get a "shave and a haircut, six bits." At 517 East Third Street, Vivian C. Chamberlain owned and operated the Family Shoe Store. Ben Franklin Variety Store was located on the other side of a vacant store to the right. Tom McCandless was the manager. Today, Moonie's Hemporium, Eve's Café, and Workforce Solutions can be found there. (Present, DP.)

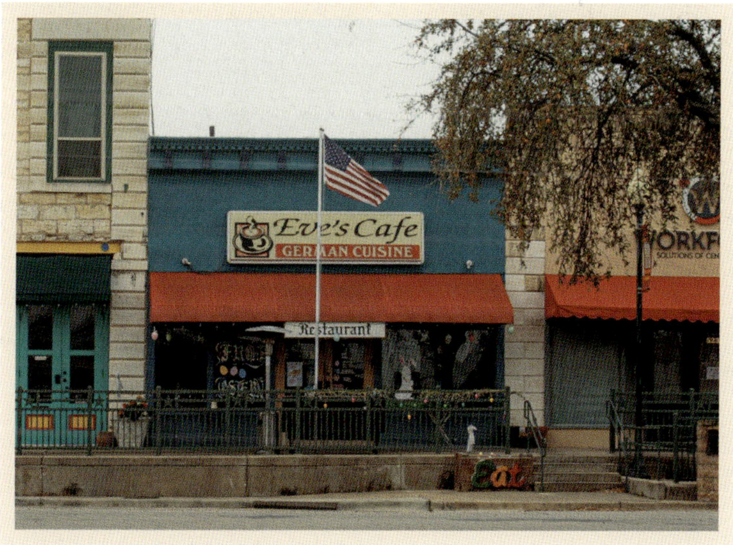

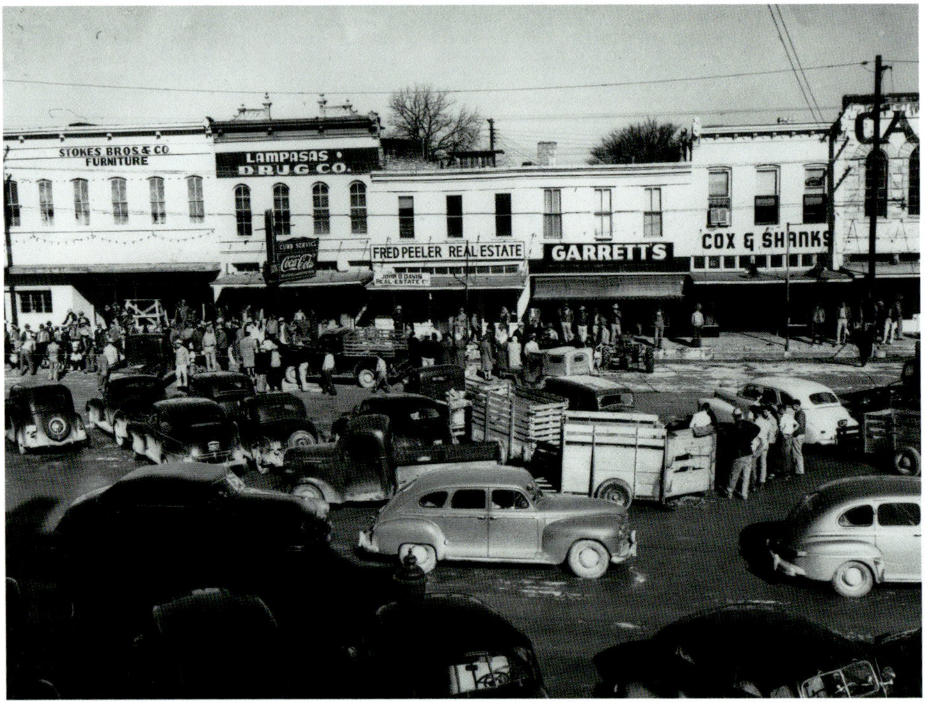

In the late 1940s, a number of businesses operated on the north side of the Courthouse Square. In the foreground, a youth livestock show brought in a crowd of interested citizens. People could shop at Stokes Brothers Furniture, Lampasas Drug Company, Fred Peeler Real Estate, Garrett's Ready-to-Wear, and Cox and Shanks men's clothing store. Today, First Texas Bank, a law office, a real estate office, and a florist can be found, along with several unoccupied spaces. (Present, DP.)

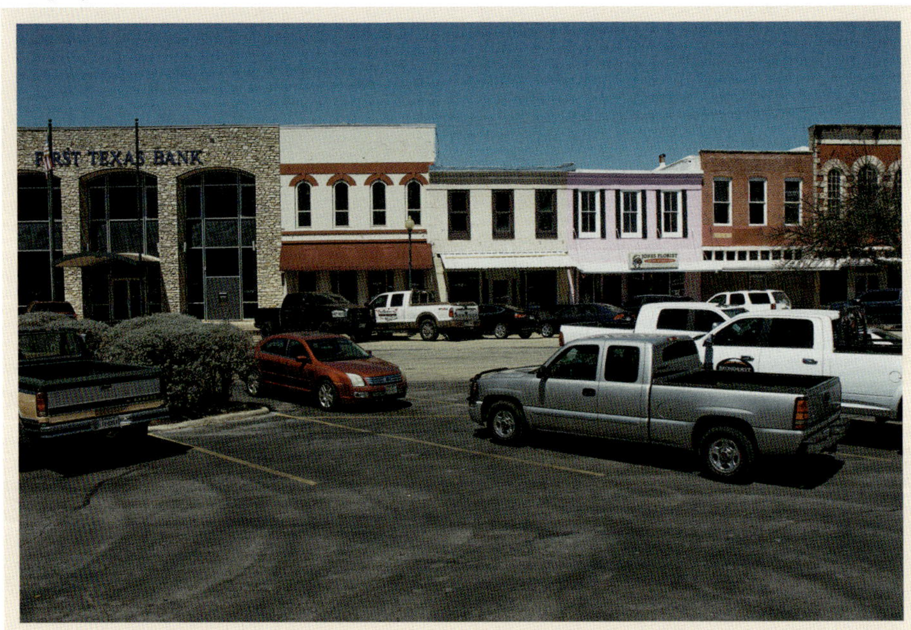

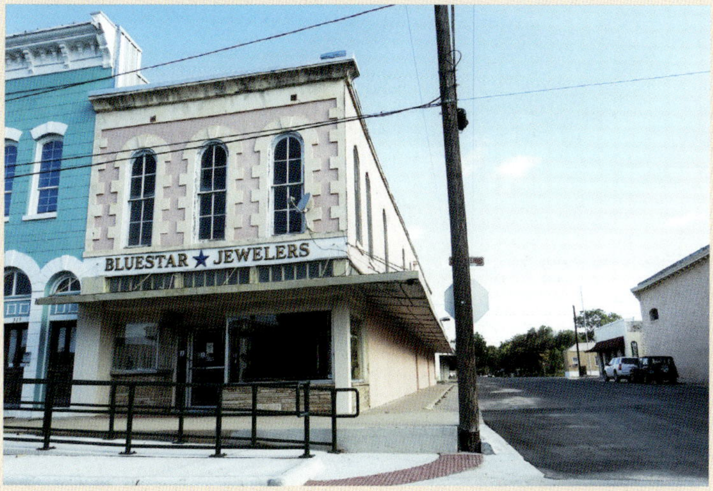

Owned and operated by Harry and Eugene Key from 1930 until 1963, when Eugene died, this store (below) was at the northwest corner of East Third Street and South Western Avenue. The Key brothers sold and delivered groceries to Lampasas residents and often went the extra mile, stocking the delivered groceries in the kitchen cabinets of their clients. Today, the building is occupied by Bluestar Jewelers, where customers can buy new jewelry and have repairs done. (Present, JF.)

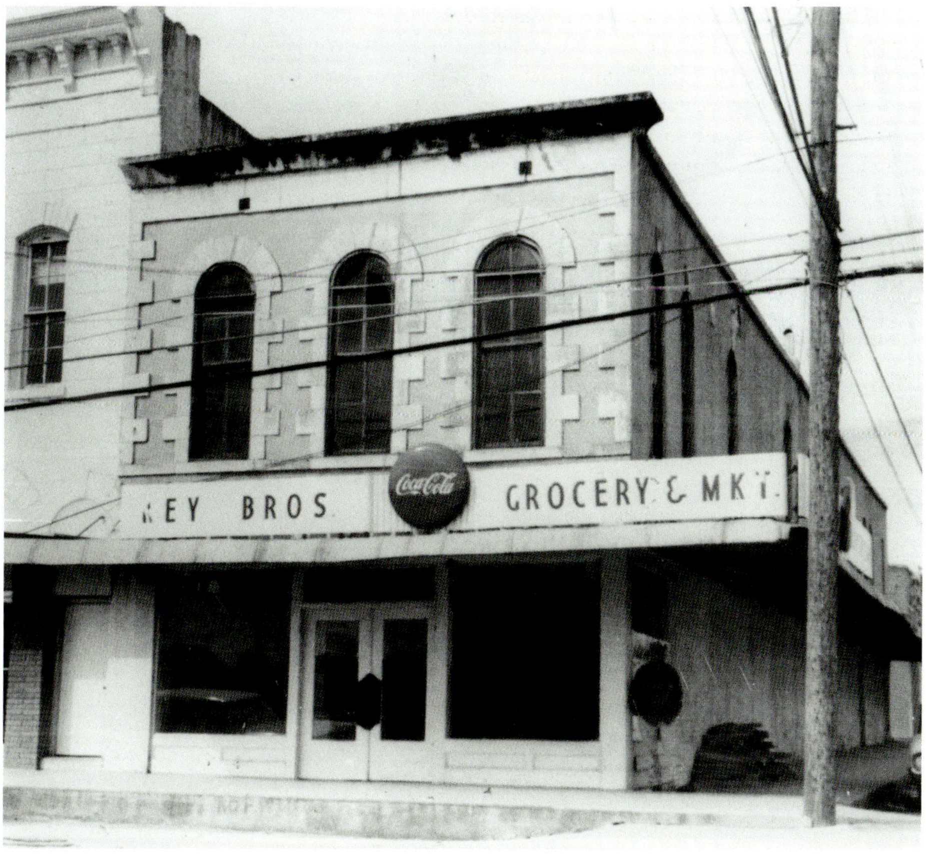

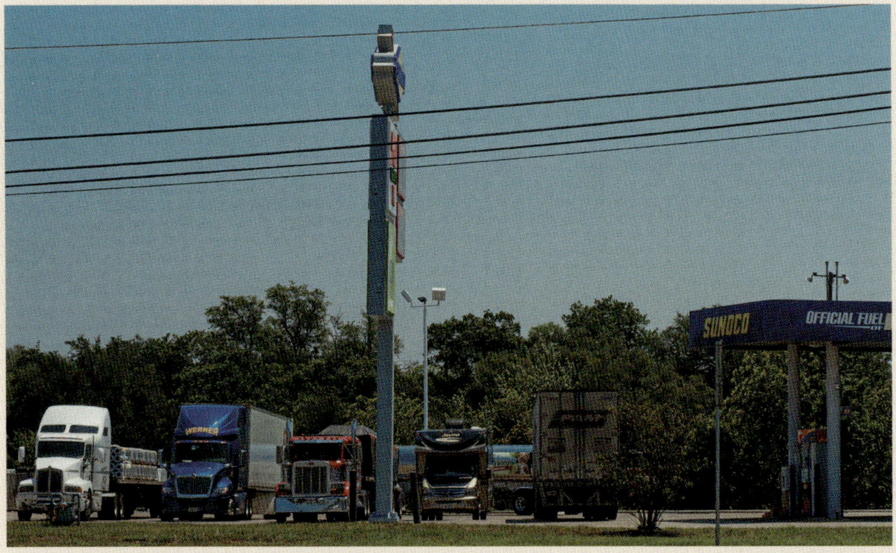

Gillen's Army Surplus Store (below) was run by Charles James "Choc" Gillen for over 45 years on North Key Avenue, where a large truck stop is today. Choc and his wife, Marie, attended army surplus conventions in Las Vegas twice a year, buying and selling surplus inventory. In 1986, he earned commendation as an outstanding member of the American Association of Surplus Dealers. Among items sold at the store were pup tents, rubber boots, baseball gloves, and slippers. (Past, collection of Sherry Gillen-Milligan; present, DP.)

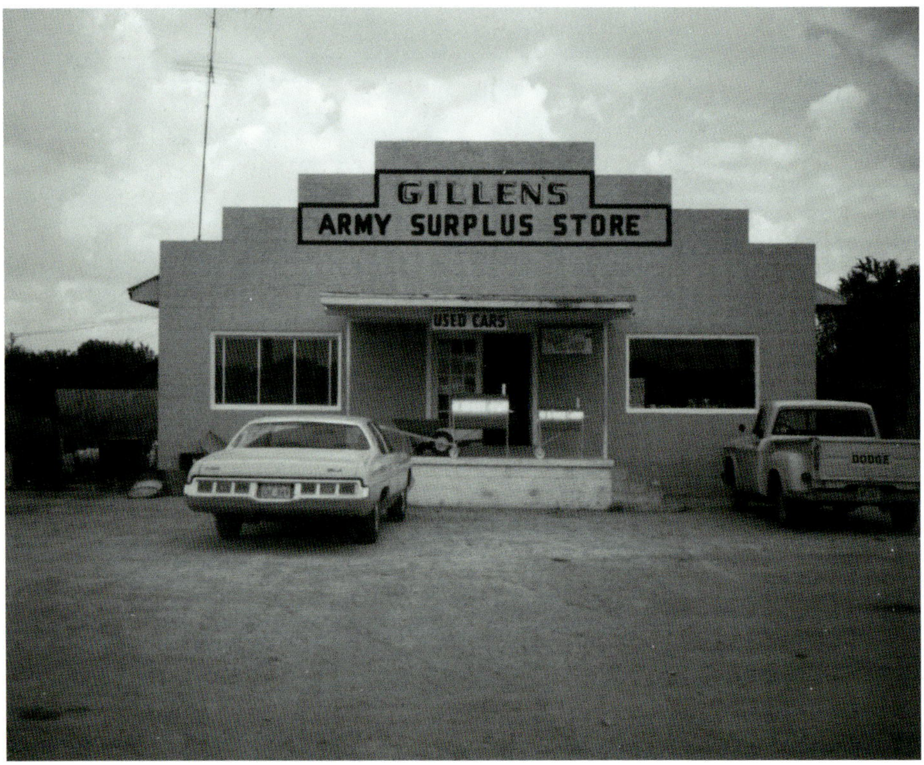

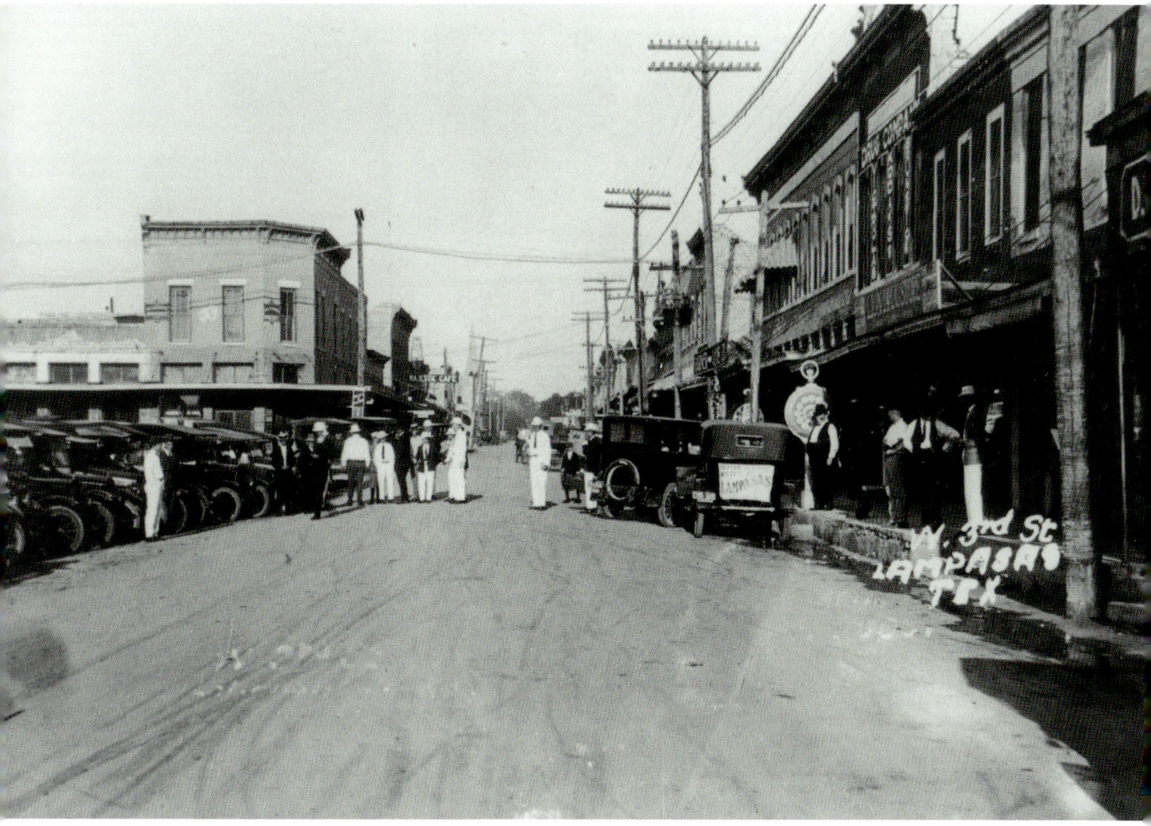

This early-20th-century view of East Third Street looking toward Grand (now Key) Avenue features businesses such as D. Culver Hardware, Lion drugstore, and an insurance company on the north side of the square. In the distance, the Majestic Café and the steeple of the First Baptist Church are visible. Today, the north side of the square is experiencing a renaissance, with new businesses such as a florist, an art gallery, and a gift shop. (Present, JF.)

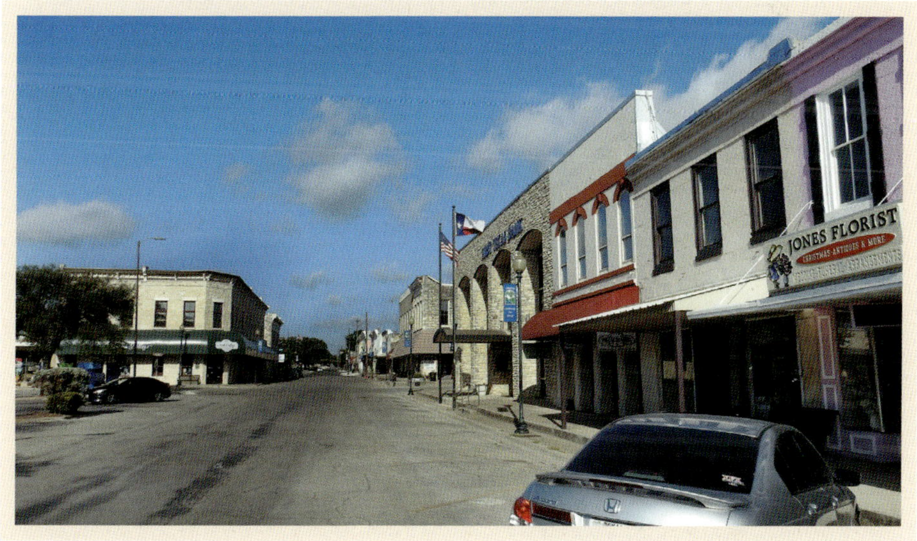

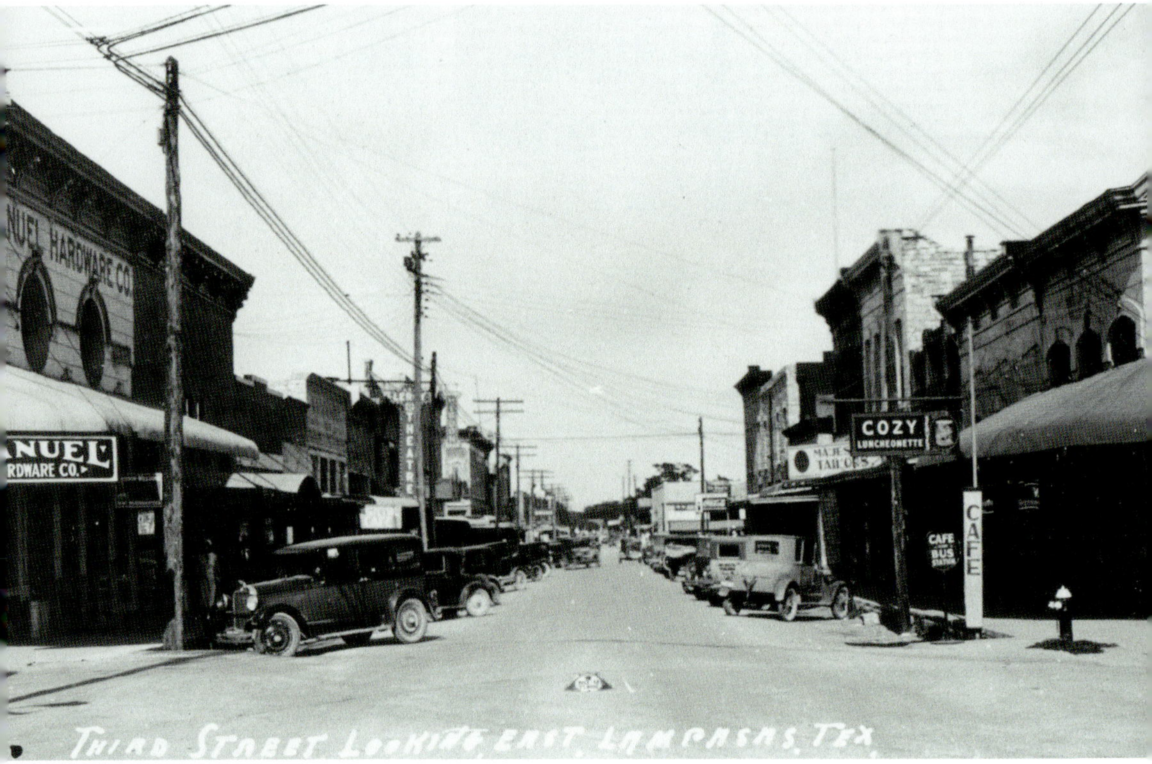

This early-20th-century view of Third Street looking toward the square was taken from the juncture of Third Street and Western Avenue. On the north side, signs for Manuel Hardware and the Le Roy Theater are visible. On the south side are the Cozy Luncheonette and Majestic Tailors, which were in the Phillips and Trosper buildings. Note the raised sign on the pavement in the middle of the street, which reads "No U-turn." The Manuel Hardware building is now occupied by M.D. Abel Company. (Present, AM.)

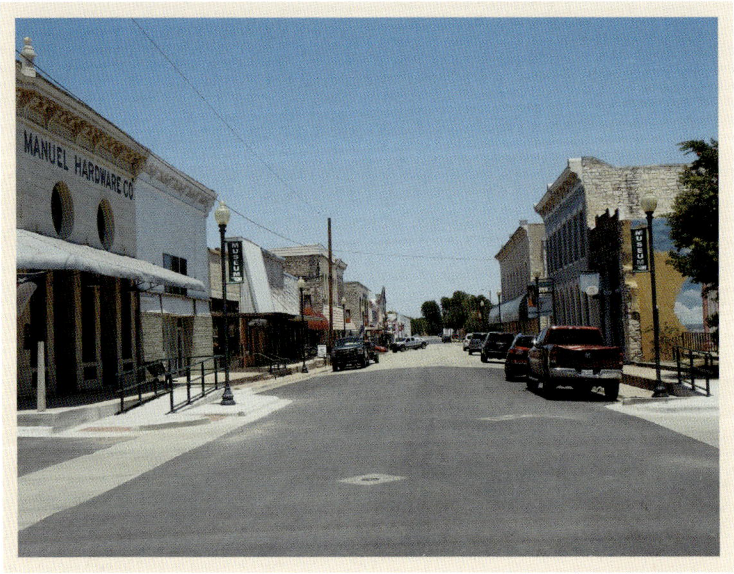

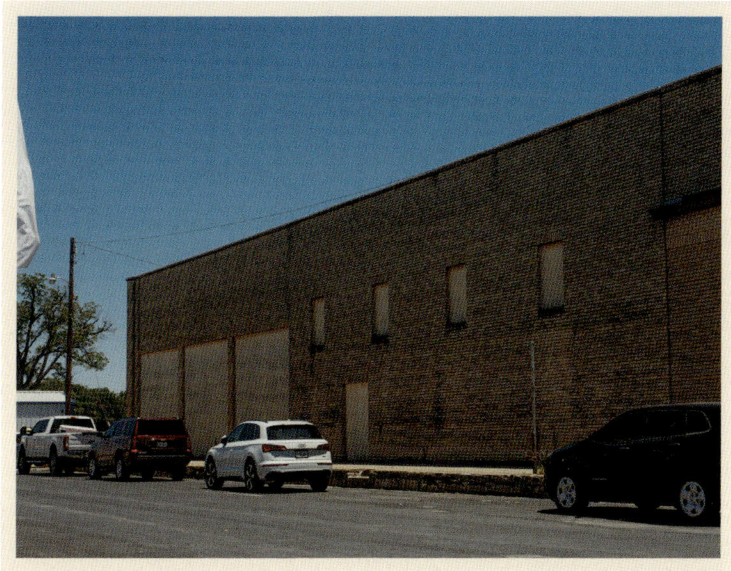

Higdon-Senterfitt Wholesale and Retail Grocers, shown below in the late 1880s advertising "staple and fancy groceries," fronted East Third Street at the corner of Pecan Street. The Dollar General is there today. The company warehouse is visible next to the store on Third Street. The original building burned in 1927, and the following year, the Lampasas men's clothing shop Cox and Shanks advertised buying men's suits from Higdon-Senterfitt-Andrew (as the store was known then) at nearly wholesale prices. The suits arrived after the building burned. (Present, DP.)

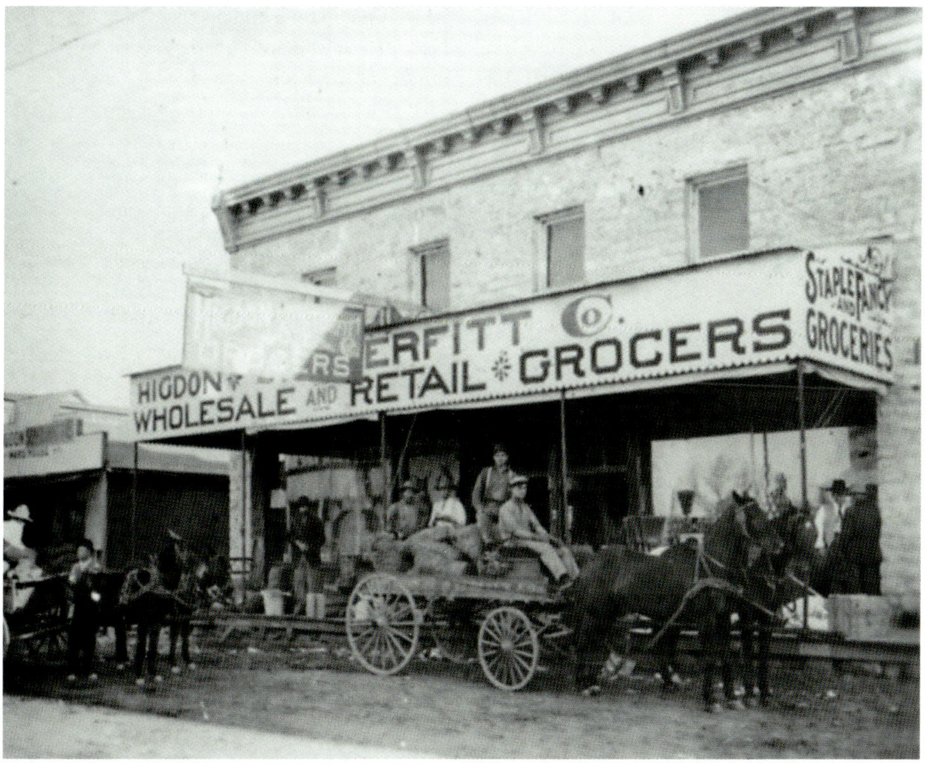

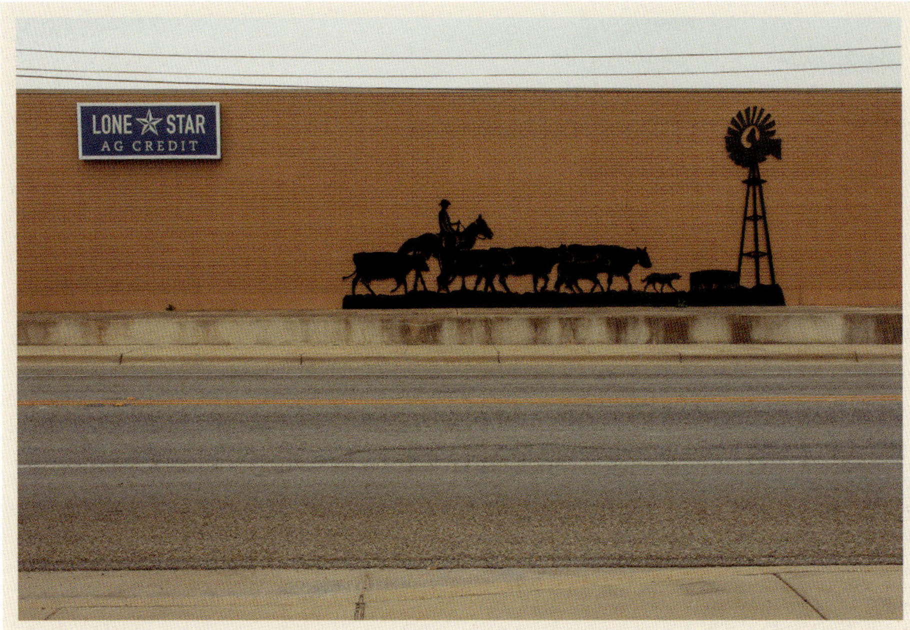

The Lampasas Ice Plant (below) was located at the northeast corner of Fourth Street and Western Avenue, where Lonestar Ag Credit sits today. In this 1940s photograph, men squat on the dock behind the spoils of a successful deer hunt. Patrons drove alongside the dock to pick up crushed ice packed in insulated paper bags or ice blocks. The building burned in July 1962, and in August, the Lampasas firemen held a barbecue to thank their counterparts in neighboring cities for help in extinguishing the blaze. (Present, DP.)

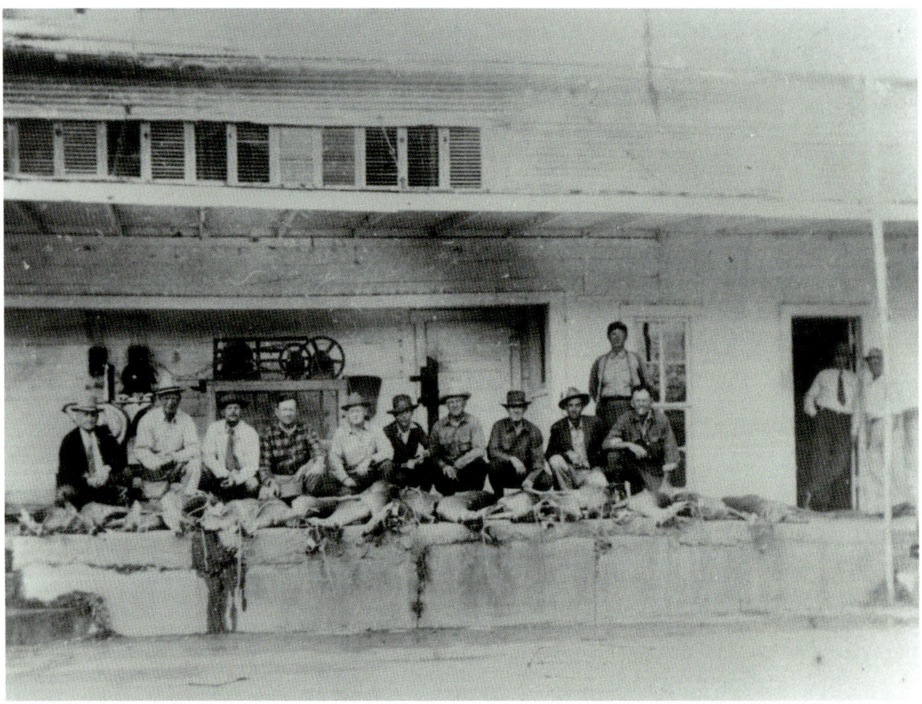

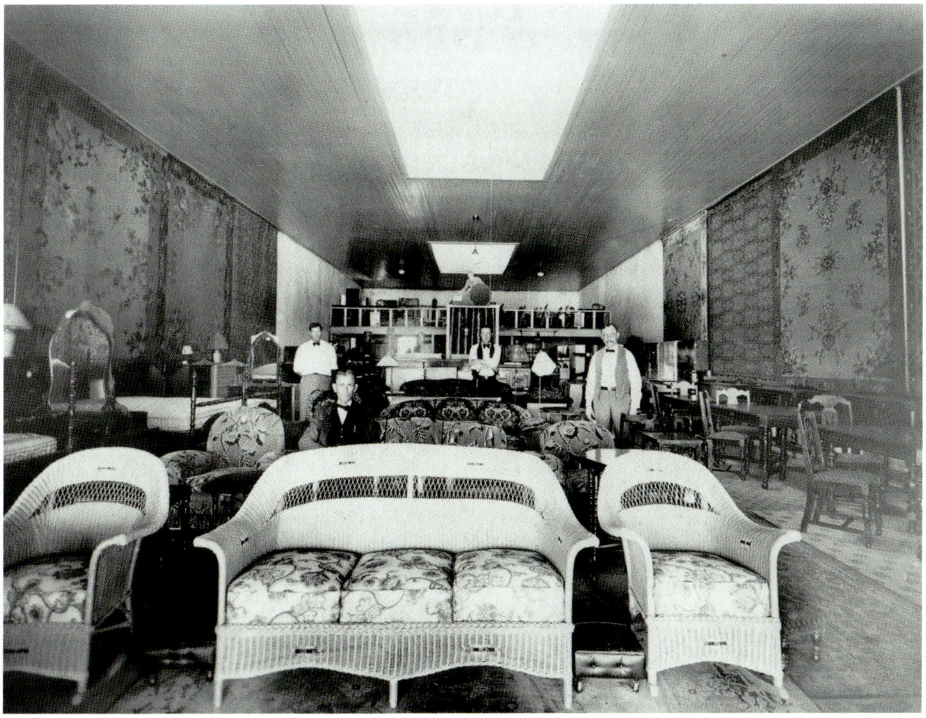

The Lampasas Furniture Company was at 416 South Live Oak Street, where a family-owned Lampasas newspaper is now. Shown here is the interior of the furniture store in the 1920s, with one of the proprietors, D.T. Briggs III, standing at right. The store sold Oriental carpets in addition to fine wicker and wood furniture. Today, the *Lampasas Dispatch Record* publishes twice weekly out of this space, covering all the news of Lampasas County. (Present, DP.)

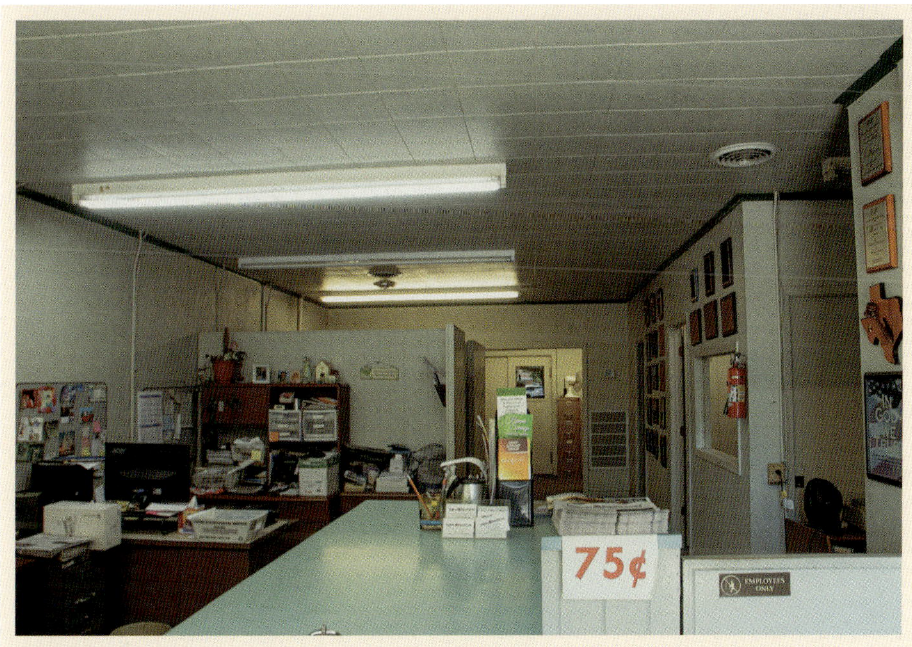

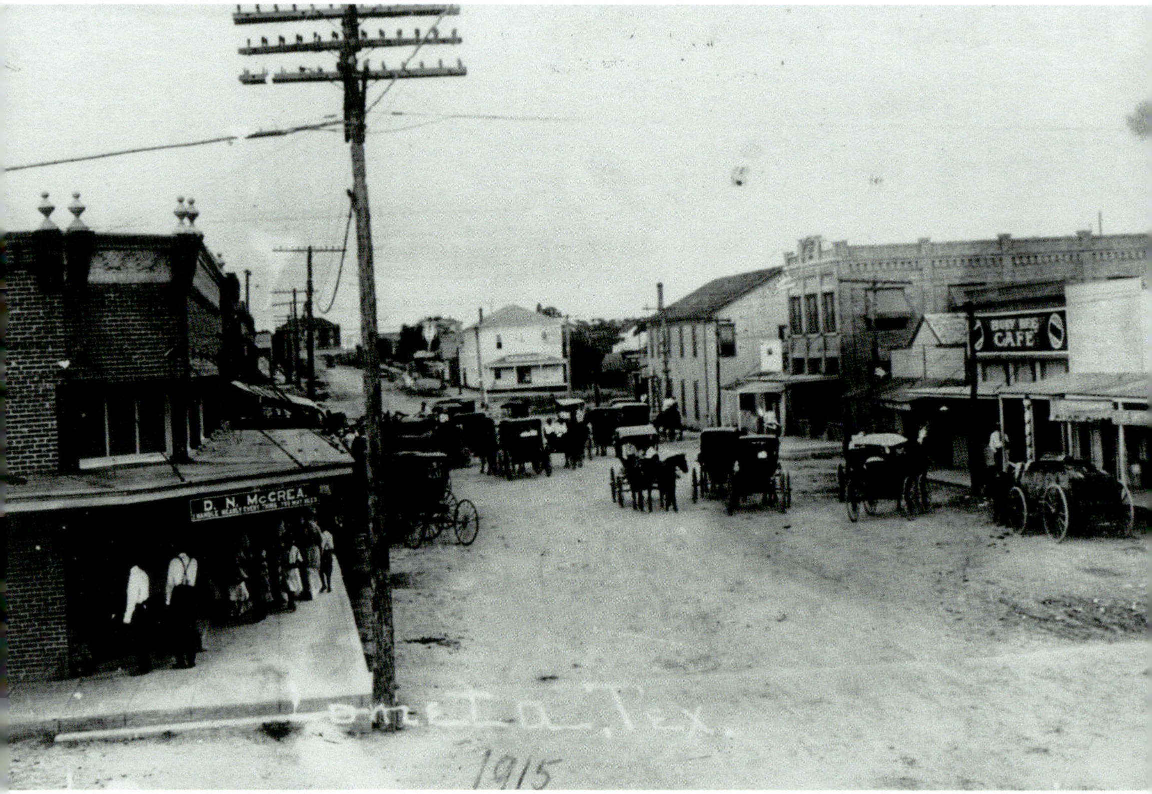

On the corner of Fourth and Main Streets in Lometa, D.N. McCrea advertised "handl[ing] nearly every thing you may need." Across the street was the Busy Bee Café. Today, the 1915 McCrea building still stands but is empty, having housed a variety of businesses over the years, including McAnelly Dry Goods, which opened there in 1945. The building has lost its finials. (Present, JF.)

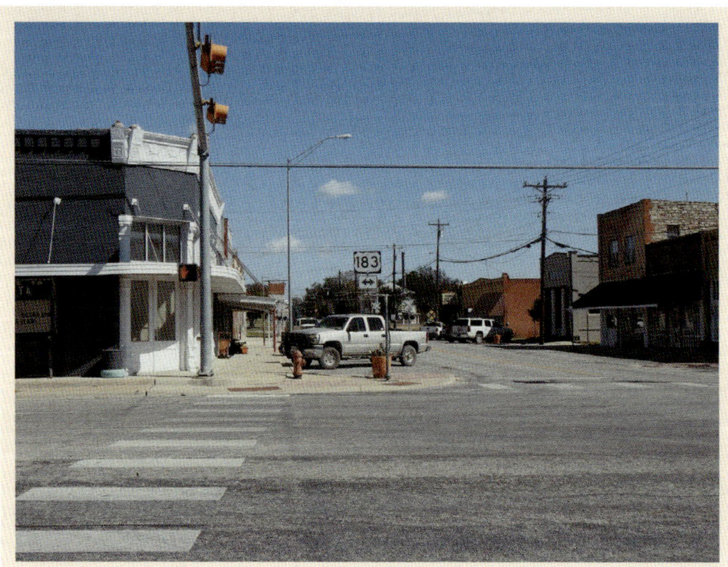

CHAPTER 4

PLACES TO LEARN

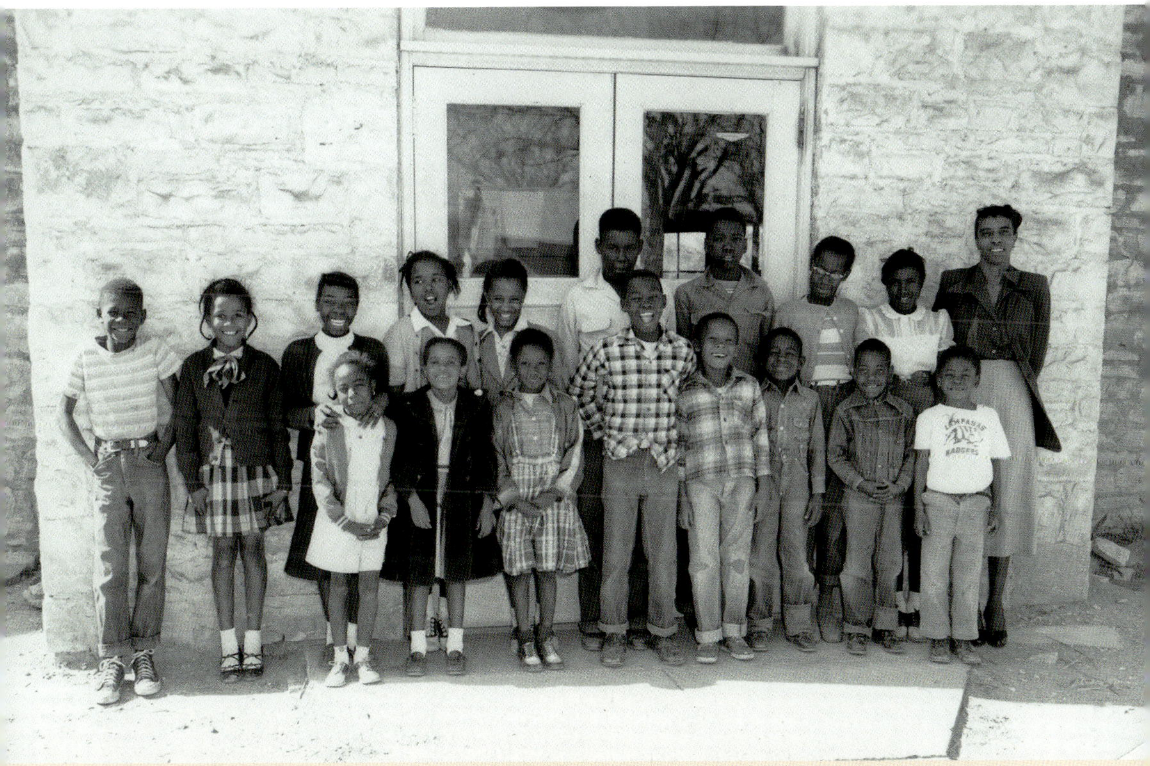

The Lampasas Colored School opened in 1898 in a wood-frame building. The limestone school, pictured here with elementary schoolchildren and teacher Ernestine Patrick, was built in 1923. In 1927, due to overcrowding, the school day was split between younger and older students. In 1963, Lampasas schools desegregated, and this school closed. It still stands and has been restored.

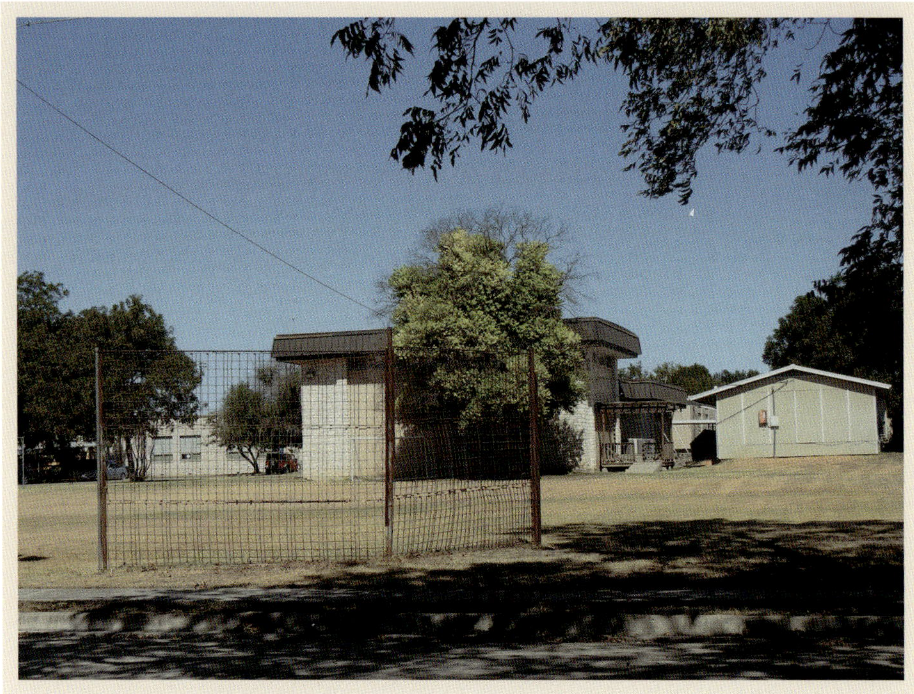

The Lampasas Grammar School (below), constructed in 1895, was the first public school building in the city. Located at the north end of Main Street, the two-story limestone structure was topped with a bell tower and surrounded by a wrought iron fence. It burned in 1977. Today, the Lampasas County Boys and Girls Club occupies the site. The original school bell and some of the original limestone (not visible here) is to the west of the club's building. (Present, AM.)

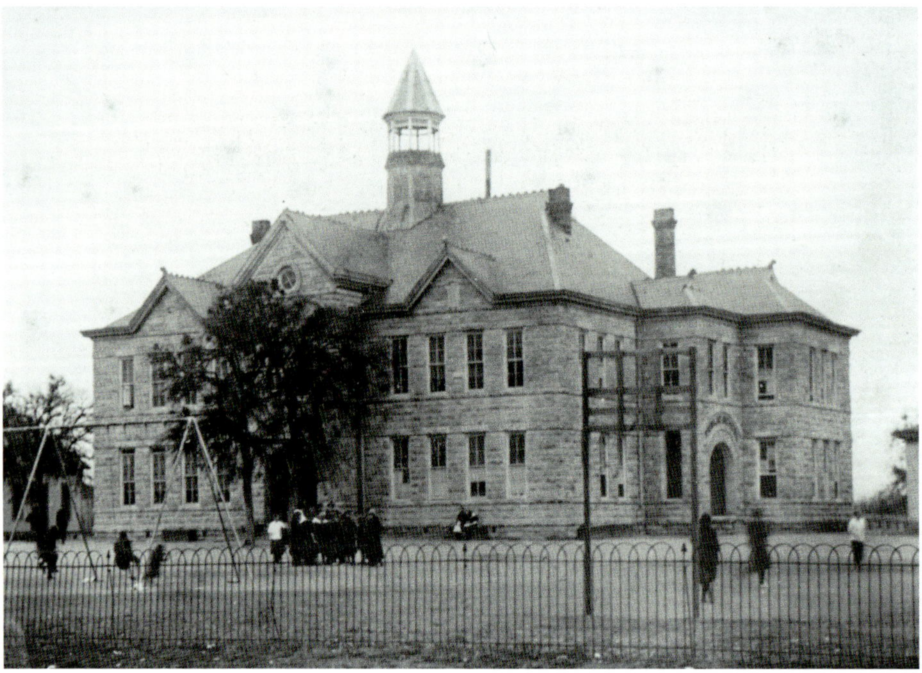

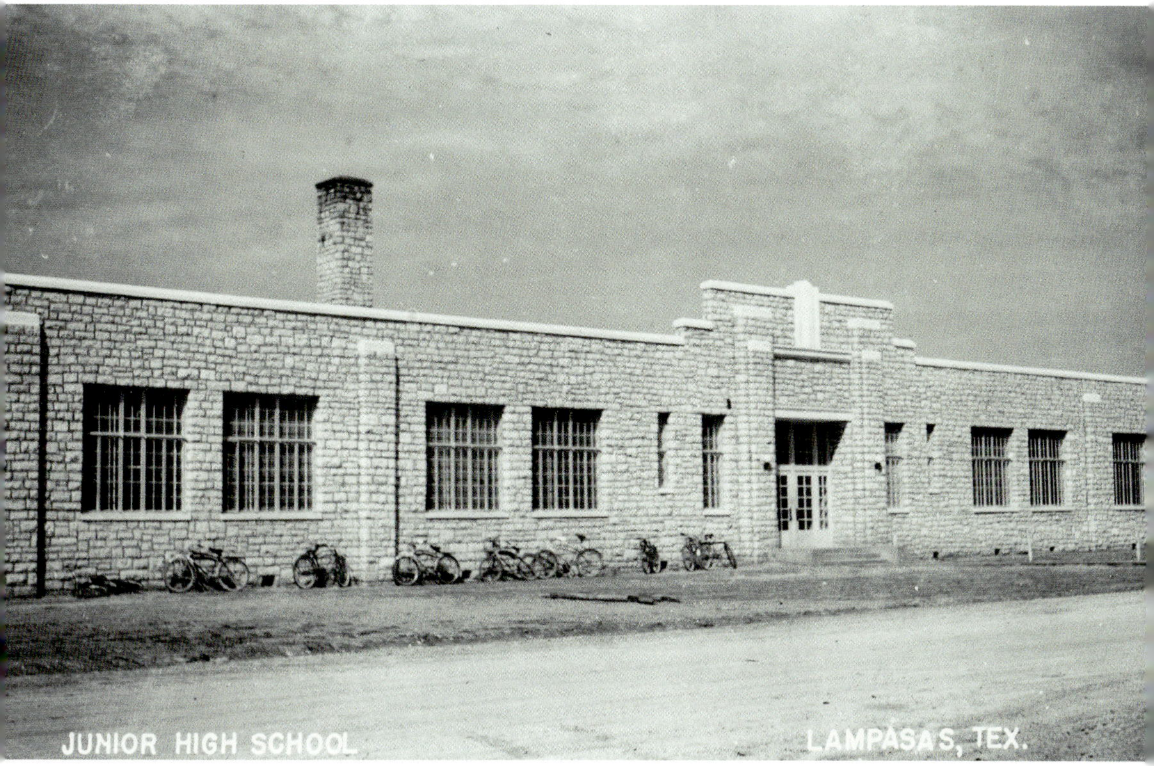

This native stone structure, built in 1938, is one of the few remaining examples of Art Deco architecture in the city. The eight-room, one-story building housed grades six, seven, and eight. It served as Lampasas Junior High until around 1950, when it became Lampasas Elementary School. Today, it is used by Lampasas County Higher Education Center (LCHEC) and Lampasas Independent School District departments, such as child nutrition, technology, and maintenance. (Present, AM.)

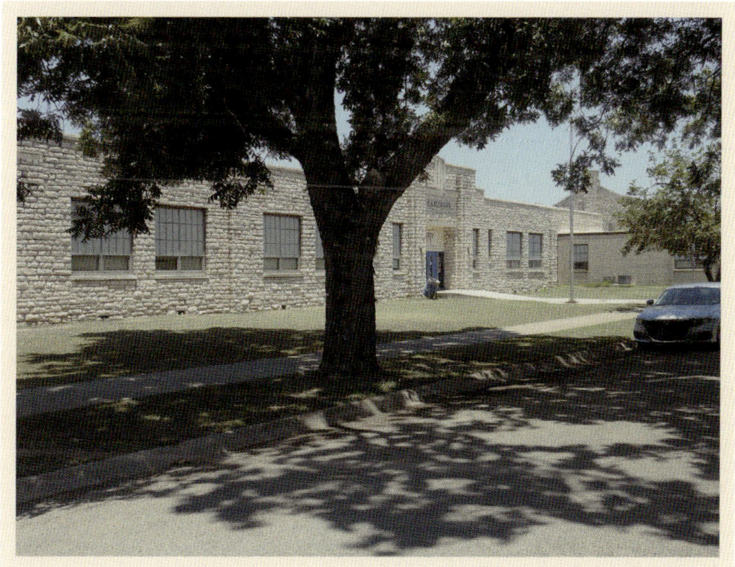

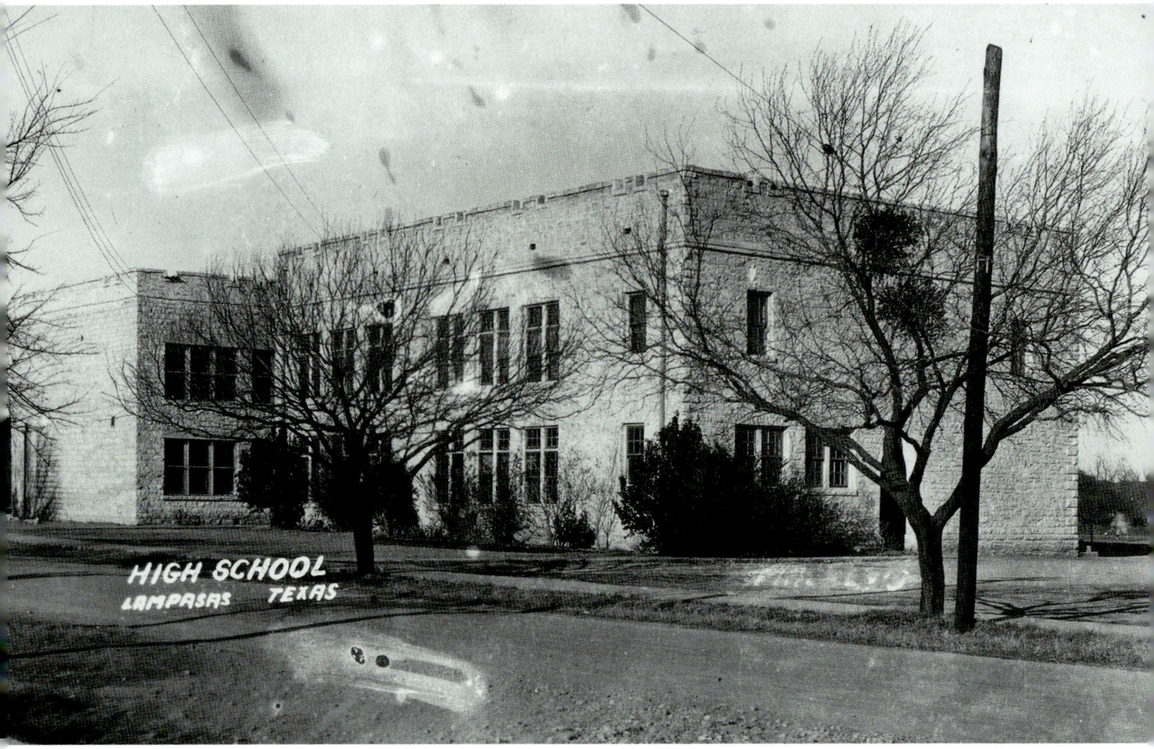

The first Lampasas High School building, erected in 1917, was an eight-room, two-story structure. It was expanded in 1922 to accommodate the growing population. The school was referred to as "ivy-covered" in the school alma mater. Due to unsafe conditions, it was razed in 1970. The Lampasas Independent School District still owns this vacant land, often used for sports practice, on Western Avenue. (Present, DP.)

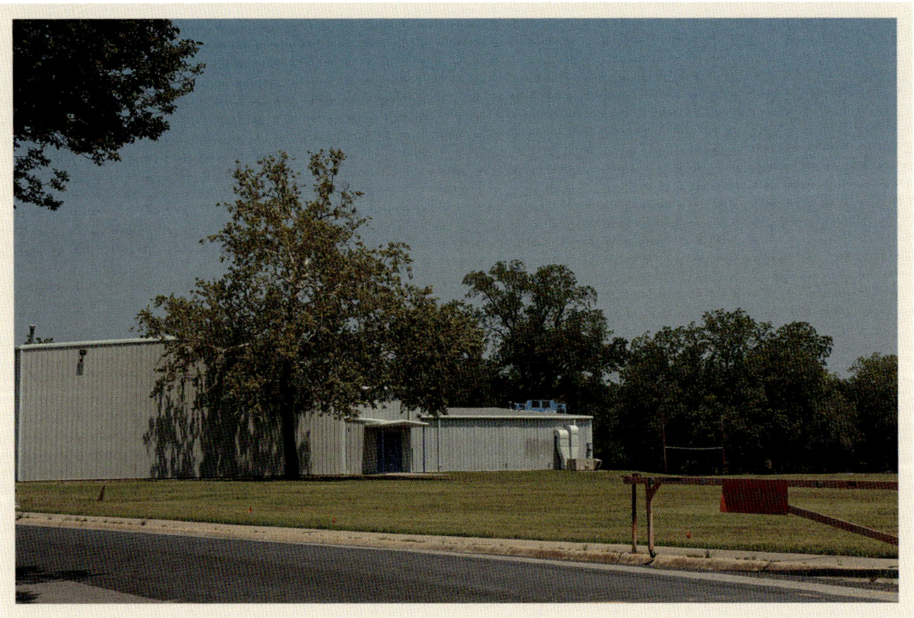

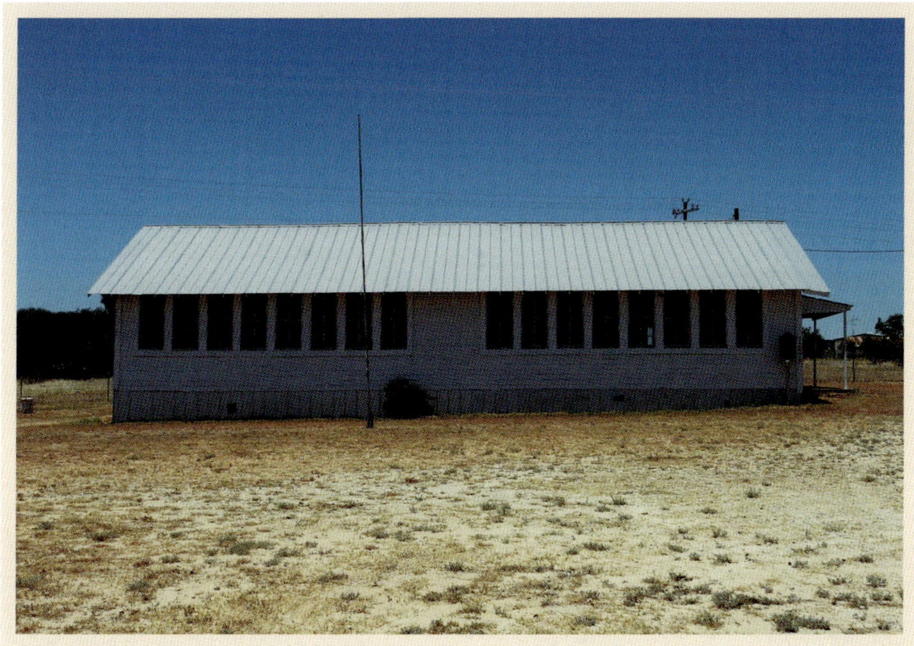

The Nix schoolhouse, pictured below, was built on Nix Road (FM 580 West) in 1920 and remained in use until 1952, at which time the school consolidated with Lampasas. The building, which incorporates lumber from the original c. 1895 schoolhouse, is now a community center. In 1878, Nix was named by an old German man who suggested *Nichts*, meaning "nothing" in his native language. (Present, AM.)

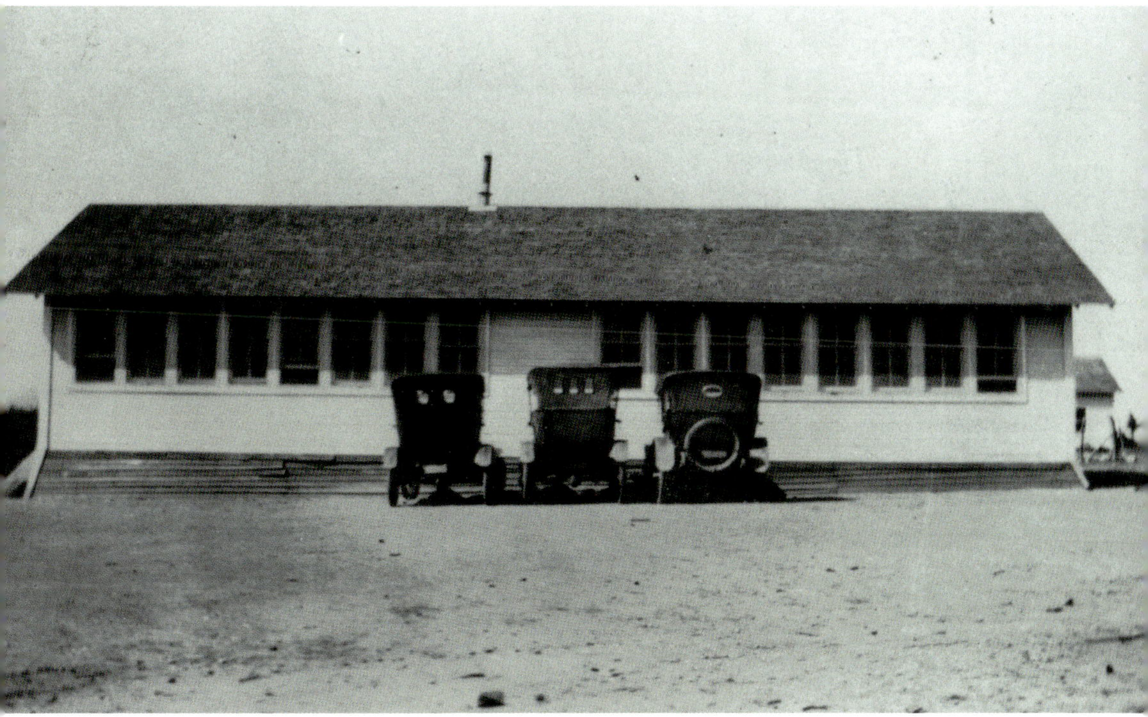

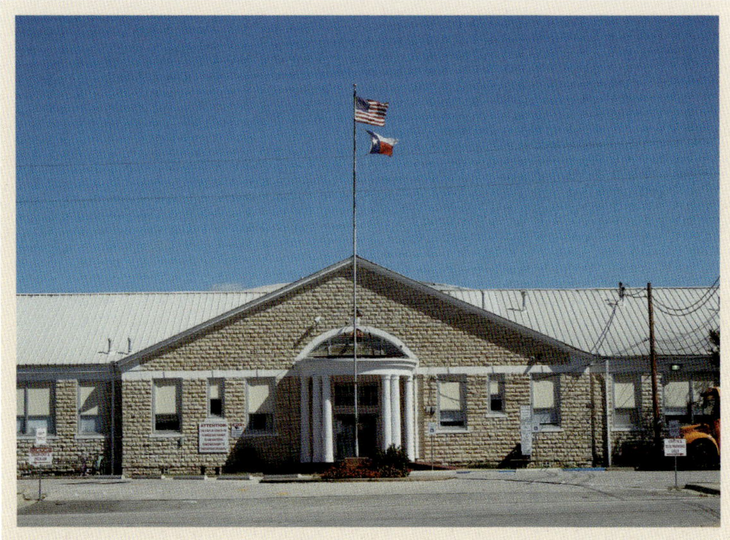

High school students in Lometa attended classes in a wooden building owned by the Lometa Educational Association (LEA) College until this two-story brick building (below) was erected in 1906. It had two large rooms on each floor and an auditorium with a stage and an organ on the second floor. The Works Progress Administration built the present one-story native limestone structure on the same lot in 1942. It was the first Lometa school with running water and indoor plumbing. Pre-kindergarten through high school classes are held here today. (Present, AM.)

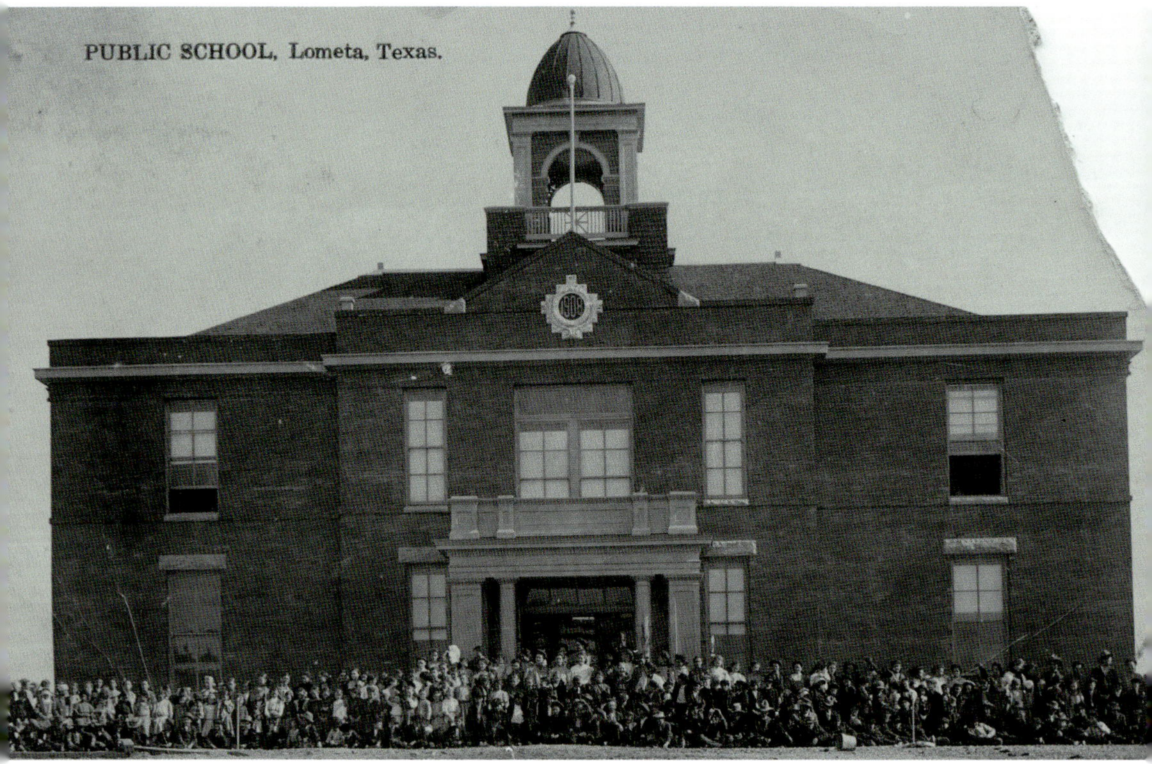

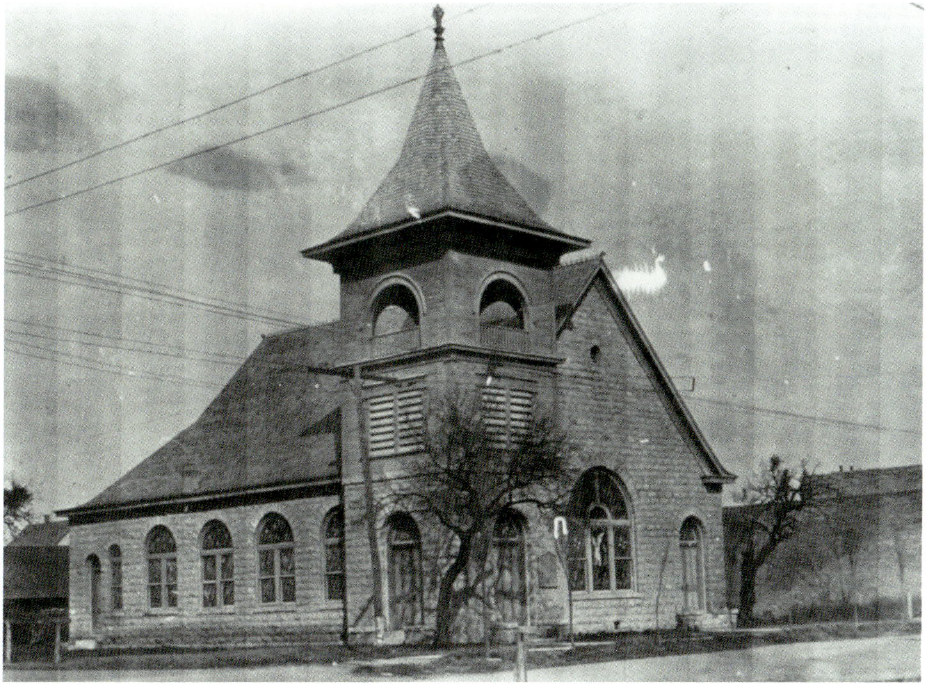

In 1905, the Disciples of Christ built the Lampasas Central Christian Church of hand-quarried, native limestone on the northeast corner of Third and Chestnut Streets. The lot was purchased by the congregation for $800, and a subscription paid for the stone. Charles Logan of Houston was hired as the architect; the Casbeer brothers did the stonework. The total cost of the building was $6,000. The Resurrection stained-glass window dominates the front. It has served as a funeral chapel since 2006. (Present, DP.)

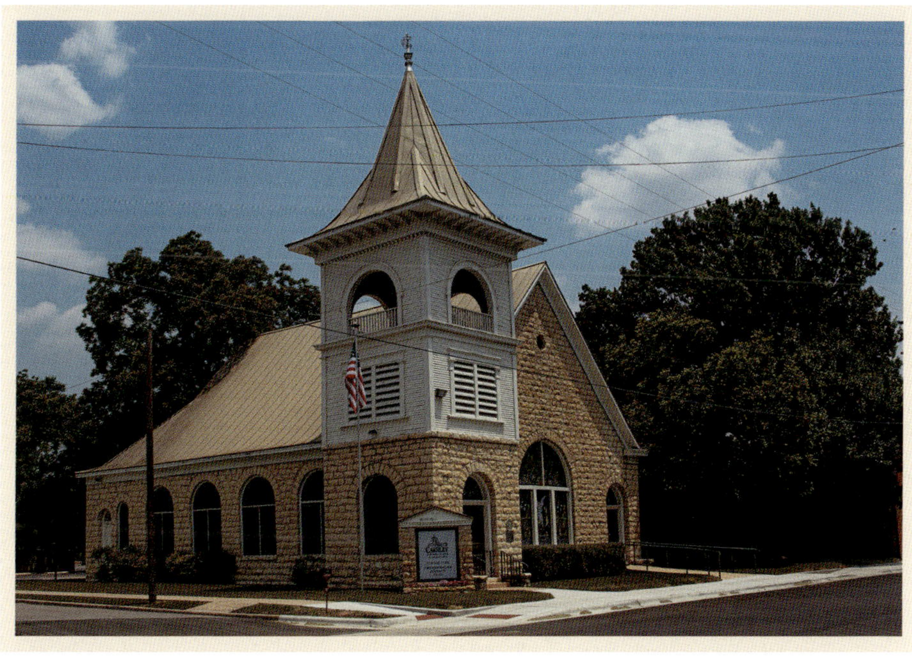

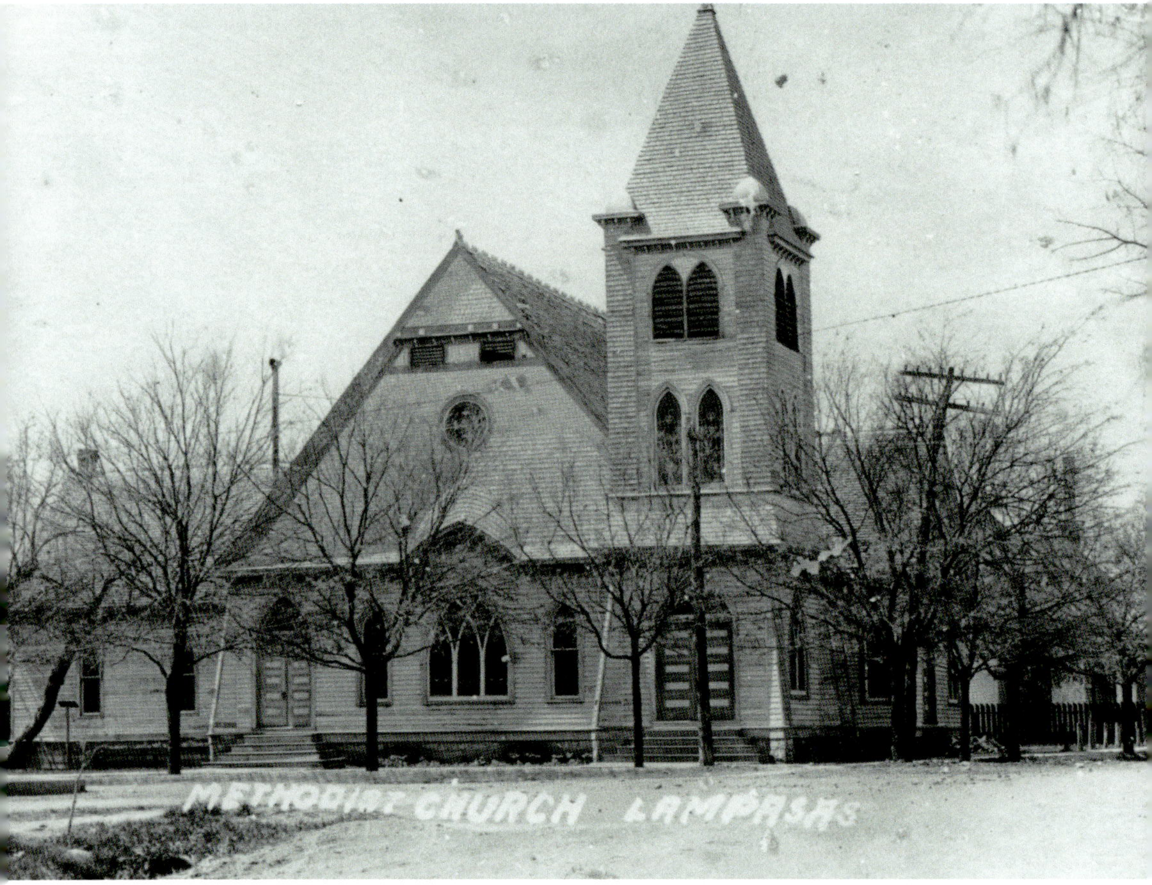

The First United Methodist Church moved into this Gothic Revival structure built for $7,500 on the corner of Grand Avenue (now Key Avenue) and Second Street in 1900. In 1947, the building was remodeled and a pipe organ was installed for $30,000. The congregation remained in this spot until 1966, when it moved to its current location on US Highway 190 East. Today, Rustler's Junction is at 302 South Key Avenue, selling a variety of Western home decor, clothing, and toys. (Present, DP.)

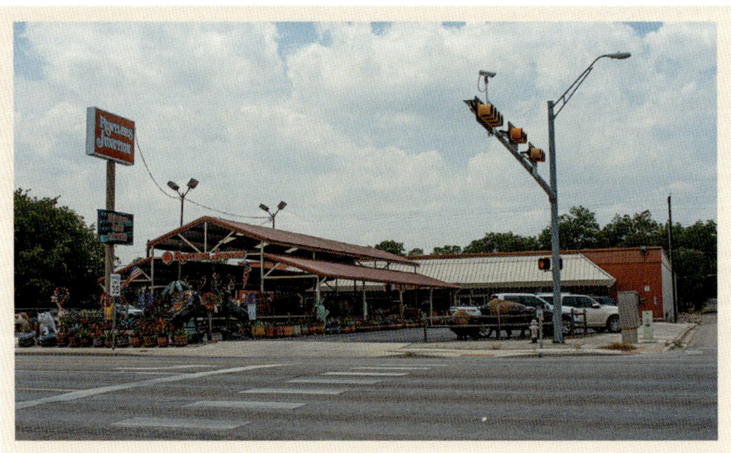

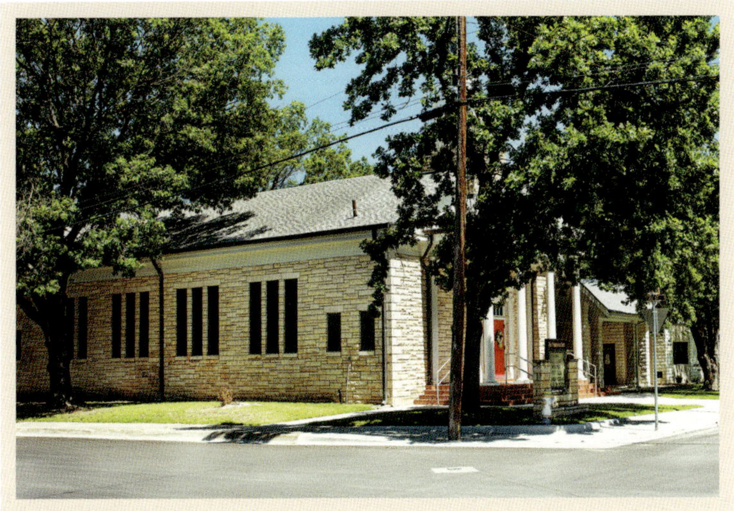

This rock sanctuary (below) at the corner of Third and Chestnut Streets was built in 1916 at a cost of $5,044. The main entrance faced East Third Street. The exterior was constructed in "rubble range" style. The opaque green and white window panes were of wavy glass. In 1959, this building was razed and the present sanctuary was constructed of native stone. The faceted-glass windows were added in 2008. The main entrance is now on South Chestnut Street. (Present, DP.)

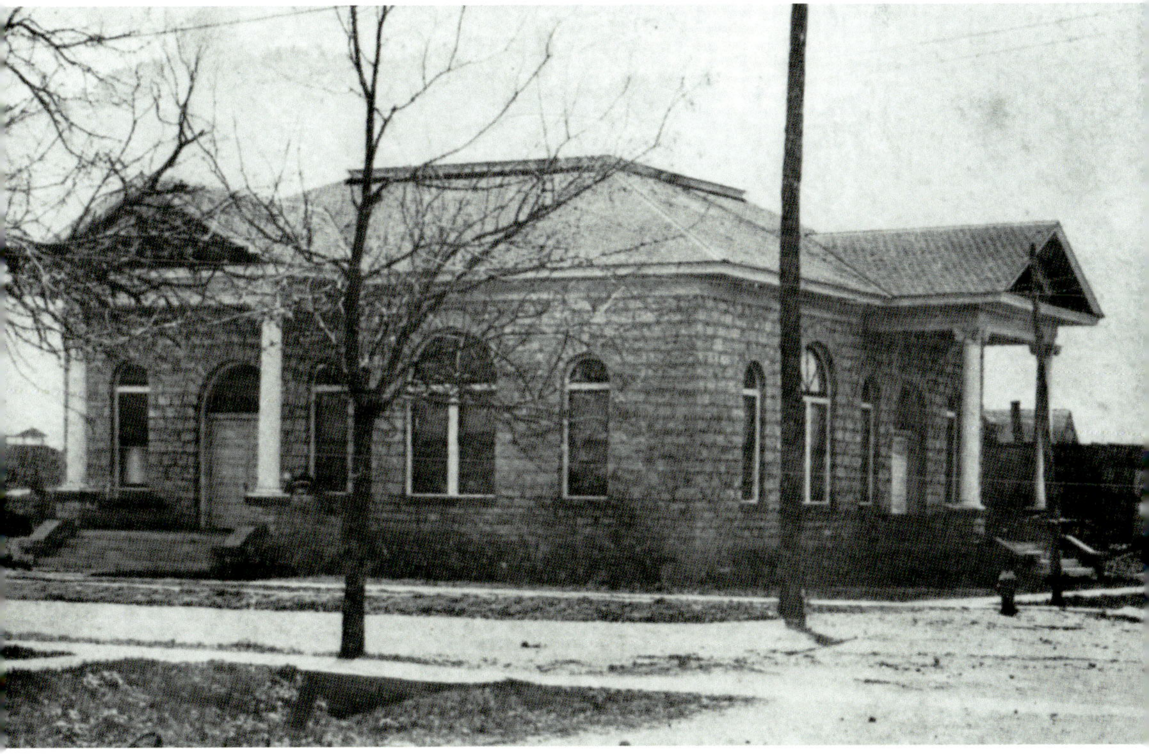

St. Mary's Catholic Church was first located on the corner of West Fifth and Broad Streets. The church moved to its present address on Key Avenue in the early 1940s. In 1949, a small parochial school and convent were built on the site (below). The native stone Mission-style sanctuary and rectory burned in 1970 and was replaced with the current brick structure in 1972. (Present, JF.)

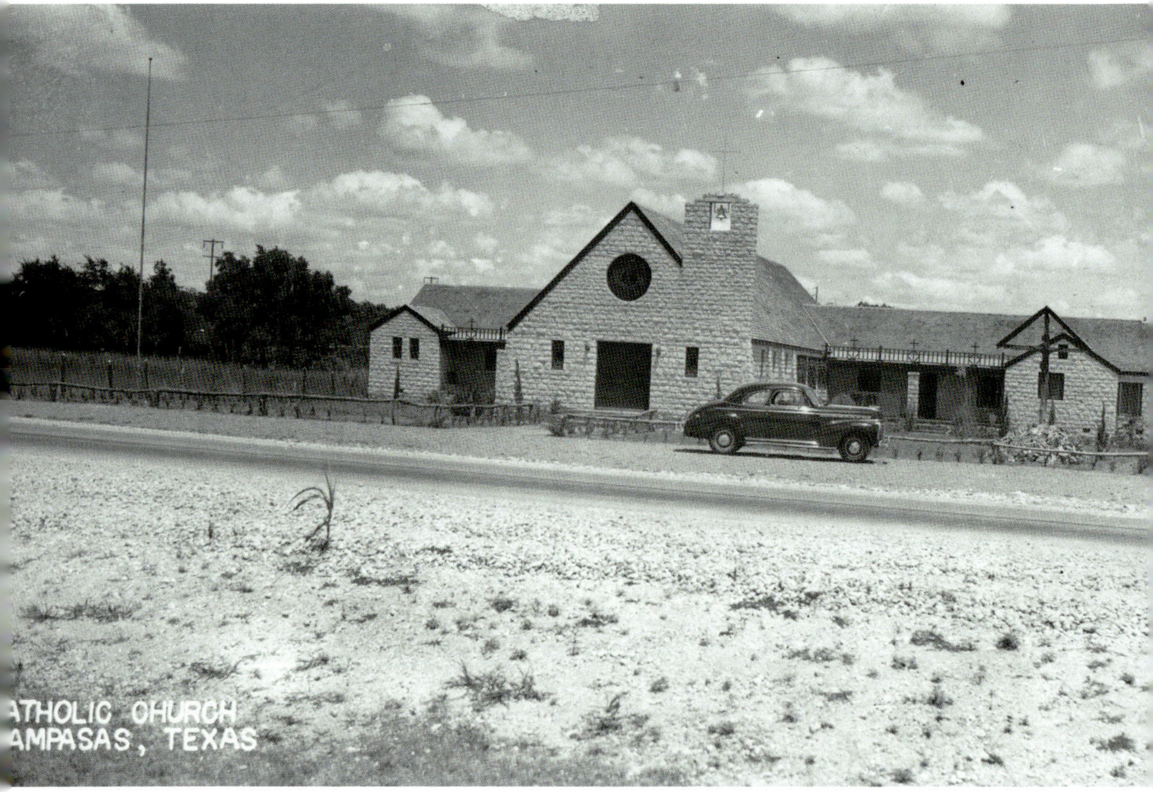

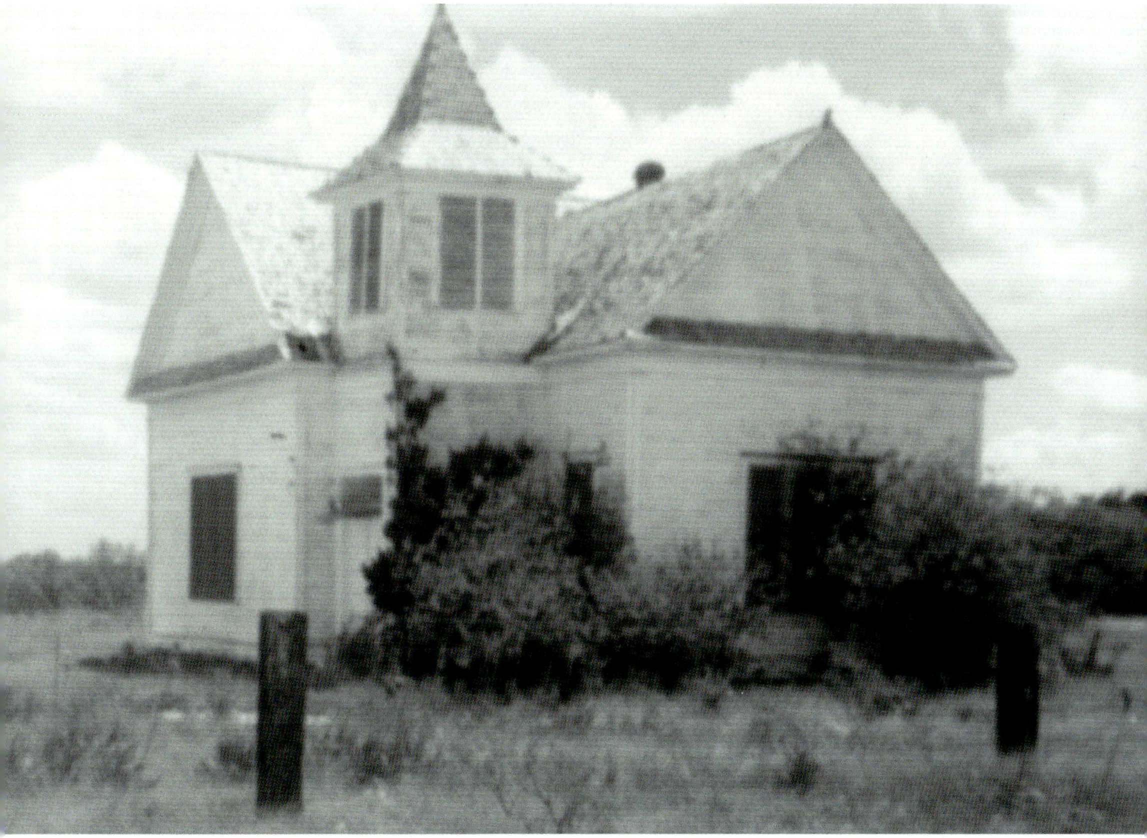

The McCreaville Methodist Church was erected in the early 1900s at the intersection of County Roads 1255 and 1299. Named for the James and Sara McCrea family, the early settlement of McCreaville was near the Burnet County line in the southern part of Lampasas County. Today, nothing remains of the old settlement; a modern home has replaced the McCreaville church. (Past, collection of Sylvia Eddy; present, DP.)

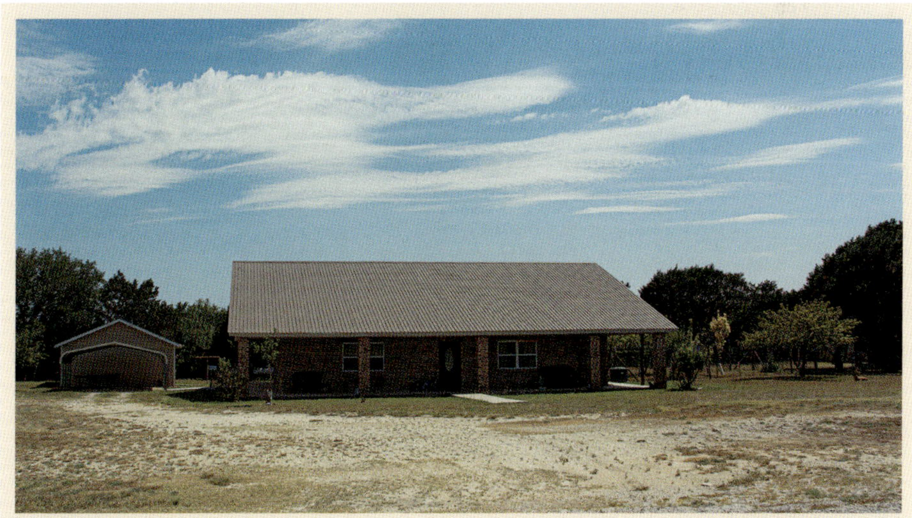

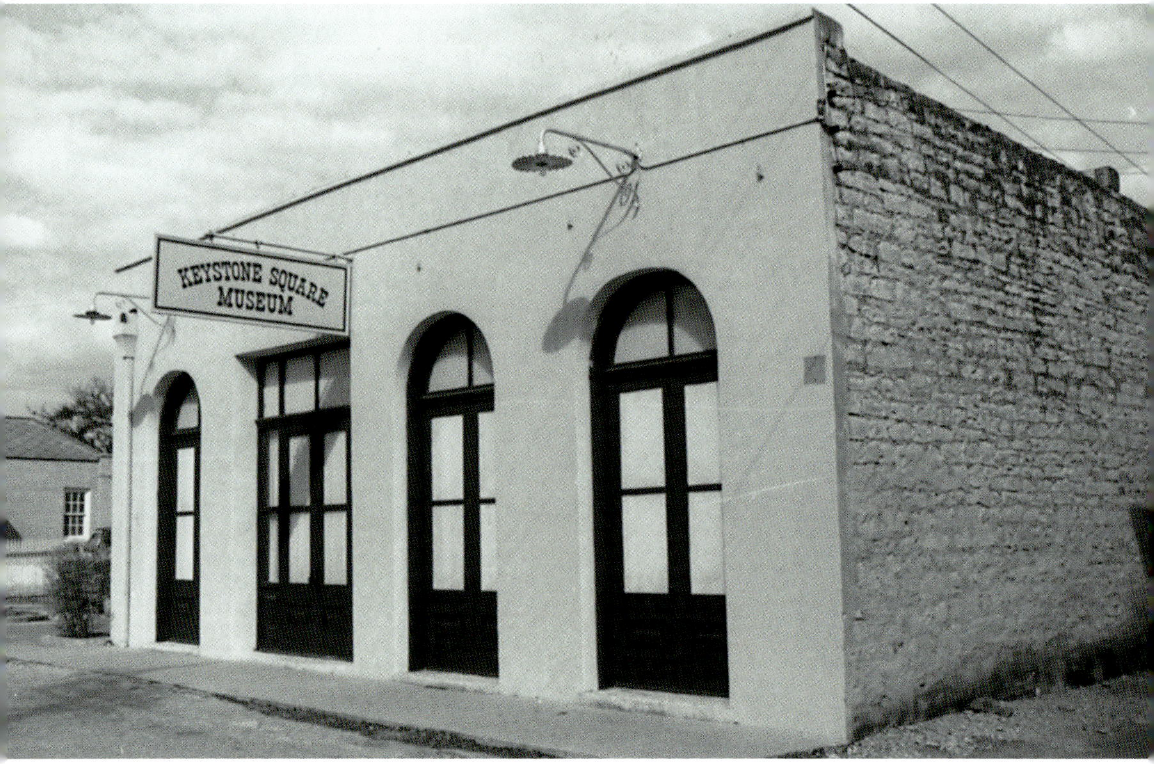

The Lampasas County Museum Foundation, Inc., was organized in 1975 as part of the Lampasas Bicentennial Committee. The museum moved to this 1890s limestone building at 303 South Western Avenue in 1982. Having recently housed Ross "Bud" Bailey's plumbing and sheet metal shop, the building's floorboards were flipped to hide the oil stains. The museum has remodeled several times, most recently in 2020. The museum changed its name from the Keystone Square Museum to the Lampasas County Museum in 2014. (Present, AM.)

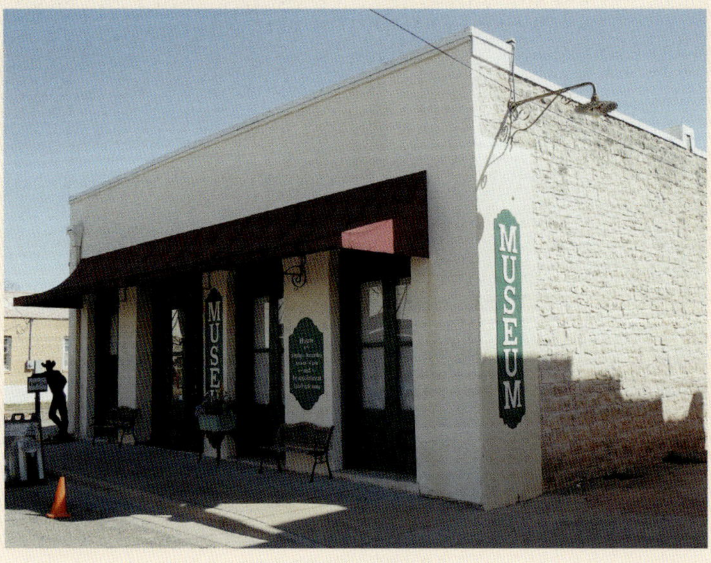

CHAPTER 5

PLACES THAT SERVE

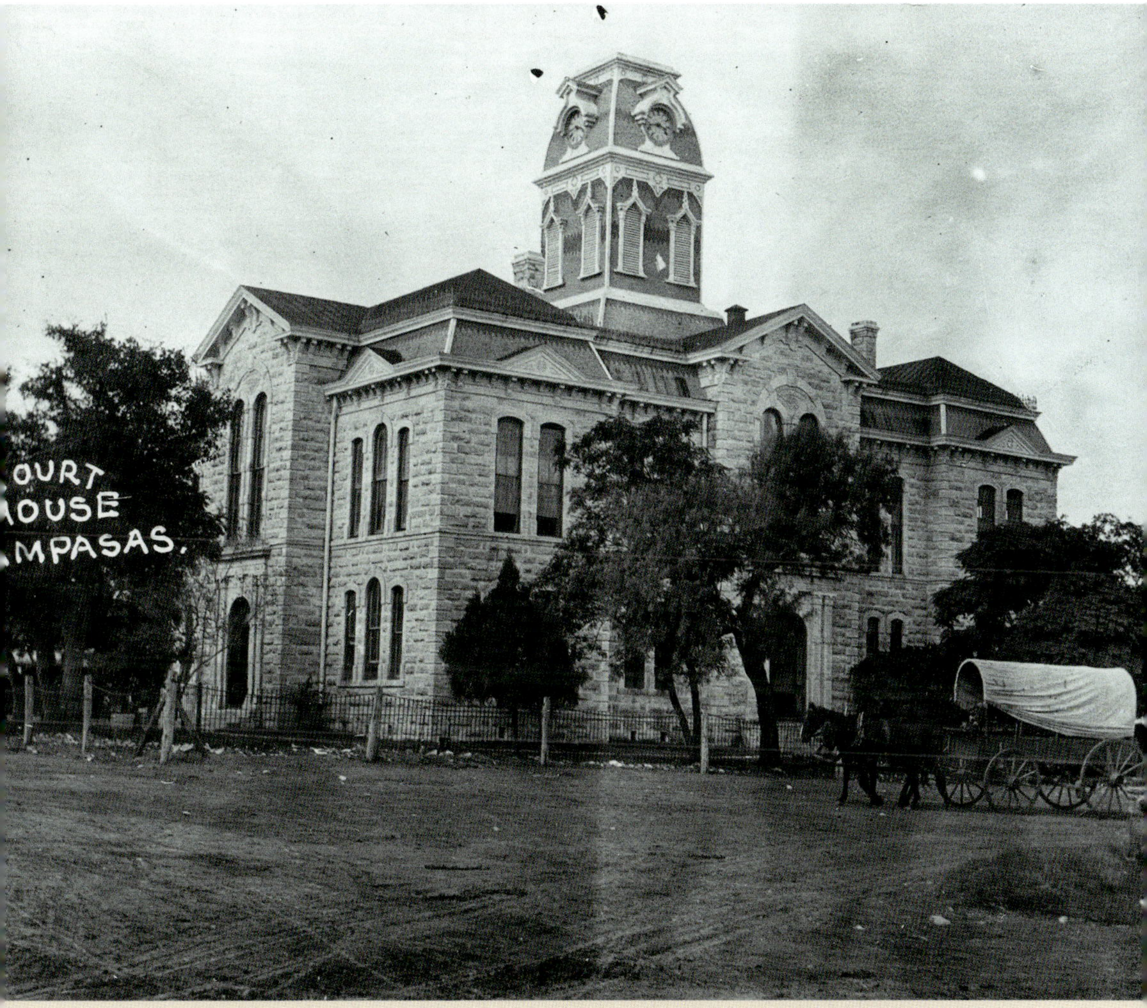

Pictured here is the Lampasas County Courthouse, which sits at the center of the town square. The city of Lampasas is the county seat. Wagon tracks are visible crisscrossing the dirt lot surrounding the building. This photograph dates to after 1884, as that is the year the clock was installed.

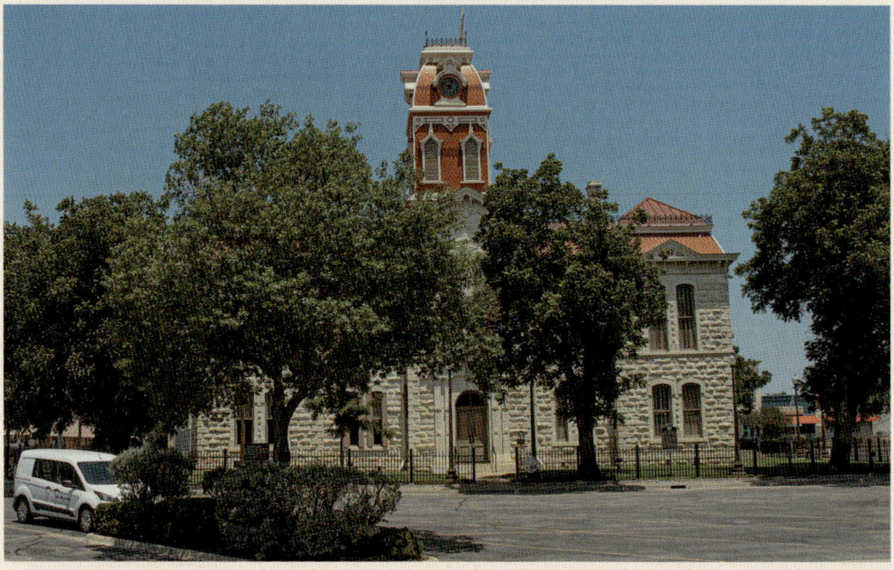

Designed by W.C. Dodson in the Second Empire style, the Lampasas County Courthouse was completed in 1884 at 501 East Fourth Street. It is the third-oldest courthouse still in use in Texas. This early view of the south facade (below) features a horse-drawn wagon and carriage parked in a dirt yard in front of the building. Aside from paved parking and an iron fence surrounding the structure, the courthouse exterior appears much the same now as it did in the 1880s. (Present, DP.)

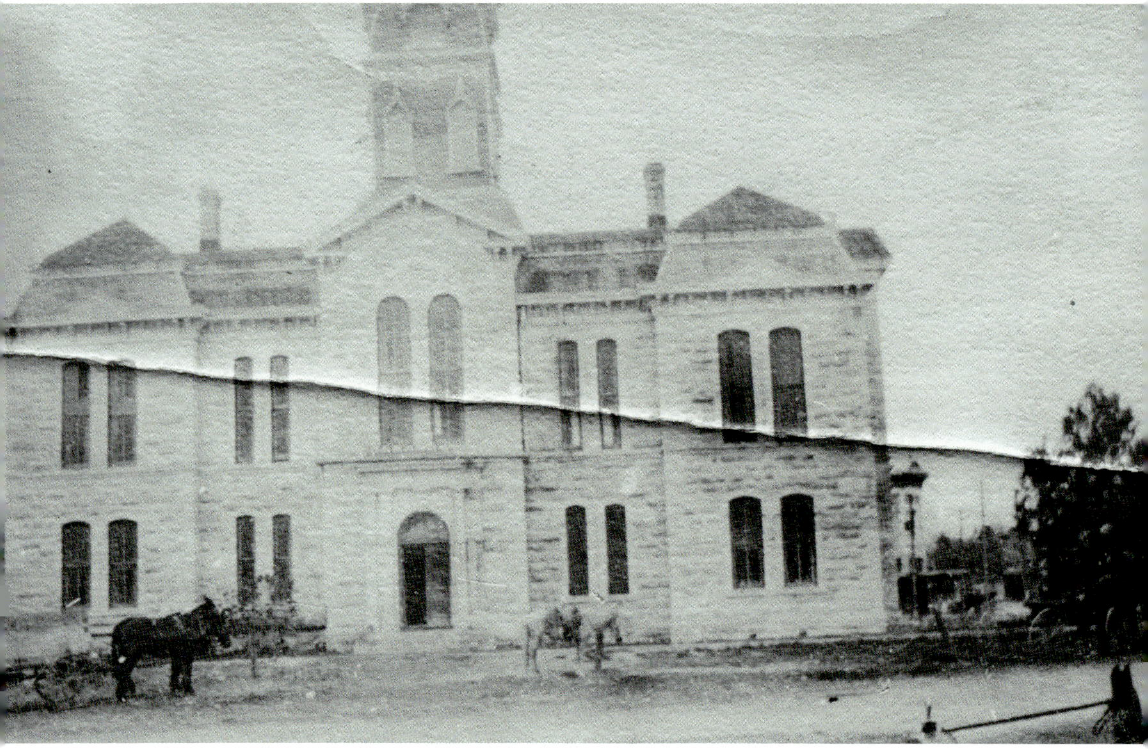

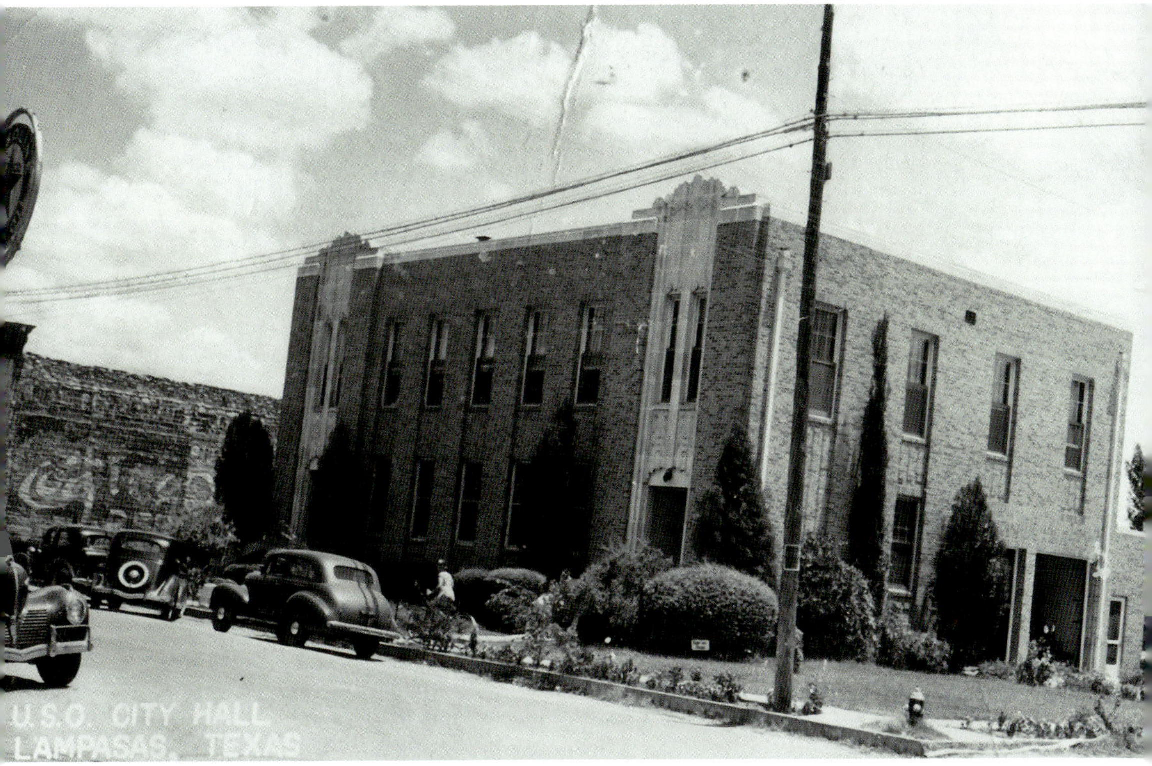

The original Art Deco city hall, built from 1931 to 1932, housed the public library, city offices, and the fire department. The library was on the second floor and city offices on the ground floor. The fire department, including the chief's residence, was on the west side. Community organizations met in the basement. Today, the building, renovated and renamed for former mayor Jack Calvert in 2020, is used for city council meetings as well as meetings of various civic organizations. (Present, AM.)

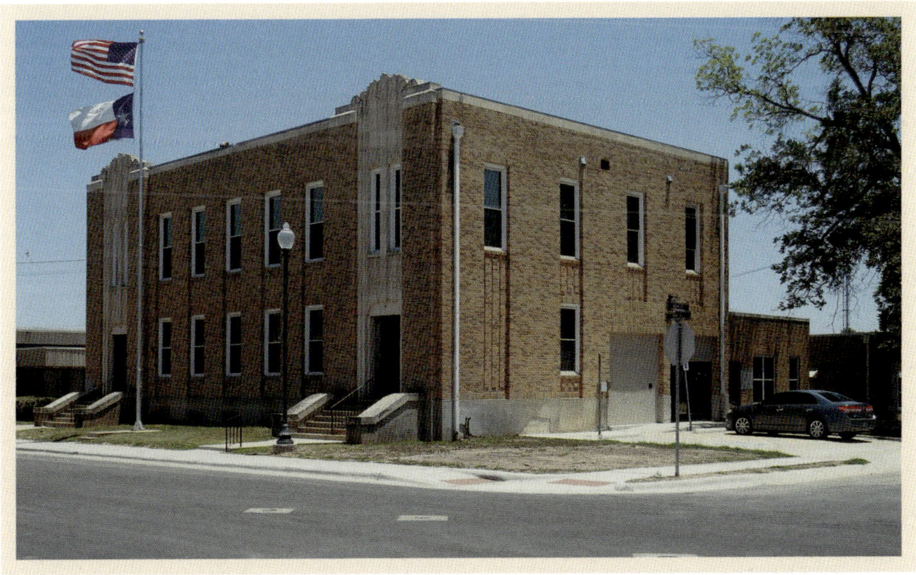

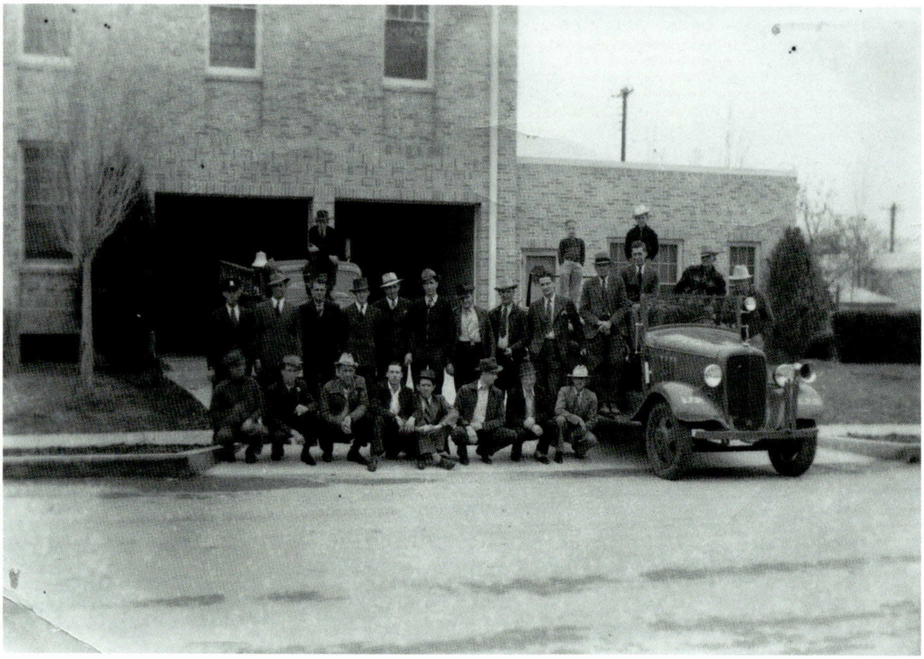

The Lampasas Fire Department moved a couple of times before landing on the west side of the old city hall at 403 South Main Street. The department remained there from the early 1930s to 1989, when it relocated to the northwest corner of East Fourth and South Main Streets. Today, the fire department is in a new building at 1107 East Fourth Street, and the Lampasas Municipal Court occupies its former spot at 403 South Main Street. (Present, AM.)

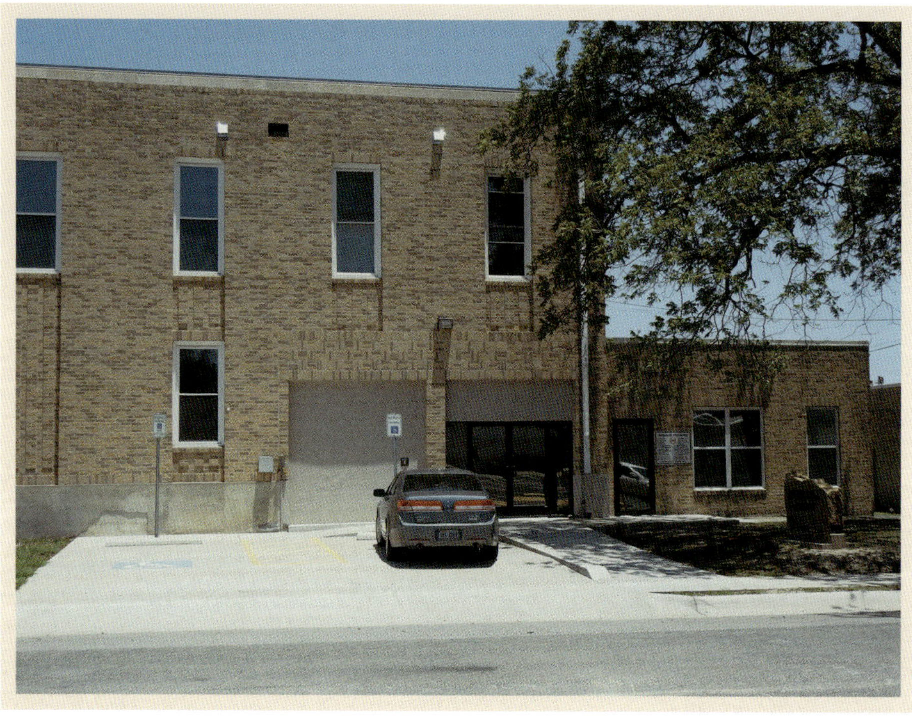

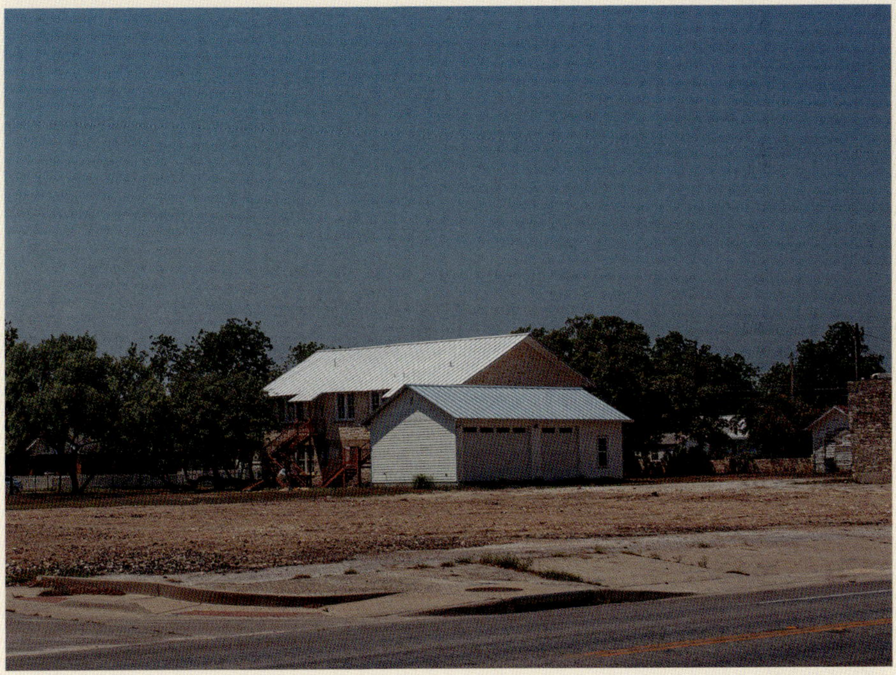

The Lampasas County Jail building was at 410 East Fourth Street. The first jail, pictured below, was built in 1883 of native stone, later covered in stucco. In 1972, the old jail was replaced with a single-story reddish-brown concrete building, which was razed in 2022. A vacant lot is there now. A new jail opened as the Lampasas County Law Enforcement Center at 1210 Barnes Street in March 2021. (Present, DP.)

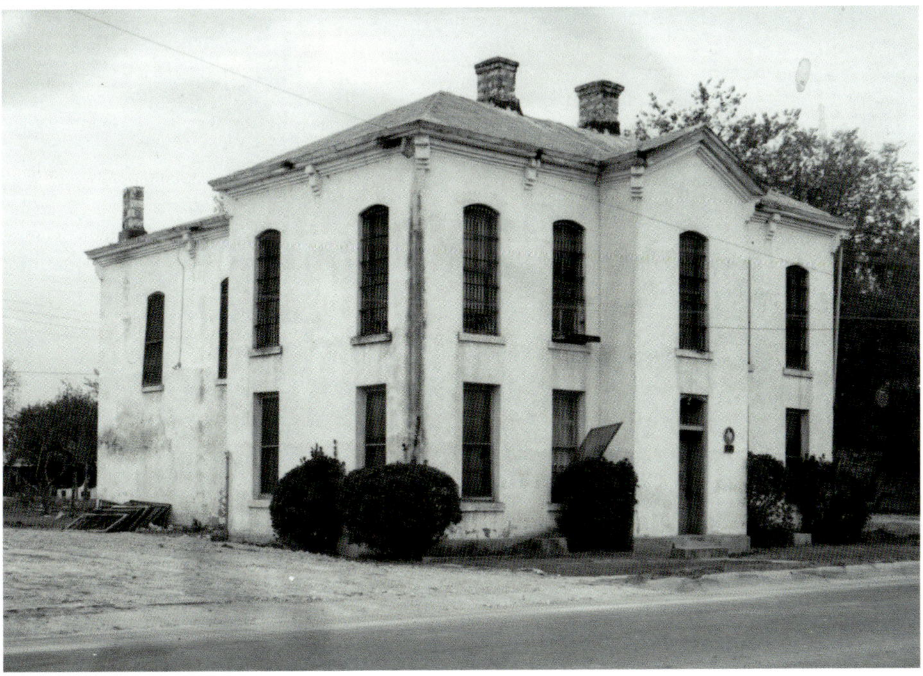

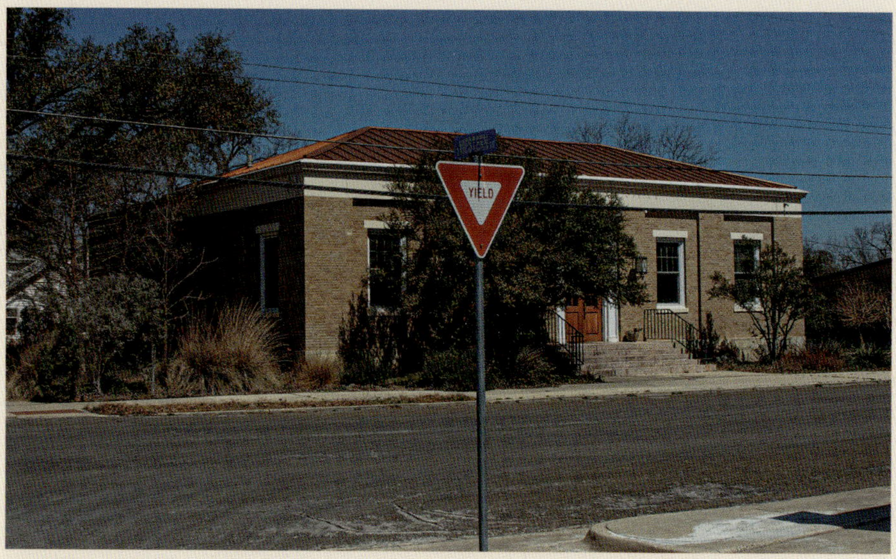

In 1939, the Lampasas *Daily Leader* reported on the new post office at 403 East Second Street and Western Avenue (below), describing it as "well located" with a workroom that "is well lighted and ventilated." The entire building had steam heat, Venetian blinds, and "every modern form of equipment." Not mentioned is the New Deal post office mural, *Afternoon on a Texas Ranch*, by Ethel Edwards now in the Lampasas City Administration Building at 312 East Third Street. The post office is now a private residence. (Present, DP.)

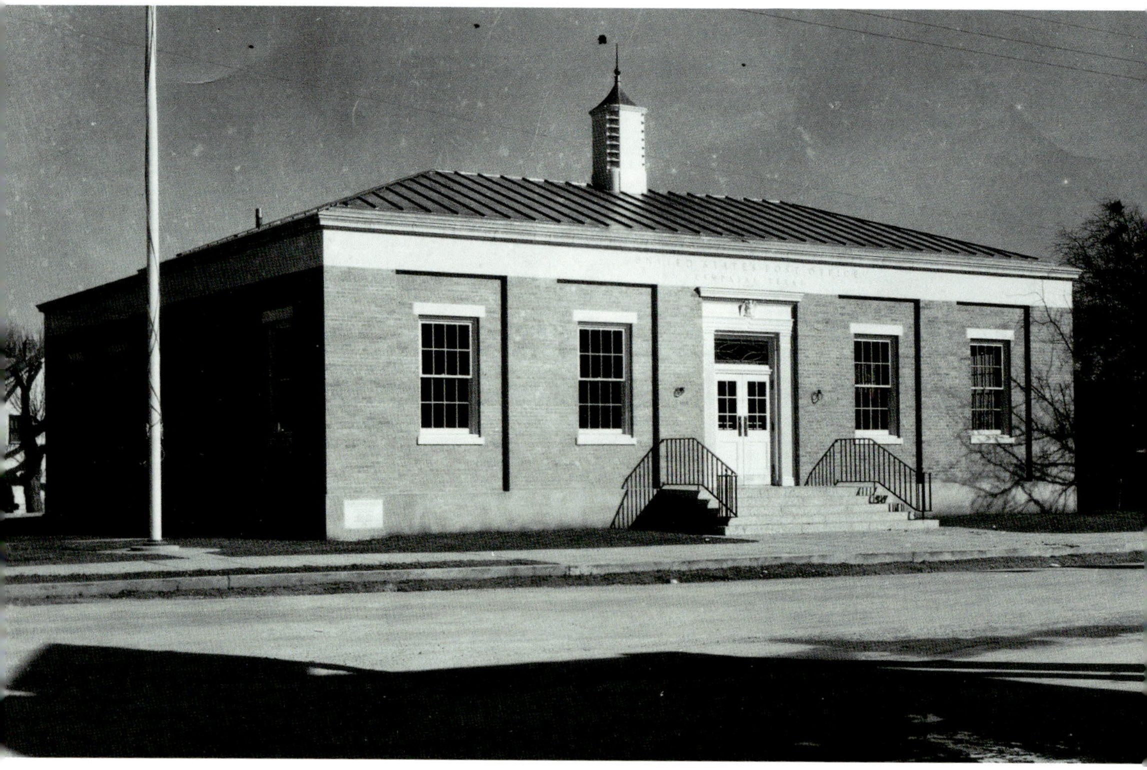

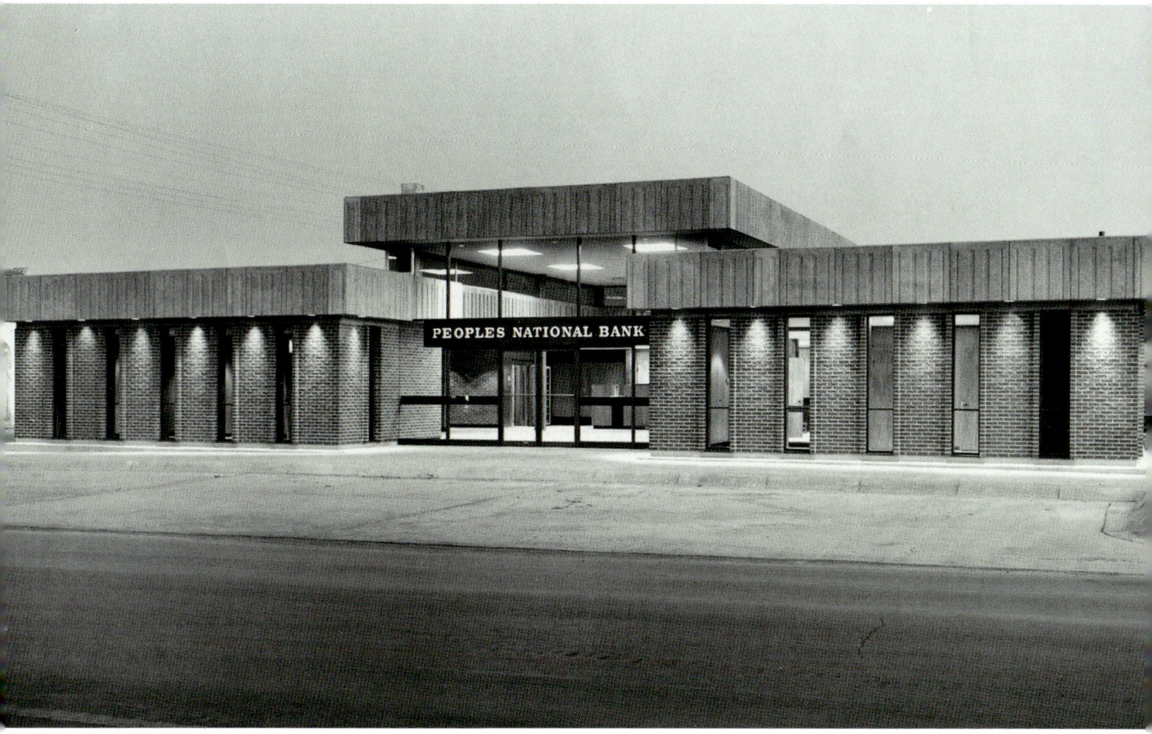

The Peoples National Bank, organized in 1905, moved in 1935 and moved again, finally, to a new building at 312 East Third Street in 1967. The bank closed in 1985. The Lampasas City Administration Building is there now. The building is constructed of glazed brick. It retains its drive-through deposit window, now used by citizens paying city utilities bills. (Past, Virgil Wooten; present, DP.)

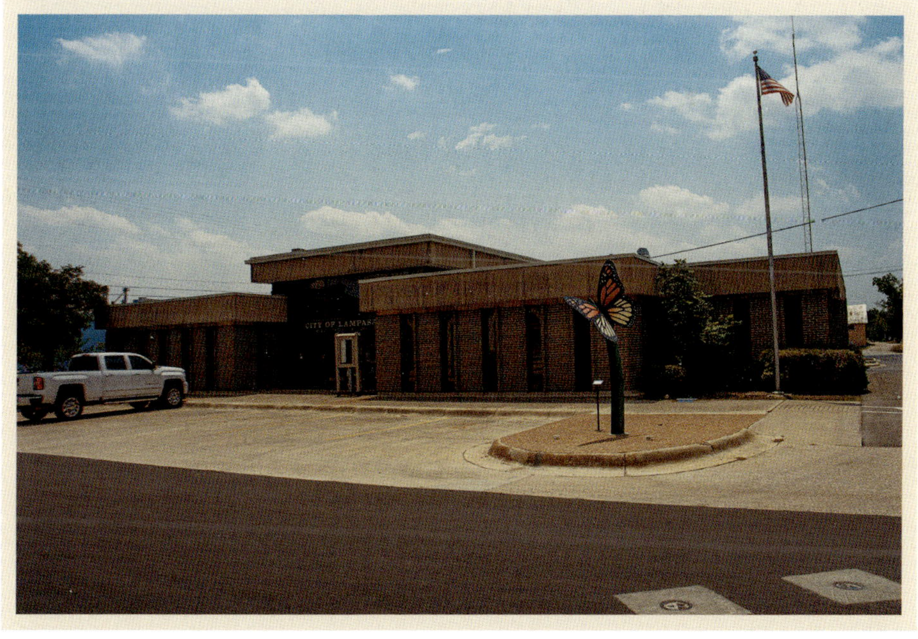

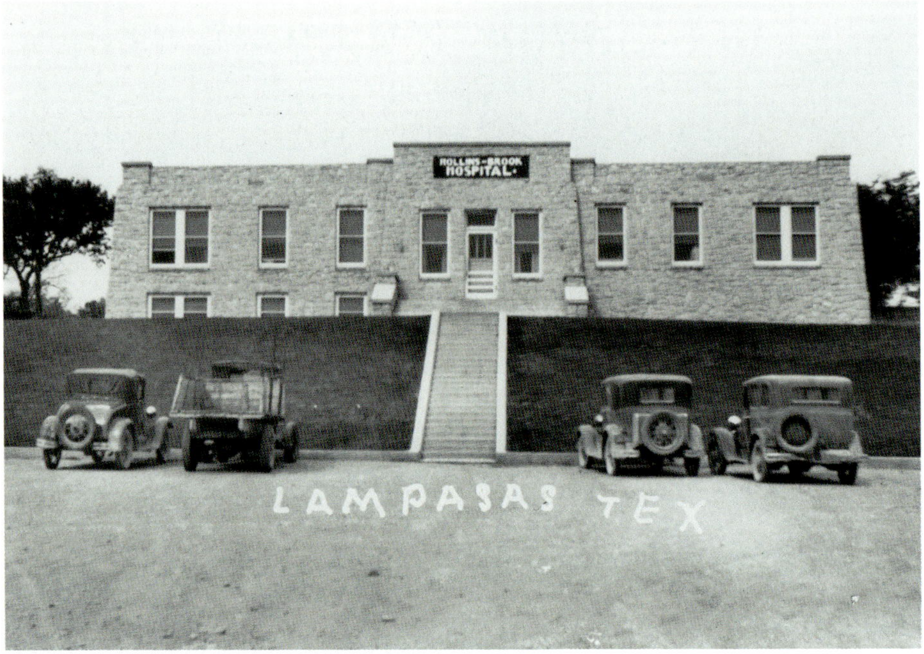

In 1935, physicians Herbert B. Rollins and W.M. Brook established Rollins-Brook Hospital, shown here in 1940. To pay for its construction, community members donated labor or materials and received certificates of credit redeemable for their first hospital charge. In 1991, the hospital closed, but Lampasans rallied and raised enough money to purchase and reopen it as the Rollins-Brook Community Hospital. Today, it is part of AdventHealth, a large nonprofit health care system. The original building, still in use, is behind the newer structure. (Present, AM.)

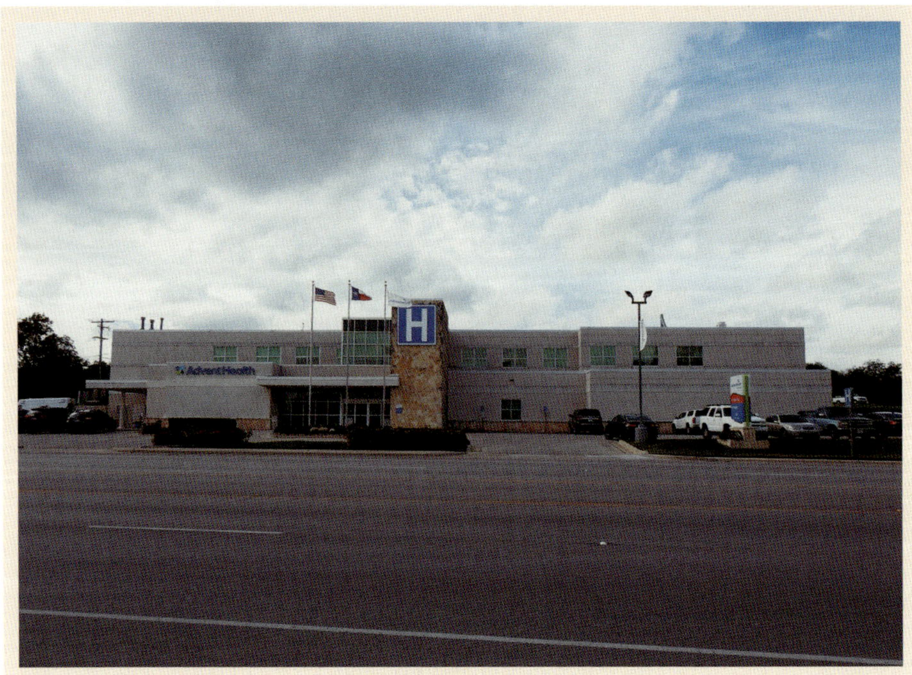

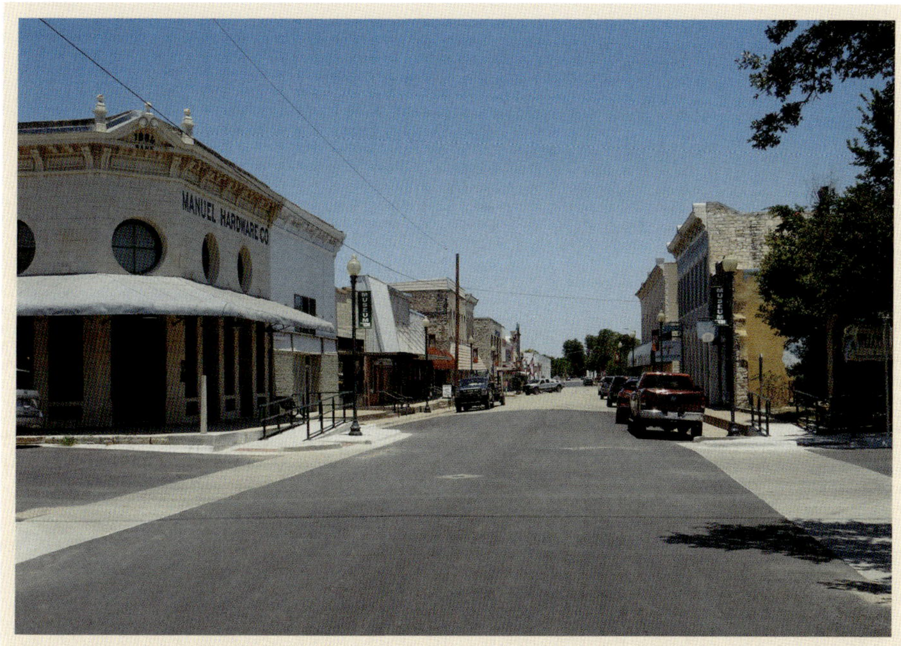

The First National Bank (below) was one of the first tenants in the building now known as the Manuel Hardware Building on the corner of Third Street and Western Avenue. The bank moved to the south side of Third Street before 1890, and subsequent tenants included Barnes and Higdon department store. In 1901, John N. Manuel, Ross W. Bailey, Eugene W. Charles, and P.E. Leatherwood incorporated as the Manuel Hardware Company and opened for business at this site. Today, the building is owned and occupied by the M.D. Abel Company. (Present, AM.)

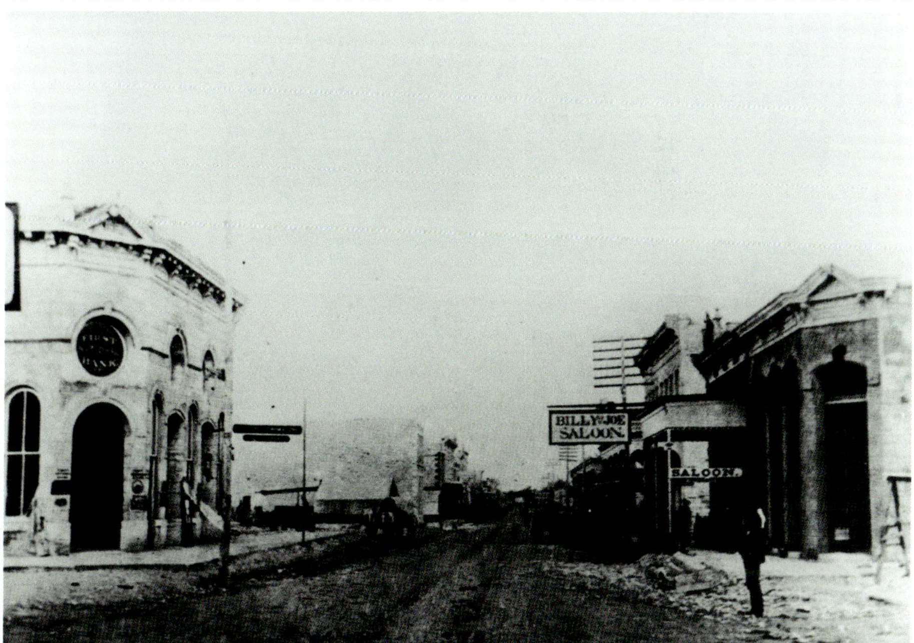

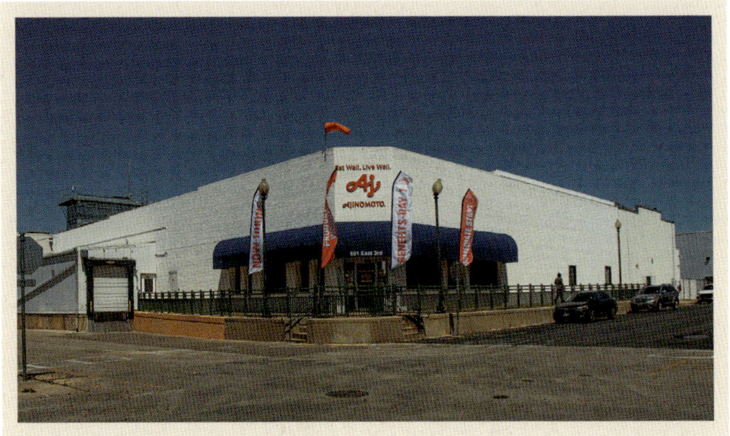

The Stokes Brothers Bank (below) at 601 East Third Street, where Ajinomoto Foods is now, was an unincorporated bank owned by M.Y. and C.D. Stokes. It was open by 1914 and moved to this address in 1922. Their primary clients were ranchers and farmers to whom they made loans. The brothers also ran a wholesale and retail business and were wool and mohair buyers. C.D. Stokes was known as the "Wool King of Texas." (Past, Virgil Wooten; present, JF.)

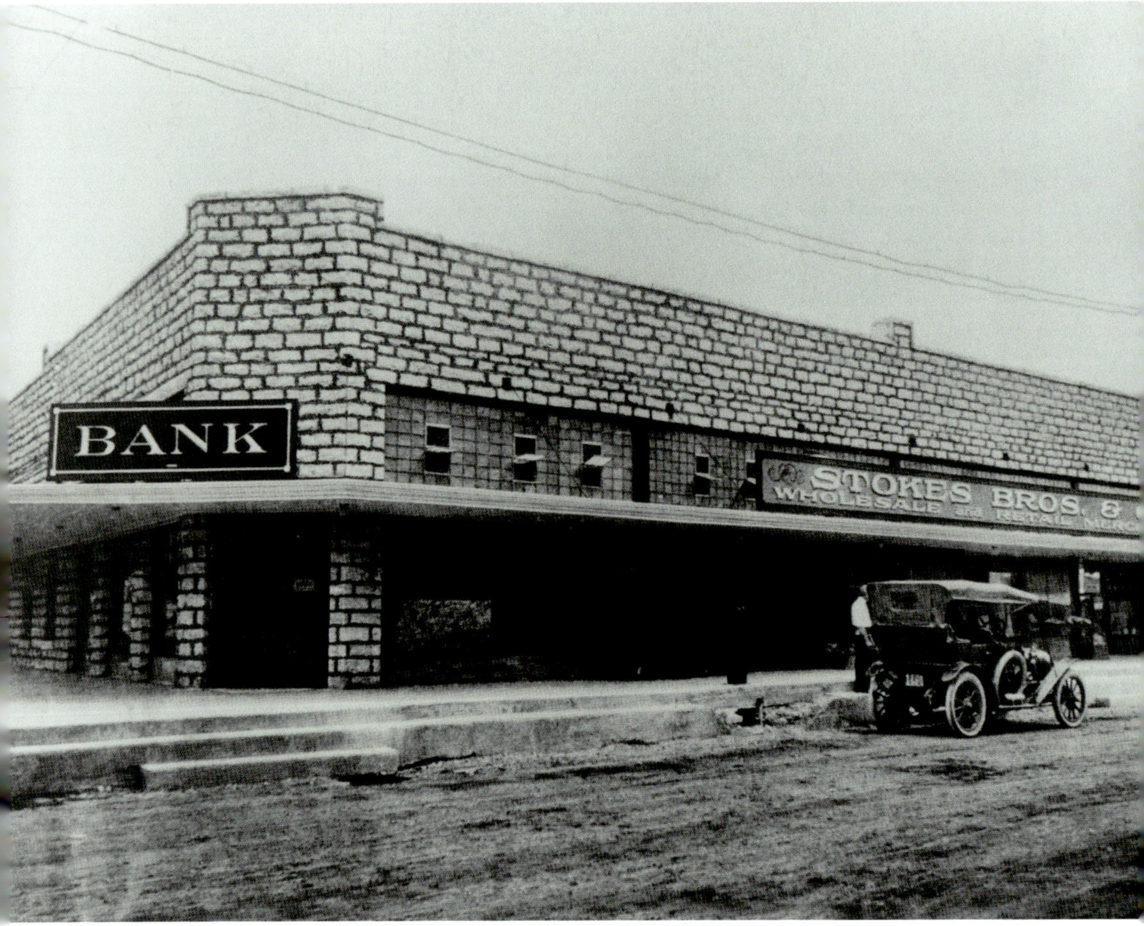

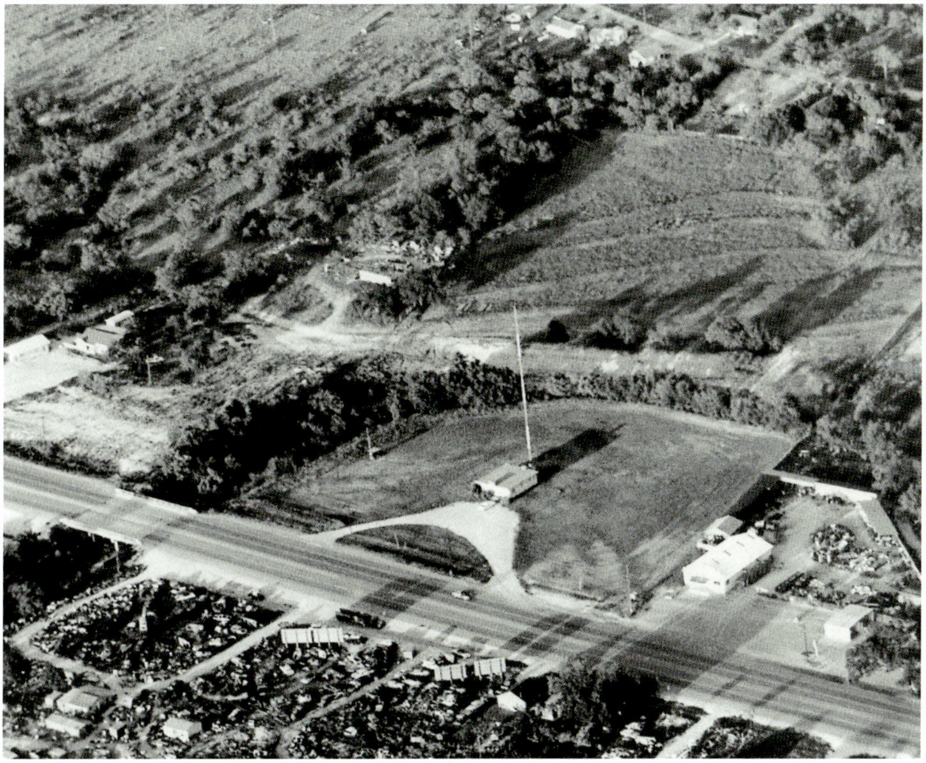

KHIT (later KCYL), the first Lampasas radio station, opened in 1948. Dean Turner (also known as Beasley J. Smith) acquired it in 1952 and operated it until his death in 1968. Gillen's Army Surplus is to the right; Burleson Creek flows along the left and back sides of the lot, where trees are visible. Across the street, June Carroll ran a salvage yard. Today, a truck stop occupies the station's spot, and across the street, the Hoffpauir car dealership is where the salvage yard was. (Past, Gladden Corbin; present, JF.)

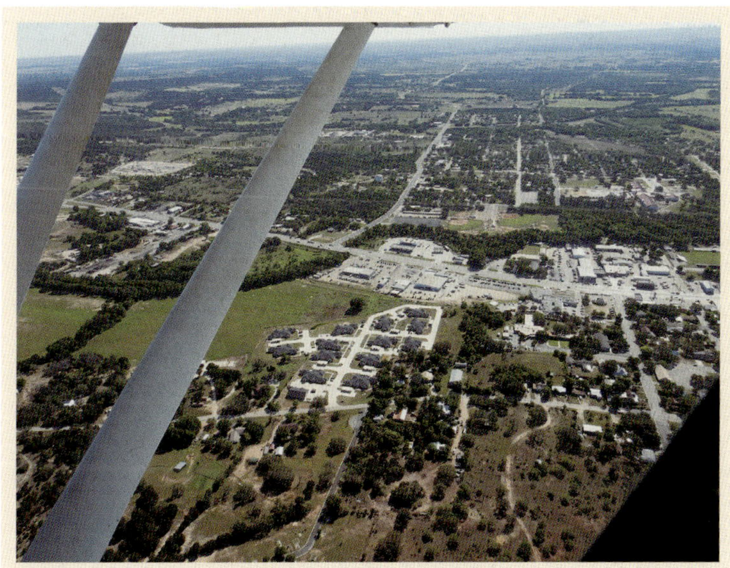

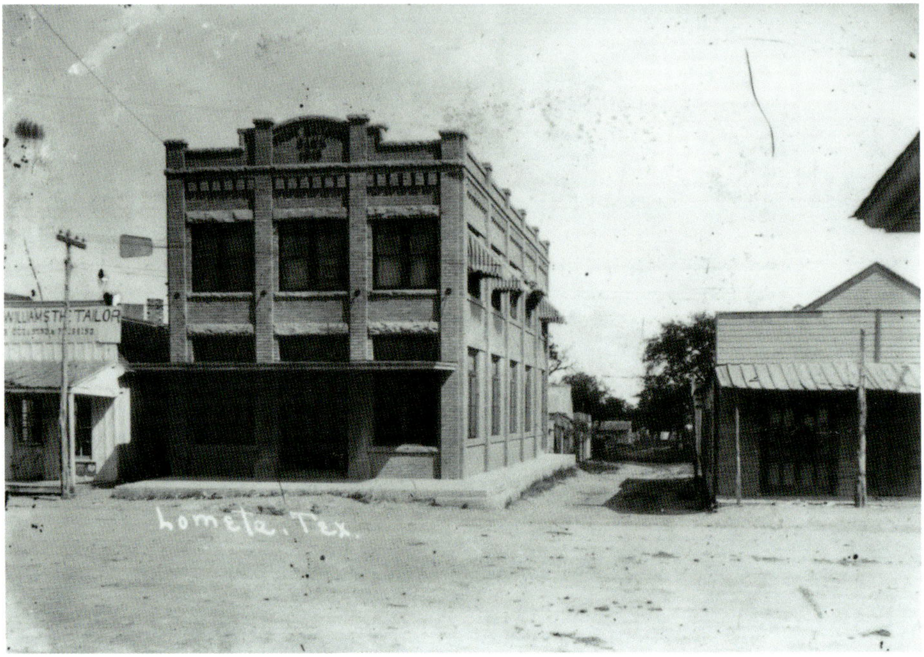

The two-story brick First National Bank of Lometa, built in 1913, stood on Main Street, where North American Coach Risk Management is today. It was the second bank in the city. The Lometa State Bank, which stood across the street, was the first. The First National Bank failed in 1930, at the start of the Depression, following the Lometa State Bank, which closed in 1925. Lometa did not have another bank until 1944, when the Citizens State Bank opened. (Present, AM.)

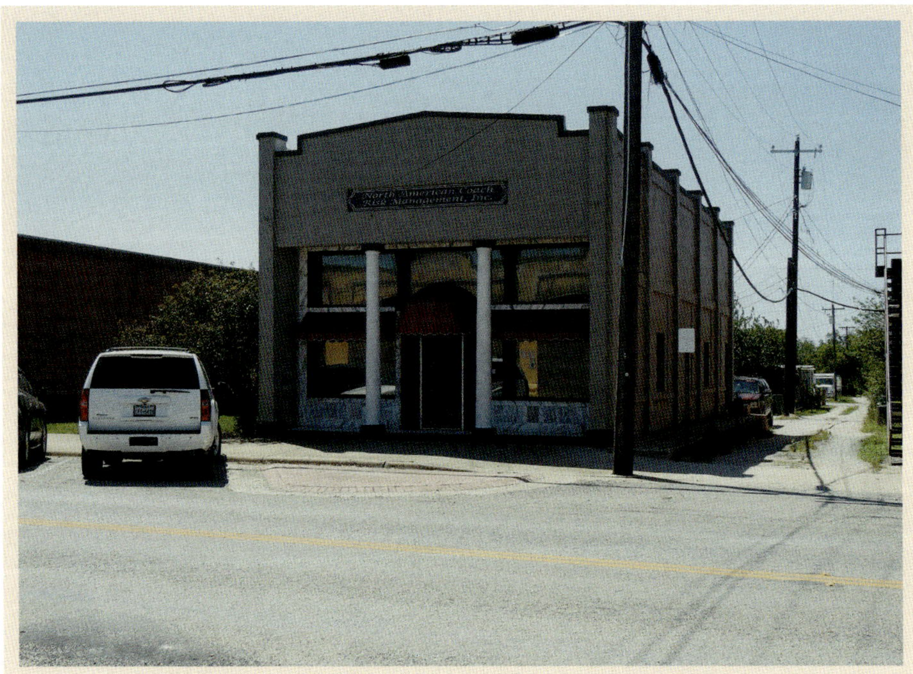

CHAPTER 6

Places to Play

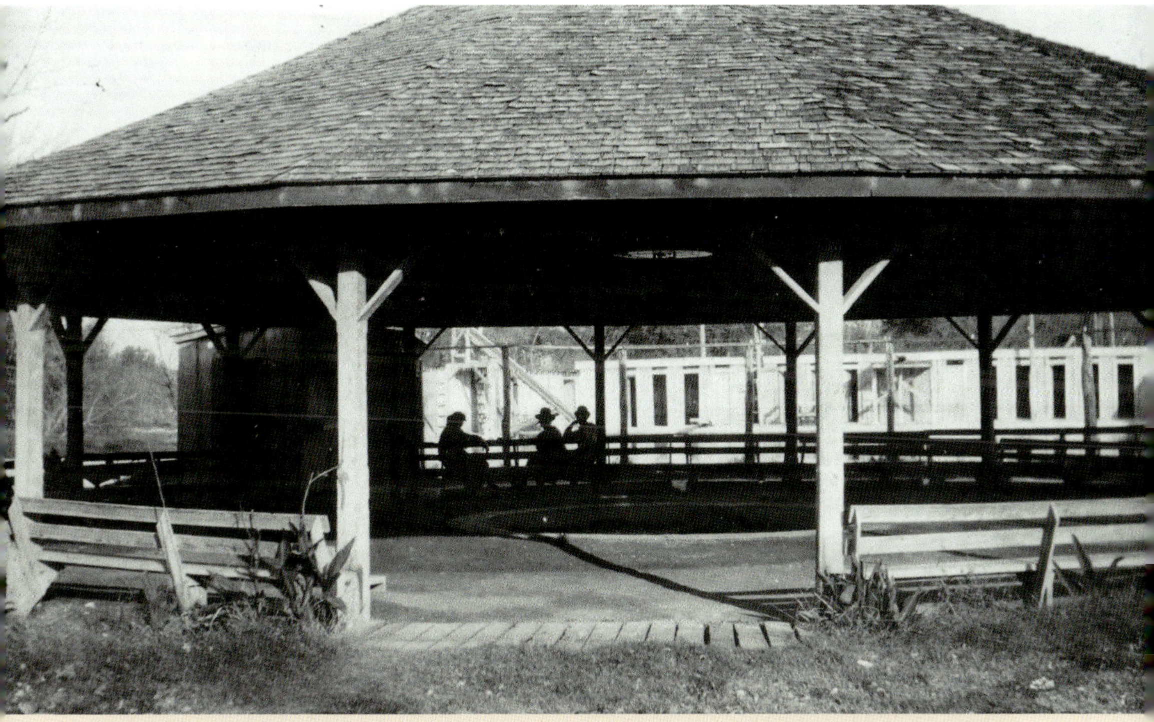

Looking across and through the shingle-roofed Hancock Park Pavilion, the Hancock Springs bathhouse and slide are visible. The pavilion was used for a variety of activities, including, in 1898, a fireman's ball in celebration of San Jacinto Day. (Courtesy, LCHC.)

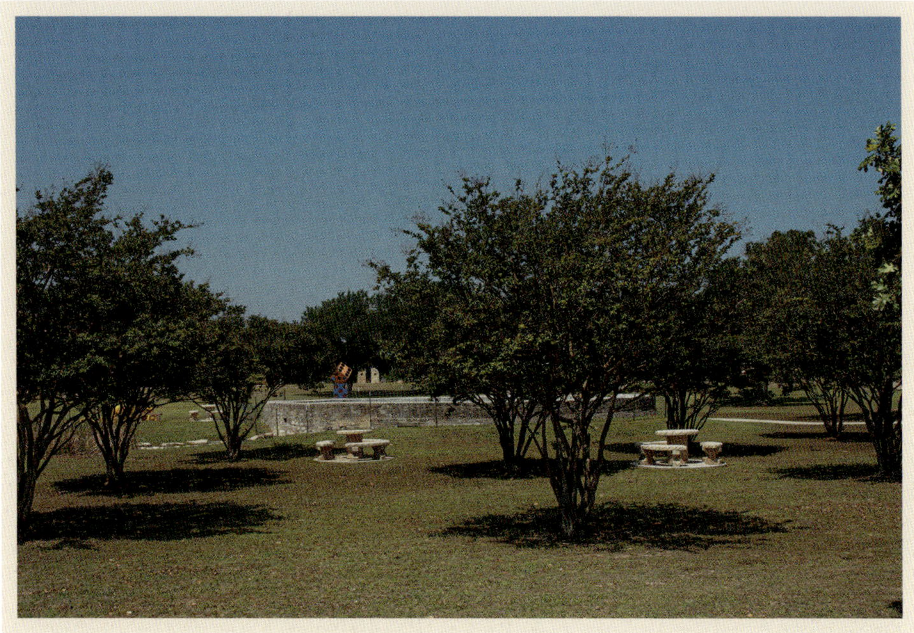

In the early view below, the circular Hanna Springs sulfur pool was level with the surrounding terrain. Today, the pool is surrounded by a limestone wall and a wire fence and is inaccessible to the public. The Lampasas County Historical Commission is working with the city to restore the pool closer to its early-19th-century appearance, with a lower stone wall topped by an iron fence. In 2005, the Lampasas Association for the Arts (LAFTA) installed three sculptures, inaugurating the Hanna Springs Sculpture Garden. (Present, DP.)

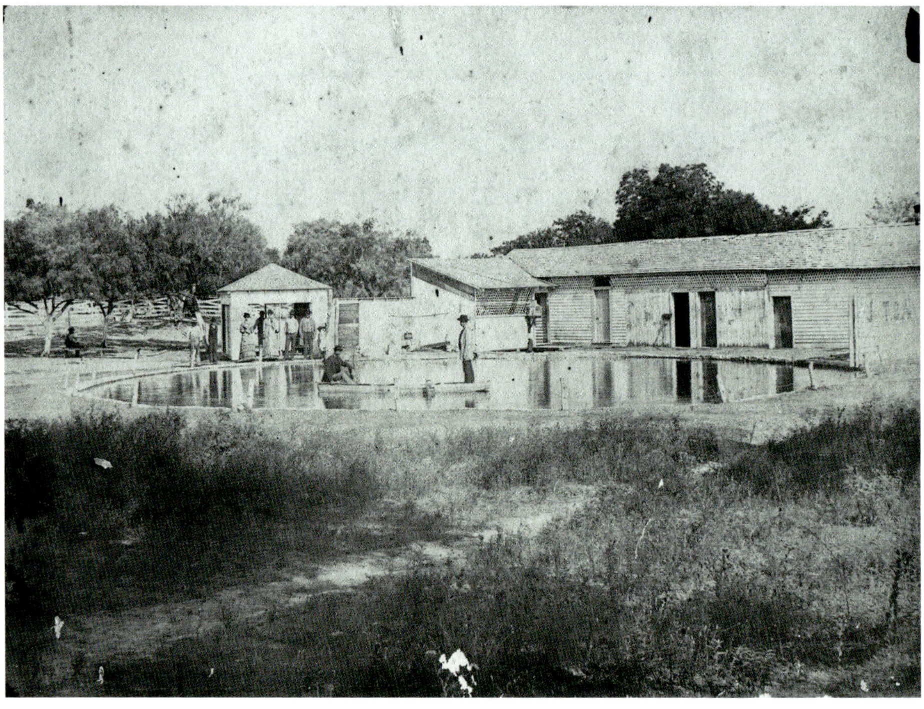

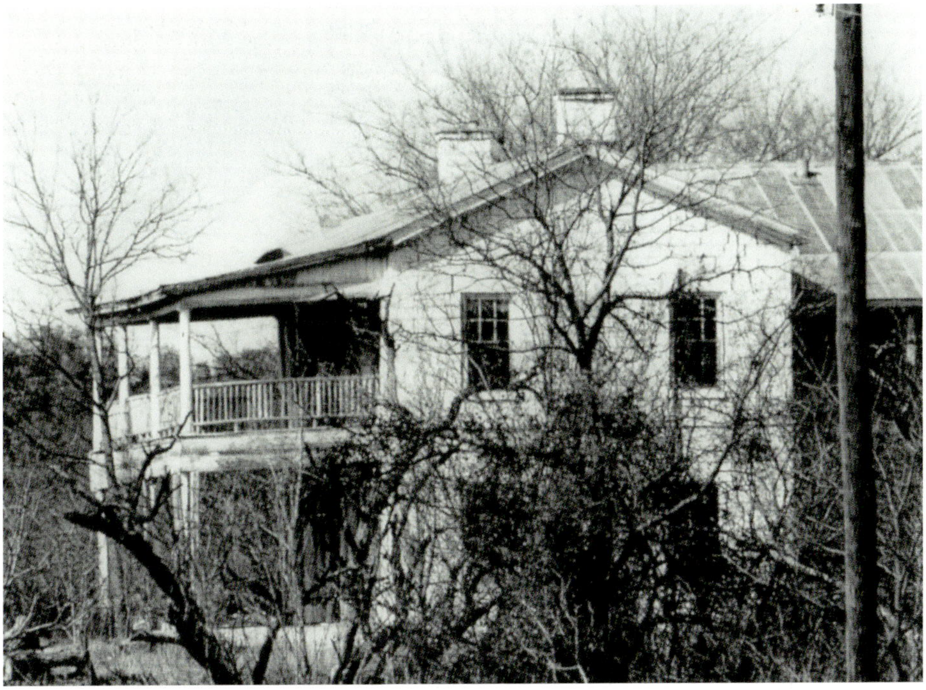

The stone Wintersteen house once sat at 103 North Hackberry Street, where Cooper Spring Nature Park is now. Originally a hotel serving Hanna Springs, it was built by the Central Texas Town Company in the 1880s. In 1920, it served as Crystal Springs Sanitarium. Twenty-six years later, Arthur and Mamie Wintersteen purchased it for their home and rented out rooms and apartments. After Arthur's death in 1982, the house was moved to Salado, where it is now a commercial office building. (Present, DP.)

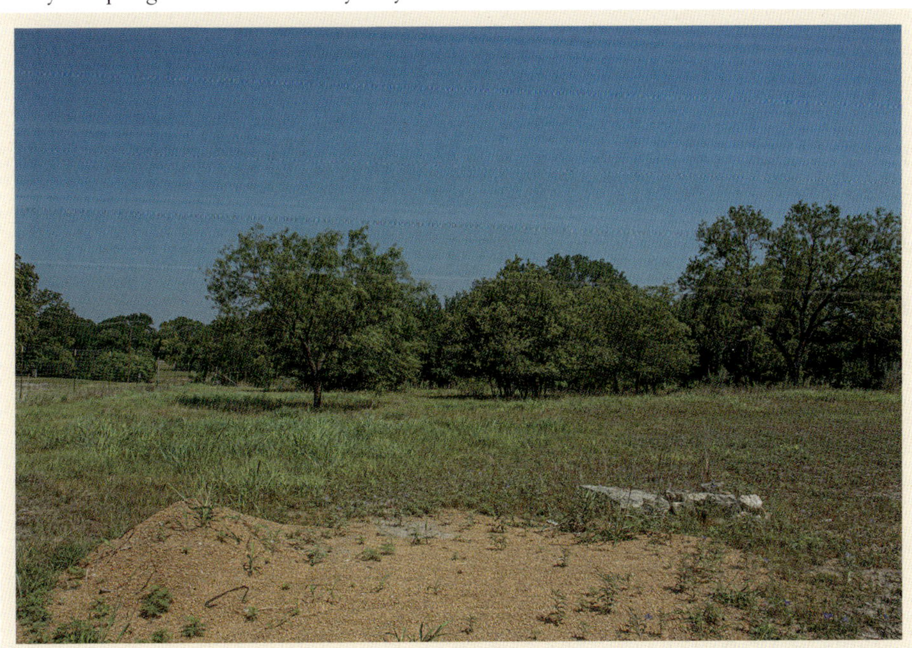

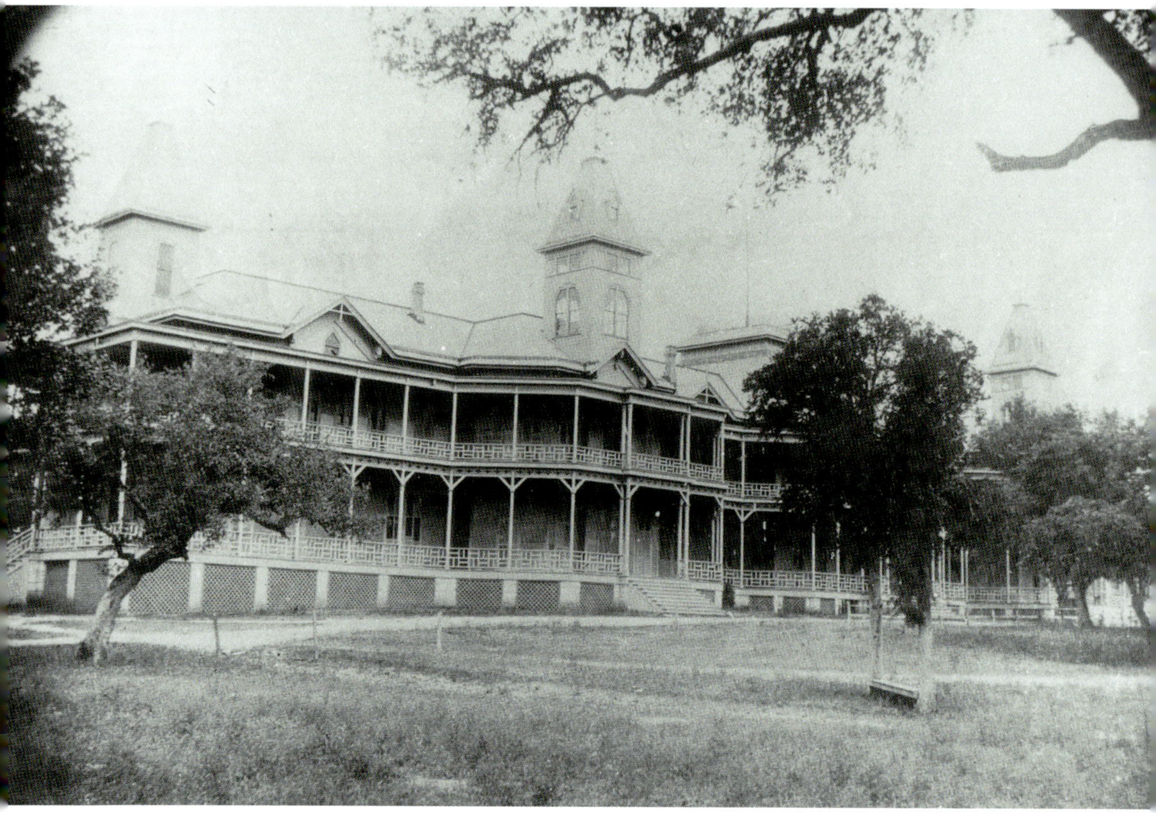

The Lampasas *Leader* (1889) described the Park Hotel, built in 1883: "About a mile from the courthouse in Lampasas on a rising elevation of ground stands an artistically designed building some three hundred and fifty by two hundred feet in size, the roof is lofty and has four towers uprising like Mussulman's Minaret." Between 1891 and 1895, the hotel was leased to the Keeley Institute and then Centenary College. In February 1895, it burned. Today, South Spring Street occupies the area. (Present, DP.)

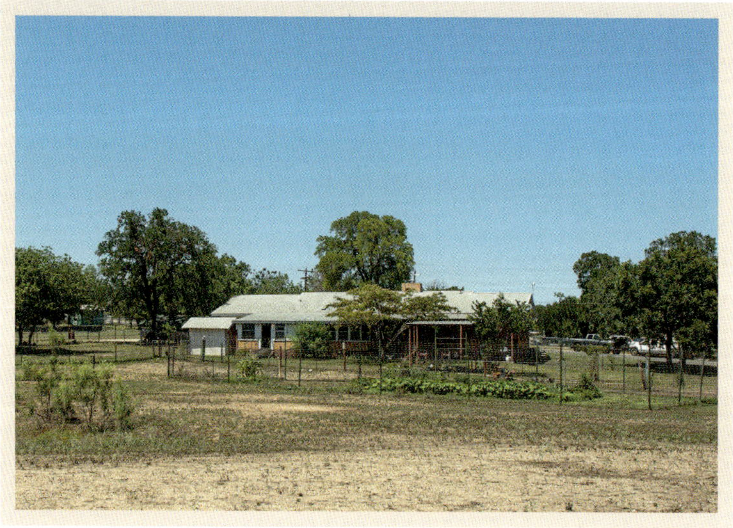

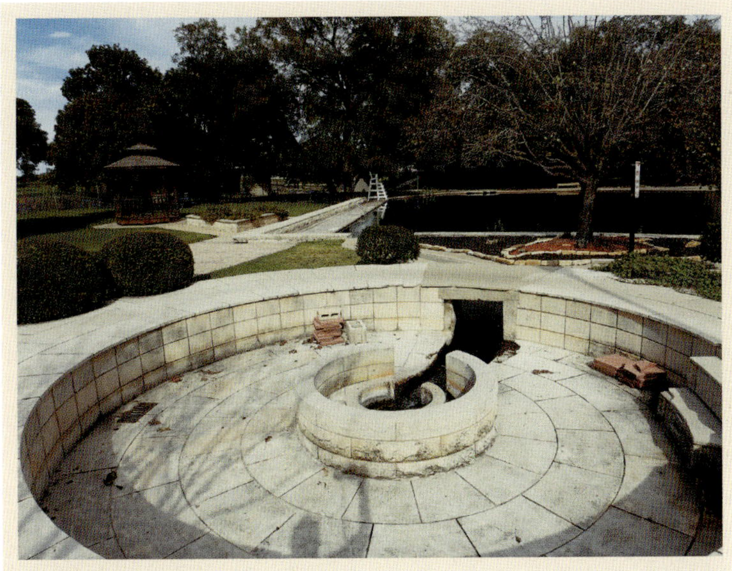

The springhead at Hancock Park is shown below in the 1950s with two local children, Martha Jane Wooten and Paul Cowan, one of whom is drinking the mineral-laced water. In the 1990s, a hydrologist advised the city to raise the springhead so that the water would cascade over the stones into a surrounding pool. The attempt was unsuccessful, but the 72-degree sulfur water continues to flow into Hancock pool to this day. (Past, Virgil Wooten; present, JF.)

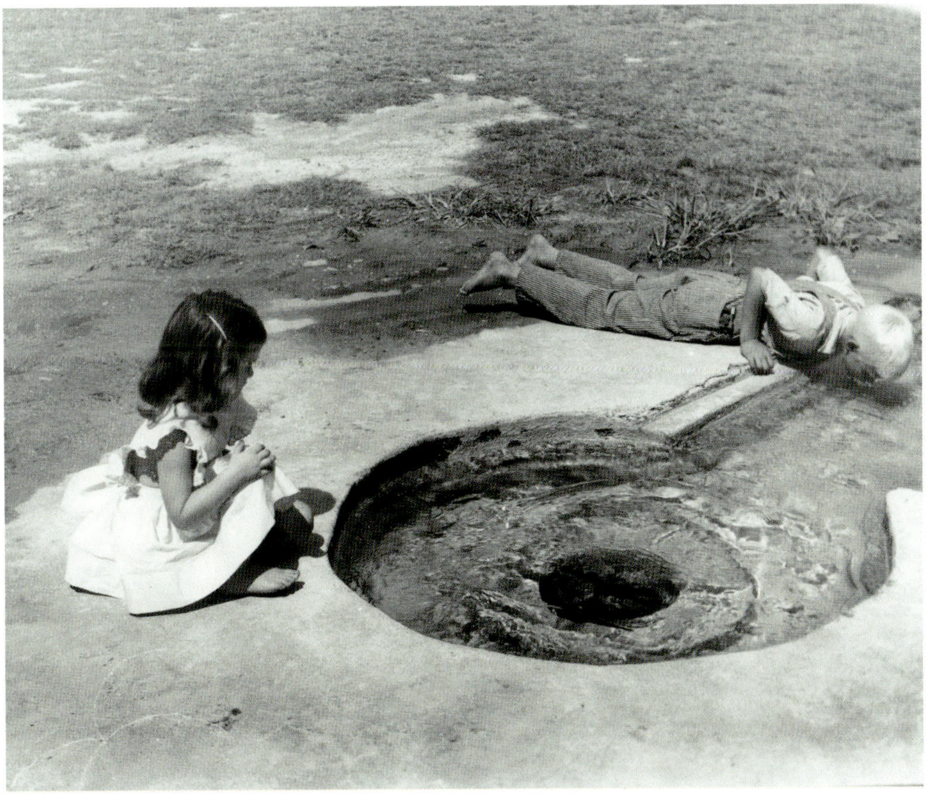

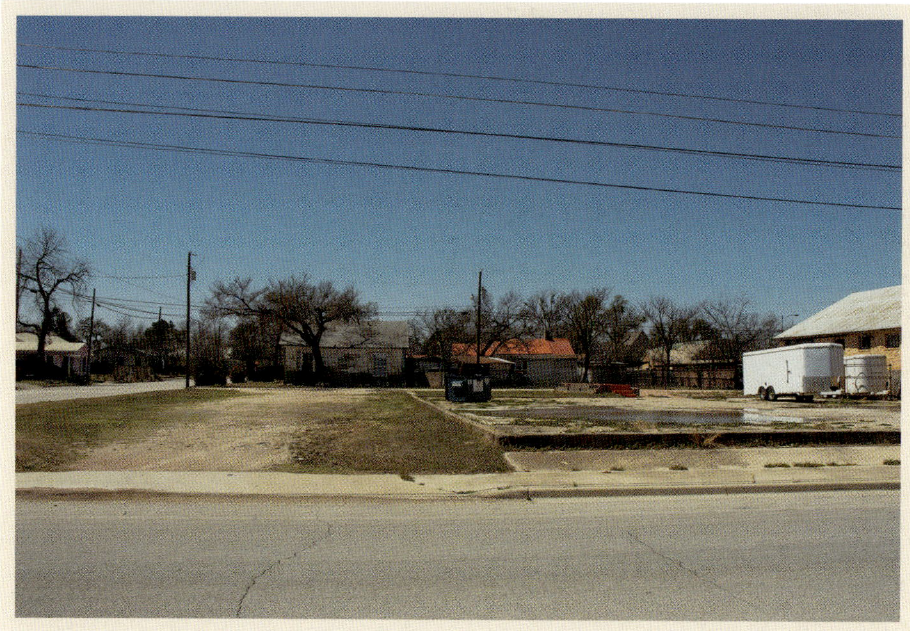

The Globe Hotel (below), built in the late 19th century, stood on the corner of Fifth Street and Western Avenue on the block where the Cloud warehouse is now. Three stories tall, it had the only elevator in town. An 1888 advertisement boasts "strictly first-class accommodation." That year, the Lampasas *Leader* reported Globe Hotel guests from cities as diverse as Boston, New Orleans, New York, Pittsburgh, St. Louis, and San Francisco. The hotel burned to the ground before 1904. (Present, DP.)

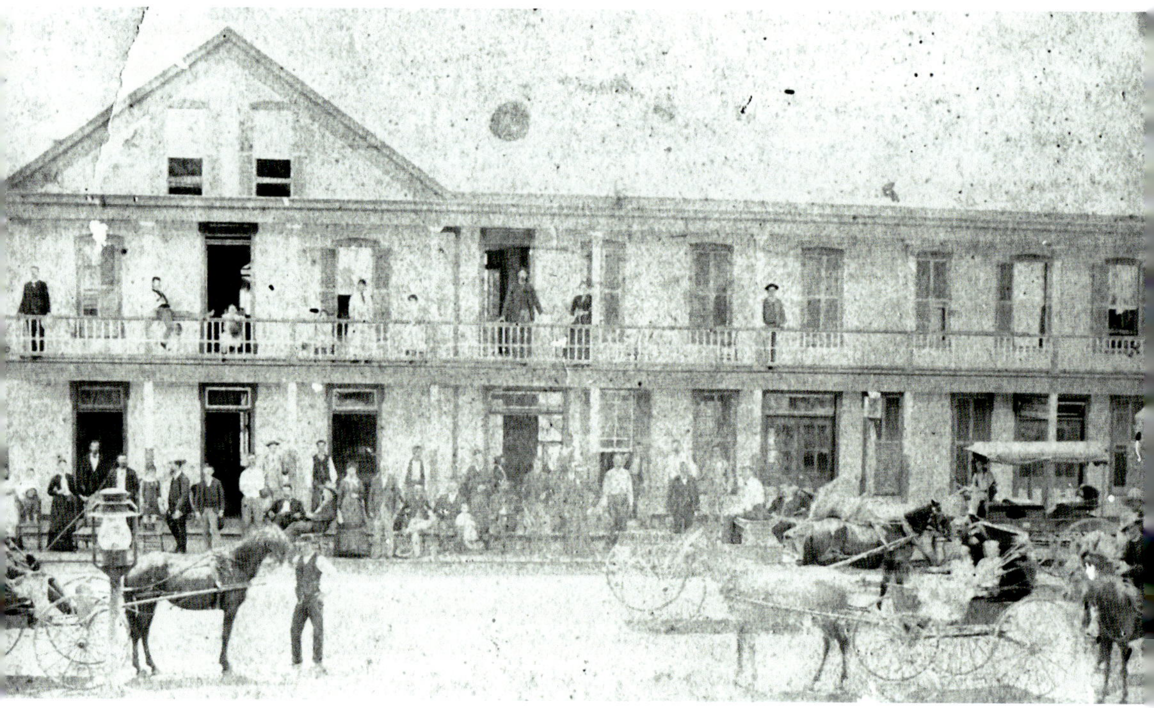

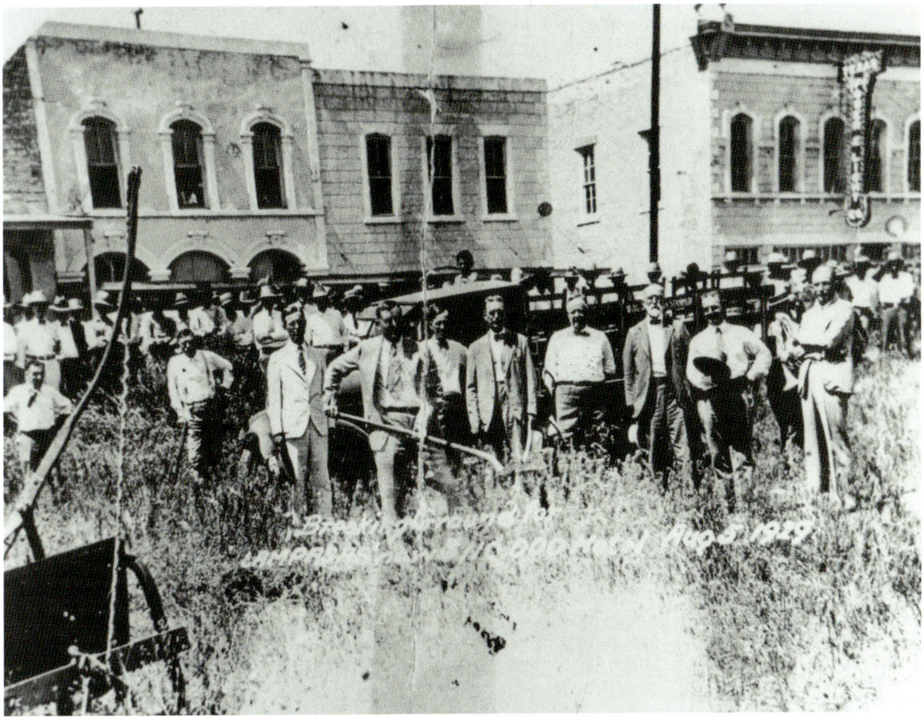

In 1929, the Lampasas *Leader* published an article about a new hotel that was to be built at Third and Main Streets, where the Calvert Building is now. The architect's rendering depicts a three-story hotel with a tile roof. A grand celebration took place, complete with a parade, speeches, and Henry Villard Campbell (pictured here) moving the first shovel of dirt. Behind the crowd are Third Street buildings, including what is now Medina's Restaurant in the center. Not long after, the Great Depression hit, and the hotel was never built. (Present, JF.)

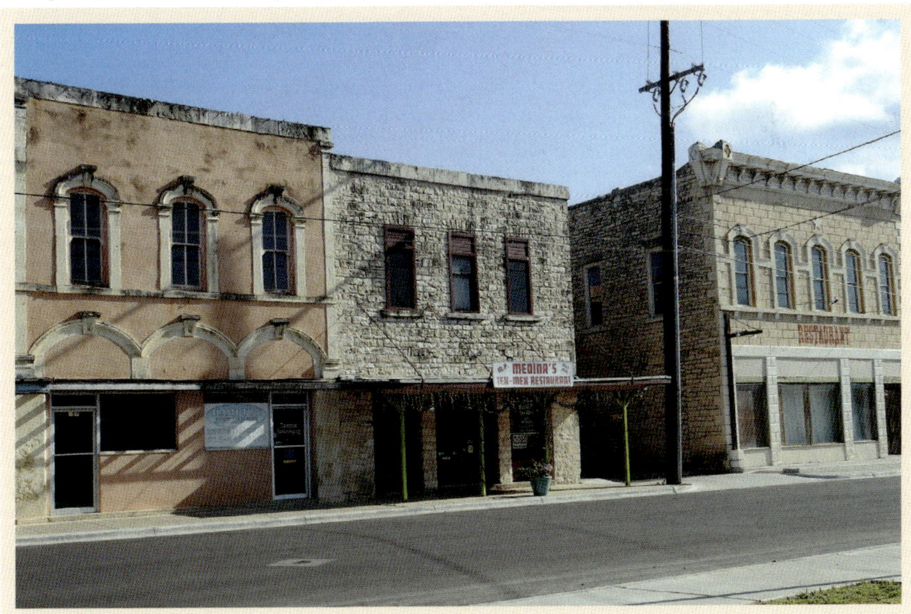

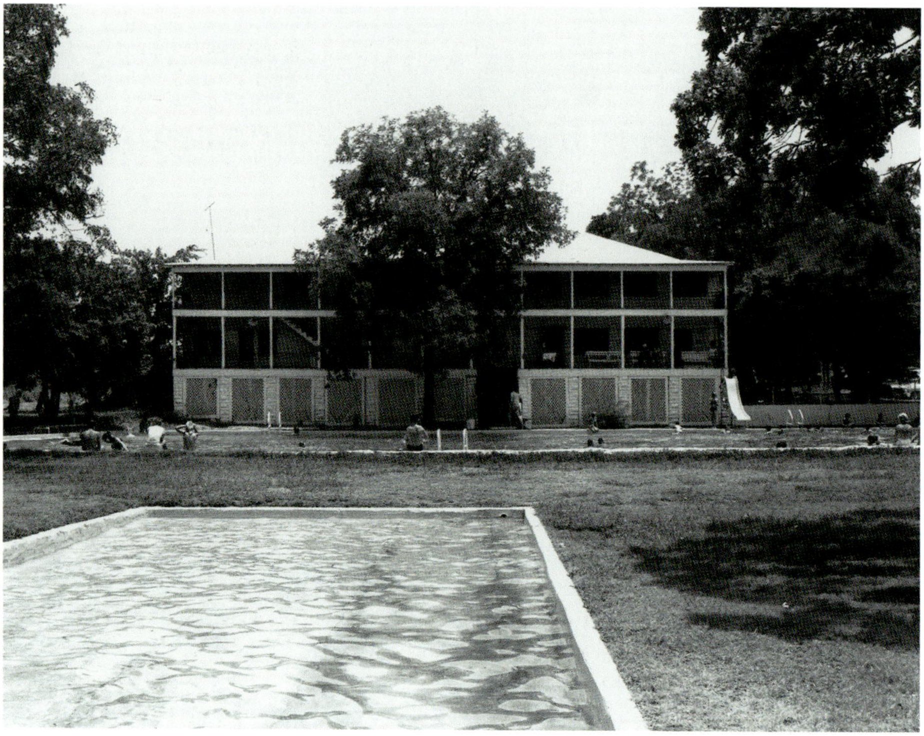

Once, children waded and played in a shallow kiddie pool (foreground) in front of Hancock Park's Hostess House and north of the large free-flow body of water (swimming pool) that remains today. The kiddie pool, installed around 1929 by Baker and Little, then owners of the park, was removed in the 1960s and replaced with a lawn for picnicking and sunbathing. A gazebo was added to the lawn in recent years. The earlier photograph dates to the 1950s. (Past, Virgil Wooten; present, JF.)

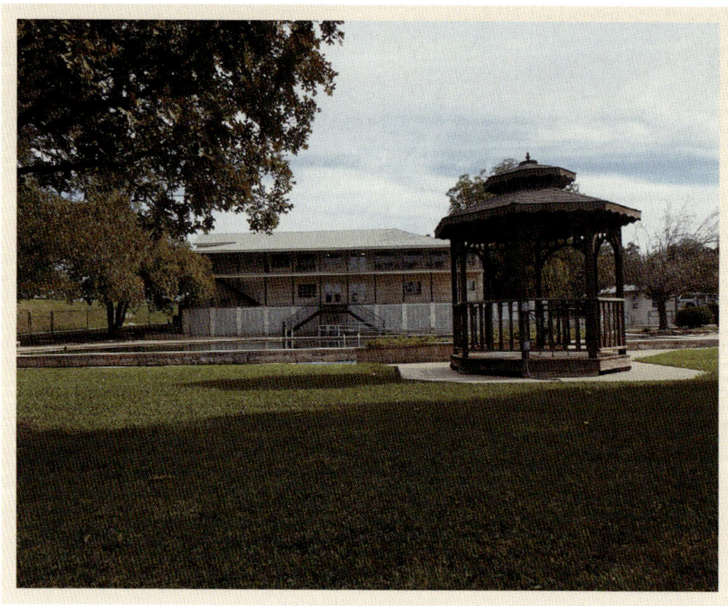

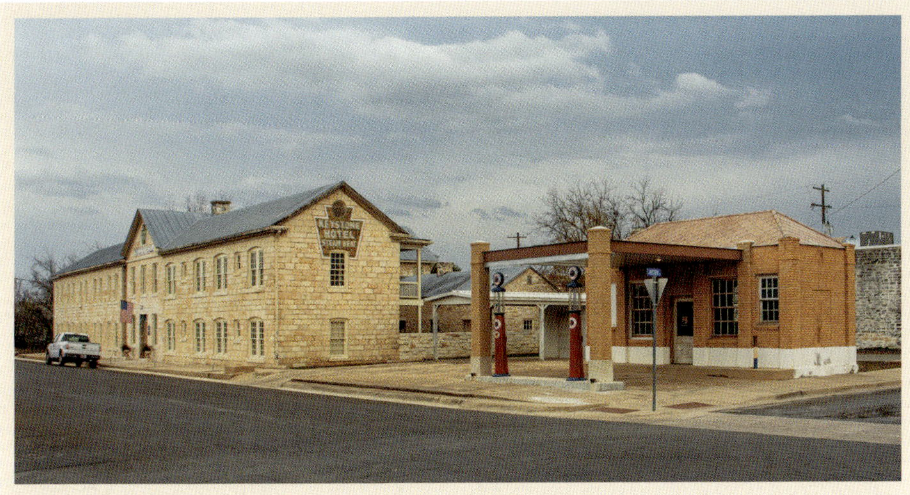

The hotel now known as the Keystone Star was built in 1856 by J.N. Gracy on Second Street. In 1926, J.R. Key purchased the building, renaming it the Keystone, and three years later, he modernized it, adding steam heat. An extension was added in 1931. Austinite Andrew Fish purchased the building in 2017, restoring it for his private residence. Fish also restored the Humble gas station next door to the hotel, which was a Gulf service station when Key owned the building. (Present, DP.)

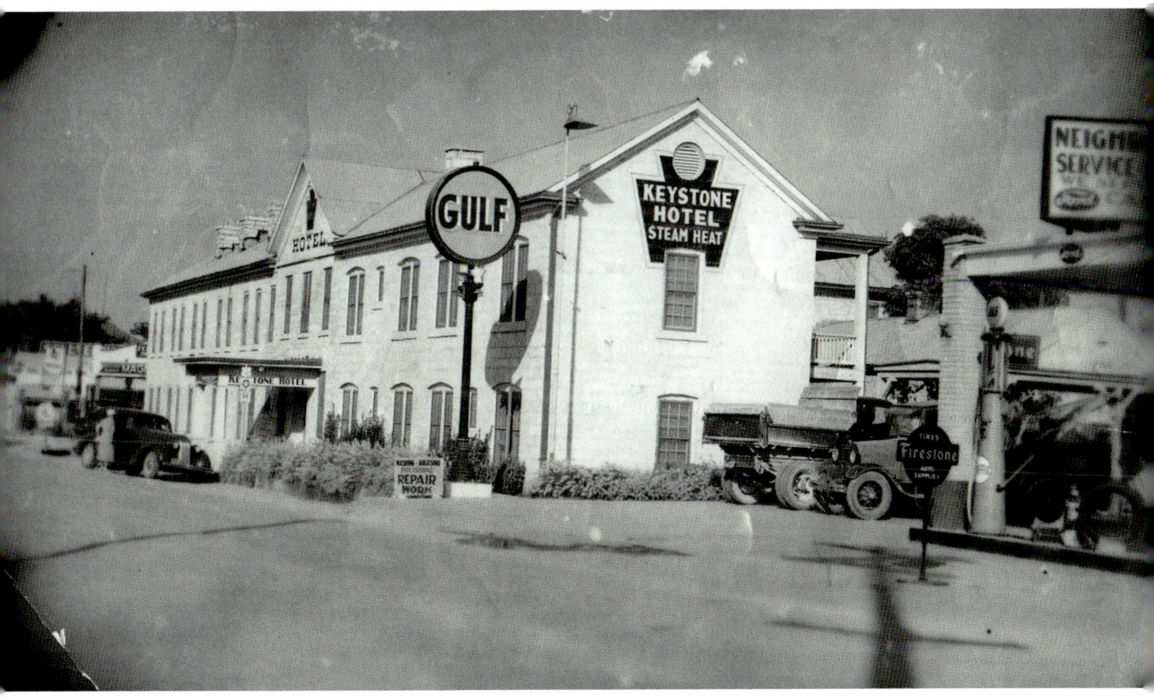

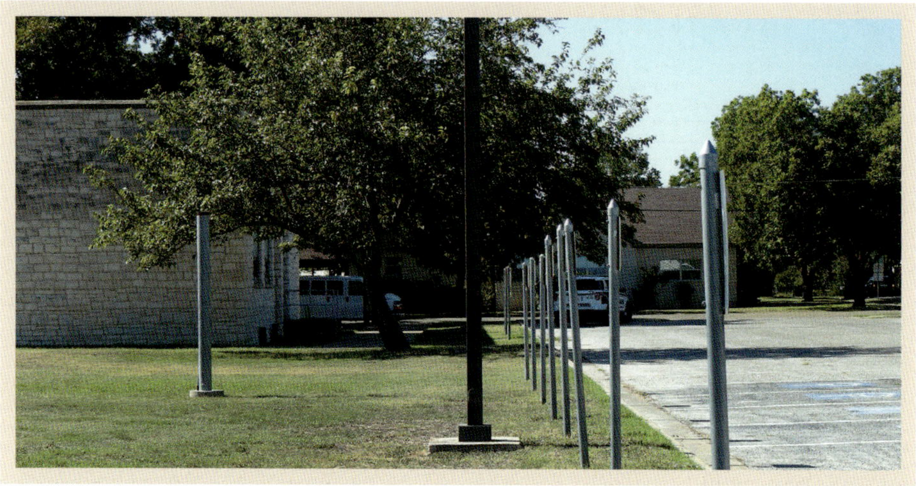

In 1903, an attempt to drill for oil was made on W.B. Abney's land on the 200 block of East Avenue B. After striking sulfur, then saltwater, and finally granite, the project was abandoned. An artesian well remained, and the mixture of sulfur and salt waters was purified for drinking. In 1906, the well opened to the public with a pavilion, pictured below, over it. The well was closed in the mid-1950s. Today, the site is next to the former middle school. (Past, collection of LCHC; present, AM.)

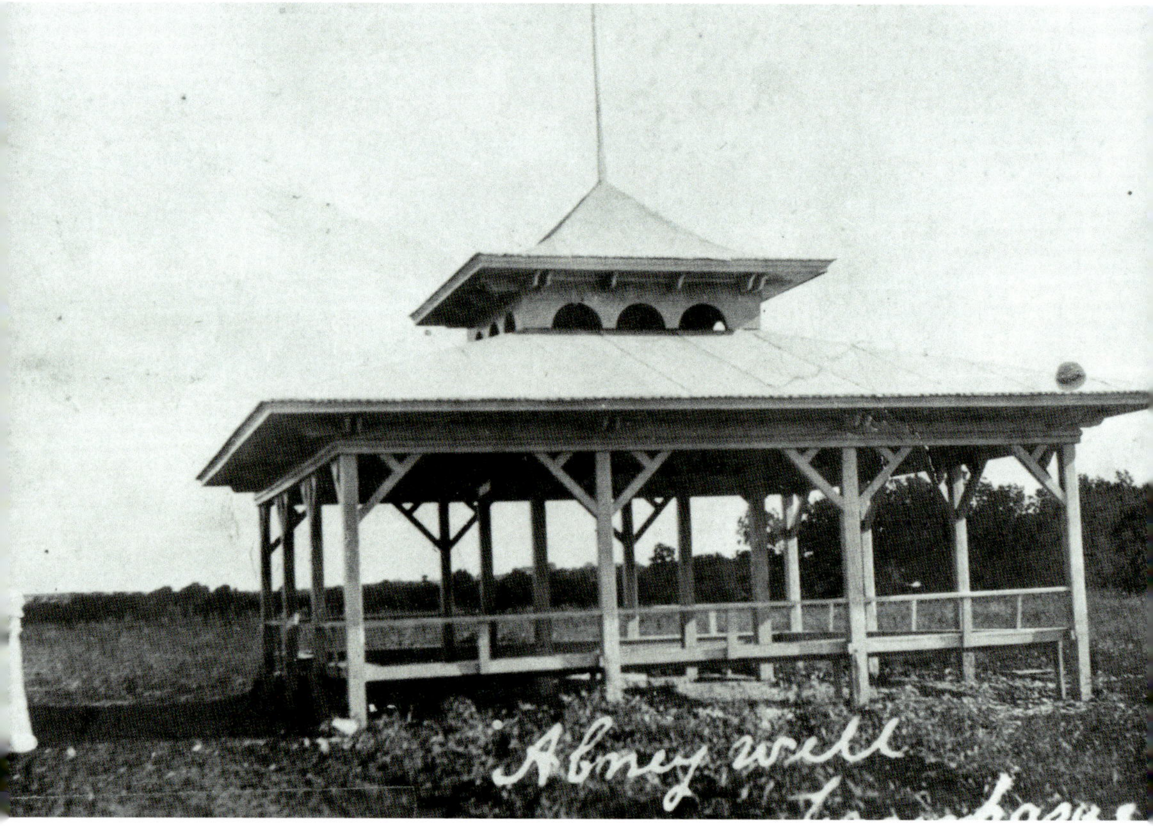

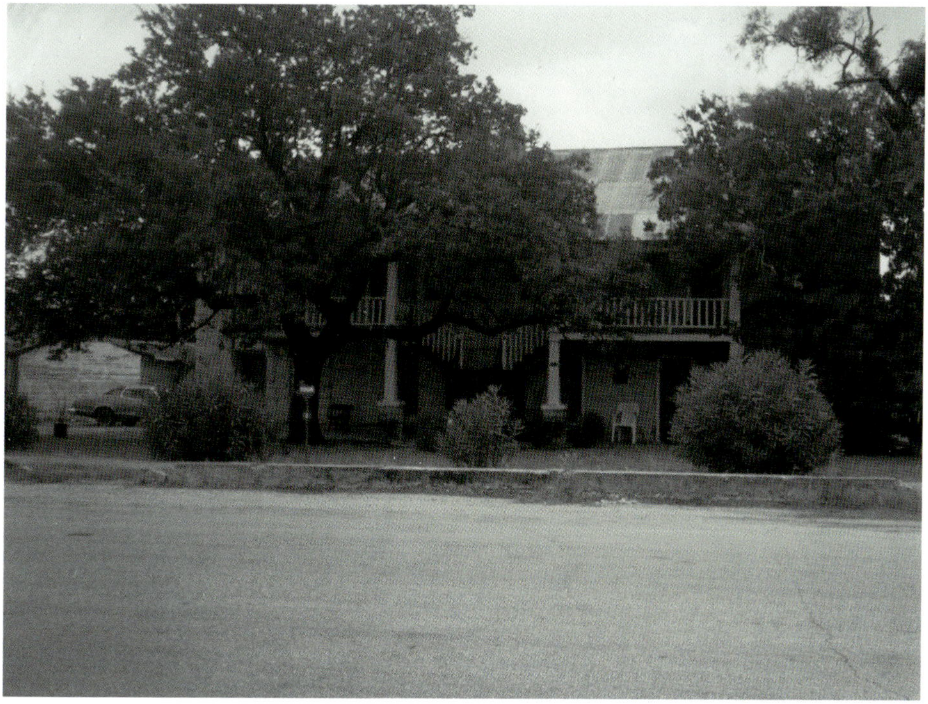

At 511 South Western Avenue, between 1865 and 1868, the two-story building now known as the Hart House was constructed. It was a stagecoach stop and hotel, later enlarged to accommodate the significant number of visitors to Lampasas in the 1870s and 1880s. In the 1970s, Mary Moore Hart Day owned the building and leased it to the Lampasas County Museum Foundation. A couple from Austin purchased the building recently; they are in the process of restoring it for their home. (Present, DP.)

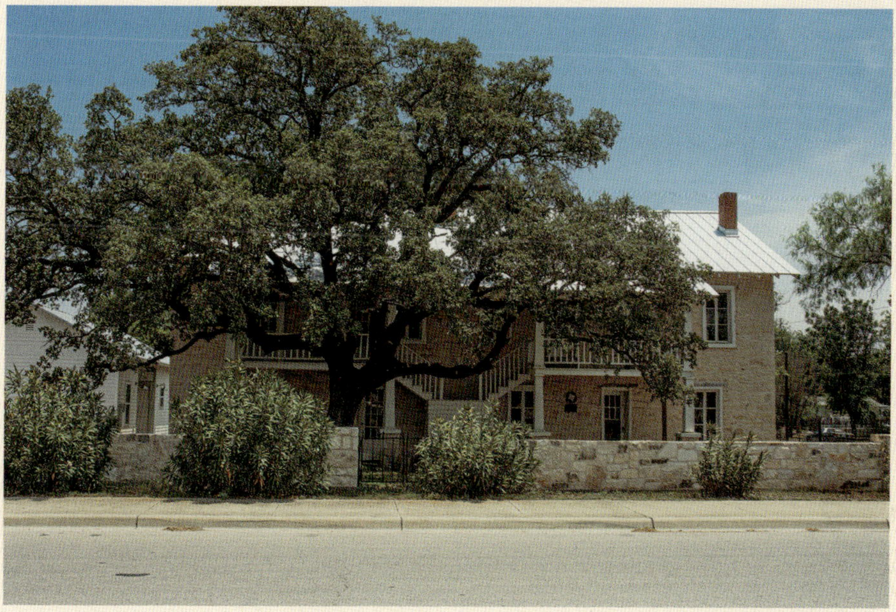

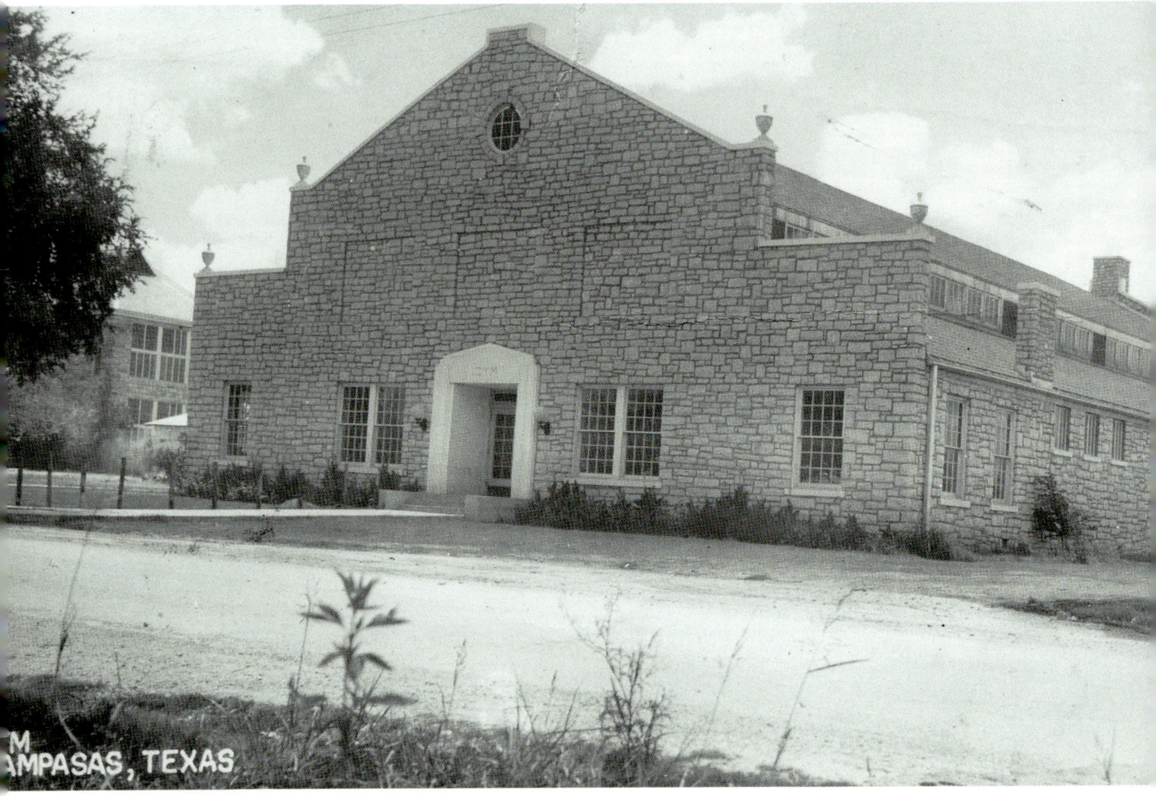

This native stone gymnasium, completed in 1939, is located on Western Avenue between Avenues A and B. The two-story grammar school, built in 1895, can be seen at the left. Today, the gymnasium appears much as it does in the earlier photograph except for the first-floor double-hung paned windows, replaced with windows of a more modern design. It is still owned by the Lampasas Independent School District but is not in regular use. (Present, AM.)

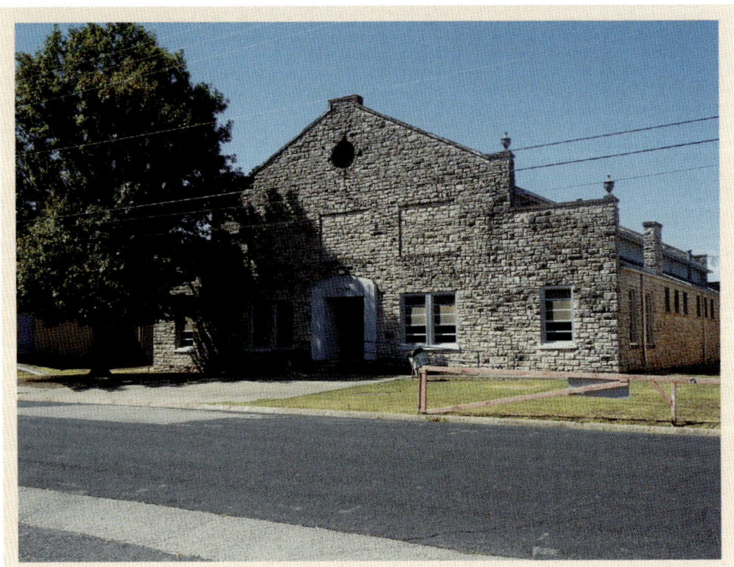

CHAPTER 7

WAYS TO TRAVEL

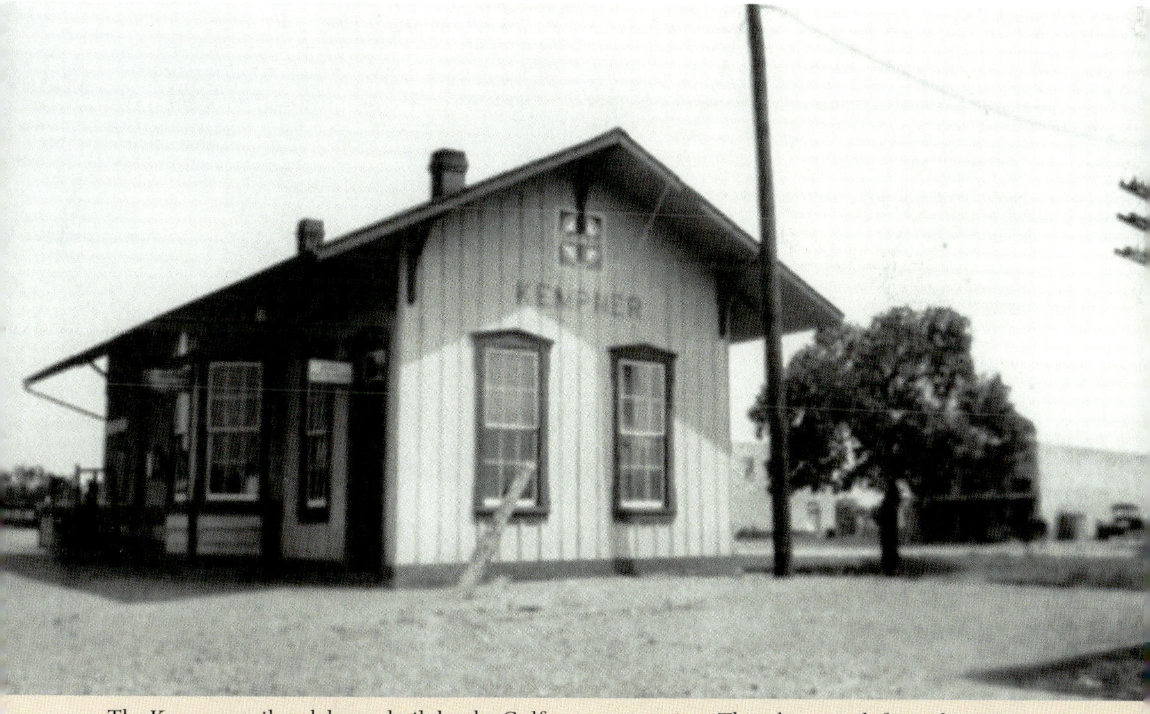

The Kempner railroad depot, built by the Gulf, Colorado & Santa Fe Railway in 1898, measured 18.25 by 47 feet and was of board-and-batten construction. This photograph from the 1930s identifies segregated waiting rooms, common at that time. (Kansas Historical Society.)

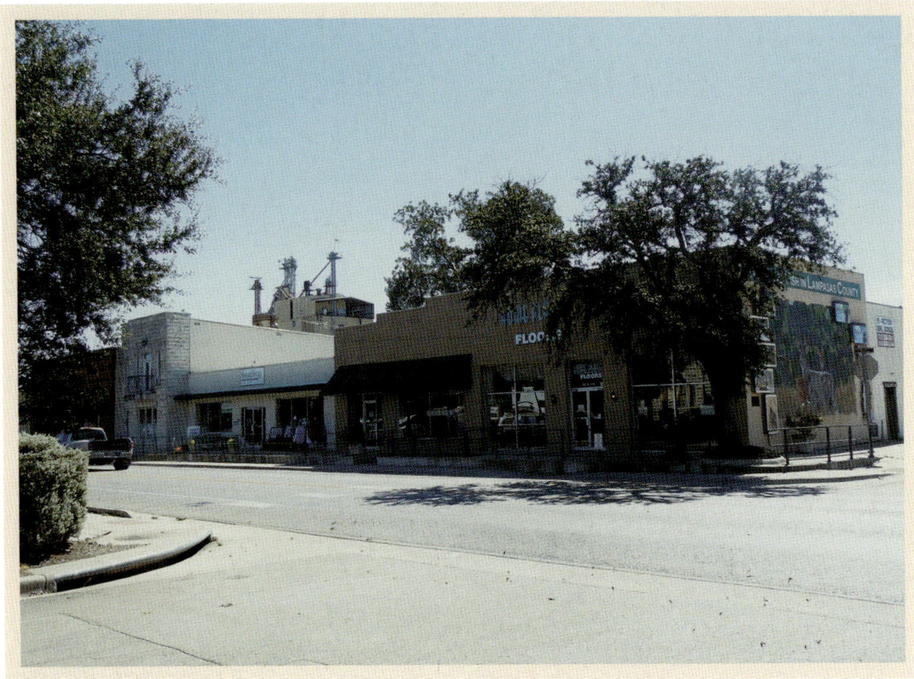

In 1935, the Holley-Langford Motor Company tore down three buildings, including a two-story structure on the southeast corner of Live Oak and Fourth Streets, and replaced them with the building in this mid-1950s photograph. In 1955, it became Burns Chevrolet, pictured below, and 10 years later, Hoffpauir Chevrolet. Note the stop sign on the pavement in the intersection. Today, the block is occupied by a variety of small businesses, including a thrift shop and a flooring store. (Present, AM.)

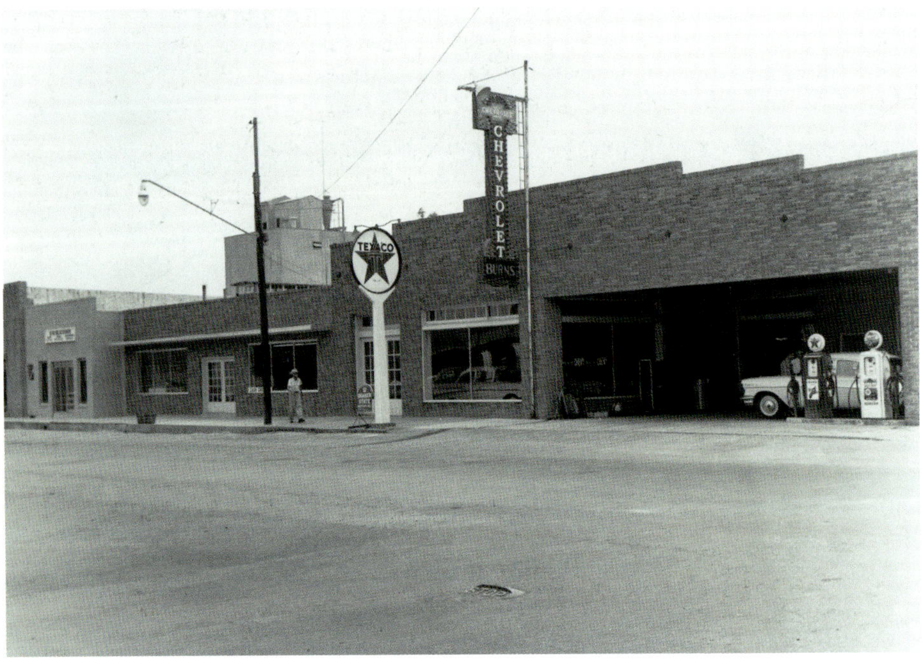

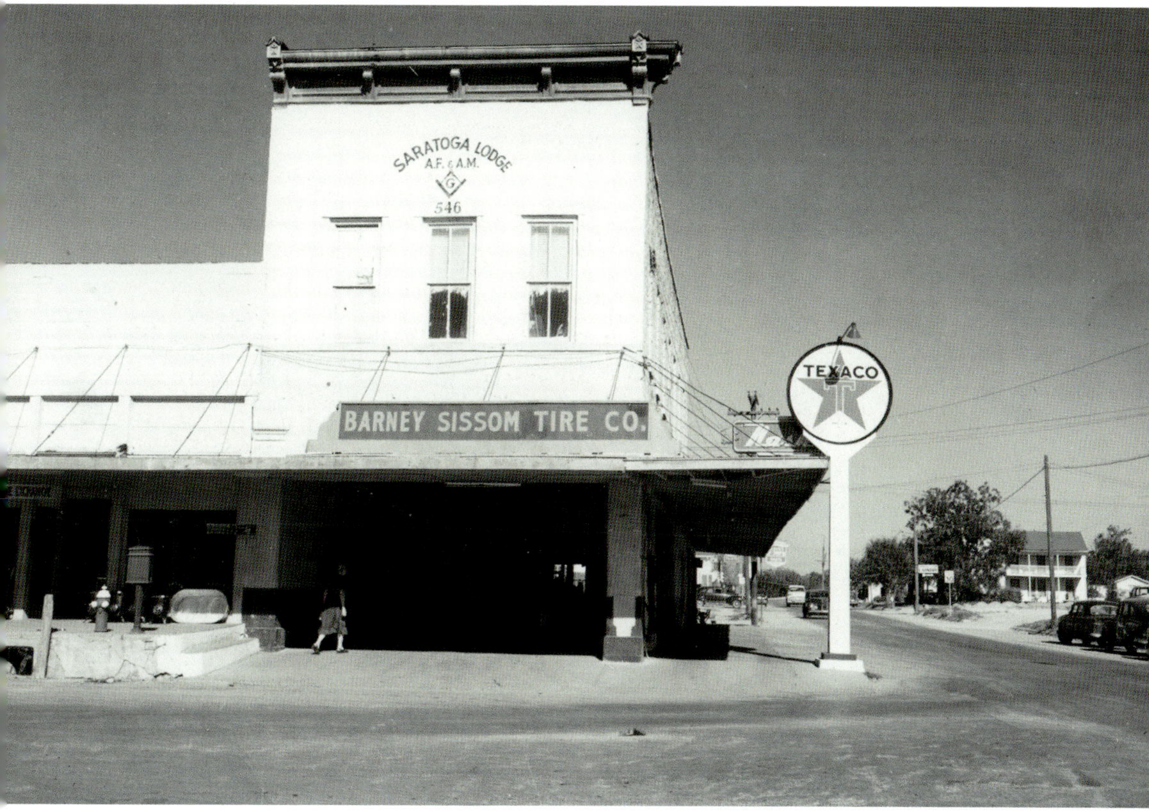

The Barney Sissom Tire Company was on the northeast corner of Pecan and Fourth Streets on the first floor of the Saratoga Masonic Lodge No. 546. Corner drive-in gas stations like this first appeared in the early 1910s, fostering the new nationwide driving culture. Before, people bought gas at a curbside pump or in a can from a blacksmith or pharmacy. Full-service stations such as this sold maps, tires, and other items to motorists. Today, the Lampasas County Annex occupies half the block. (Past, LCHC; present, AM.)

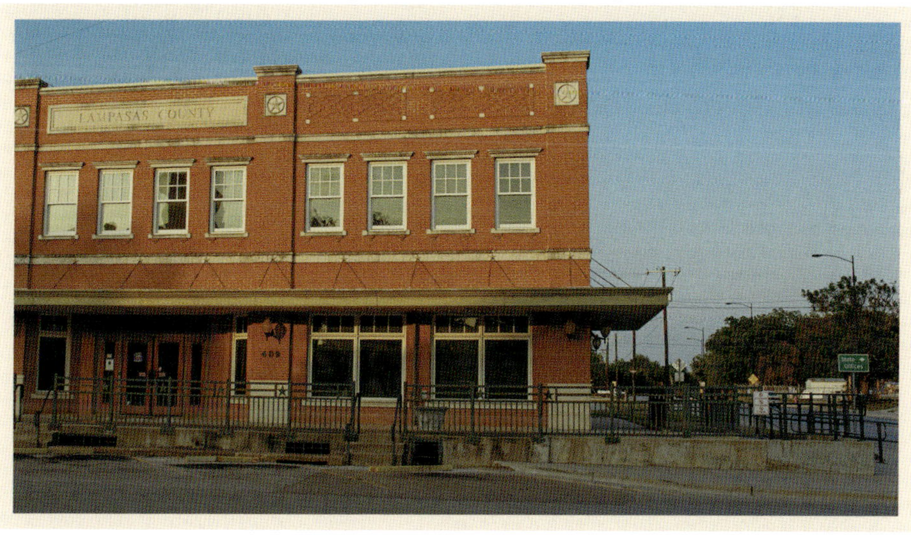

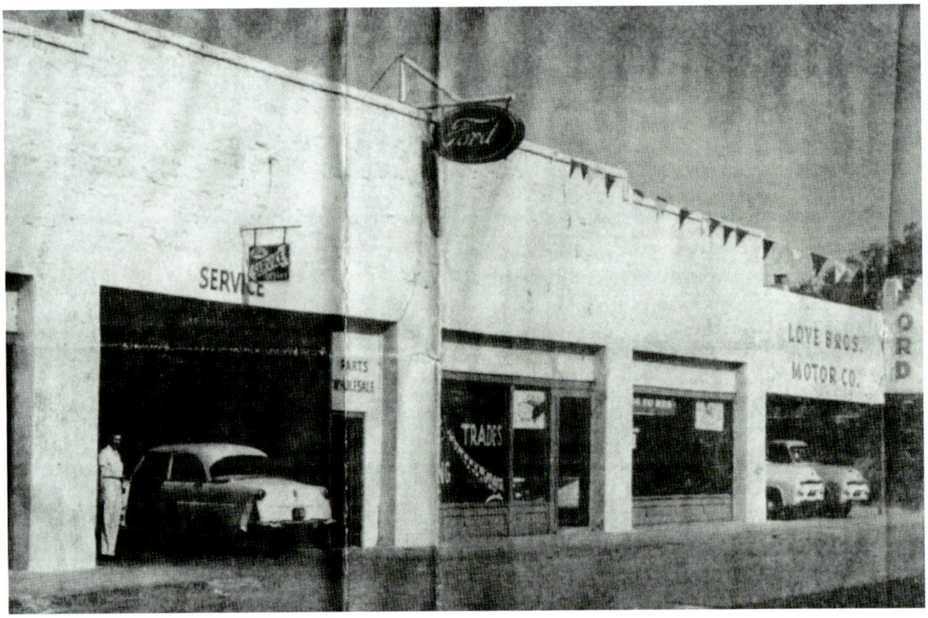

The structure at 302 South Western Avenue housed a variety of businesses over the years, beginning with the Texas Trading Company, as is documented in a mural painted by Vision Lampasas on the Second Street side of the building. One of these was the Love Brothers Motor Company, pictured here. Opened by brothers Cyril and Olen Love in 1951, they later moved their business to Key Avenue. Today, the building houses the Lampasas Auto Company, which includes a portion of Andy Fish's vintage automobile collection, featuring antique Fords. (Present, DP.)

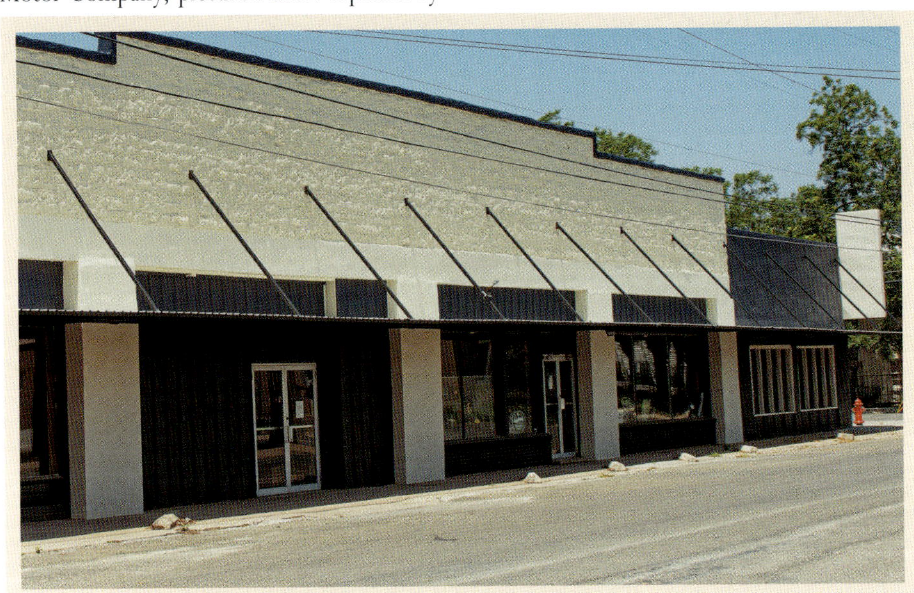

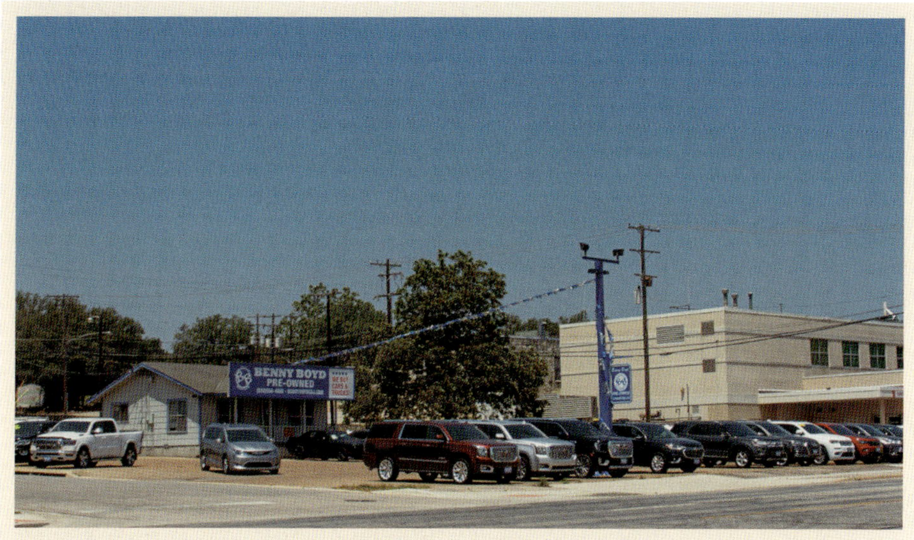

Gillen's Service Station (below), opened around 1938 by Choc and Marie Gillen, was located on Key Avenue, where Benny Boyd's used car lot is now. This full-service station sold Goodrich tires and Gulf gasoline. It also boasted a café featuring Coca-Cola. Both Choc and Marie worked there, with Choc doing some of the cooking and Marie waiting tables. She once waited on Lyndon Johnson before he became a Texas senator. They both said it was the hardest work they had ever done. (Present, DP.)

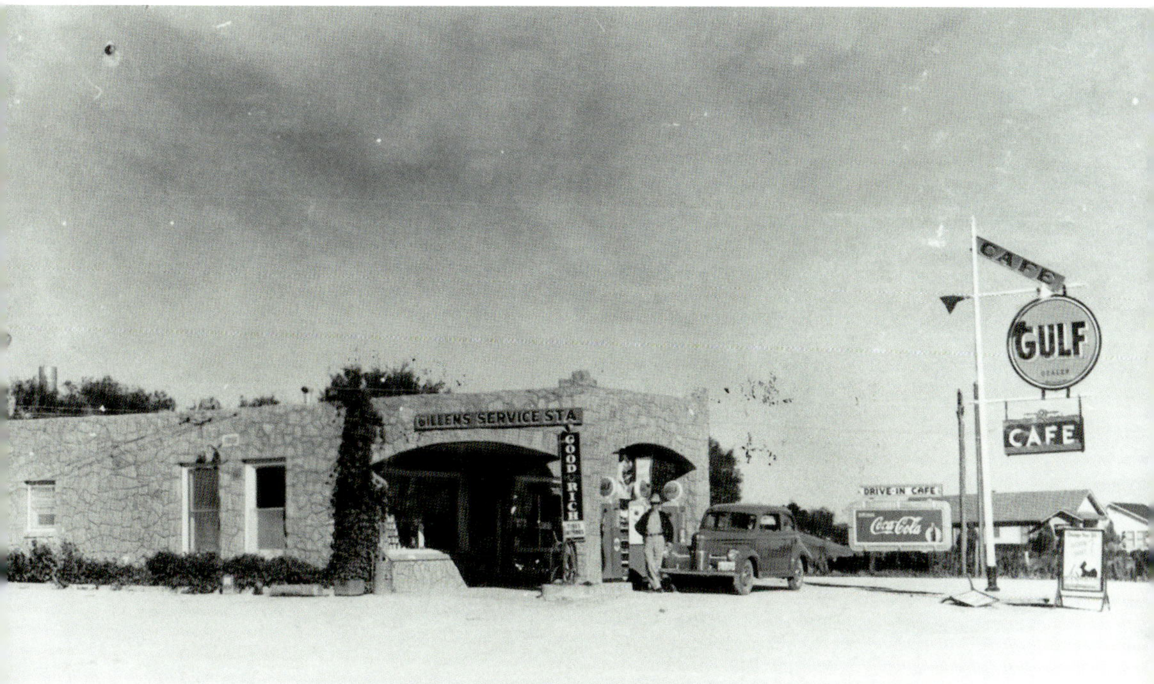

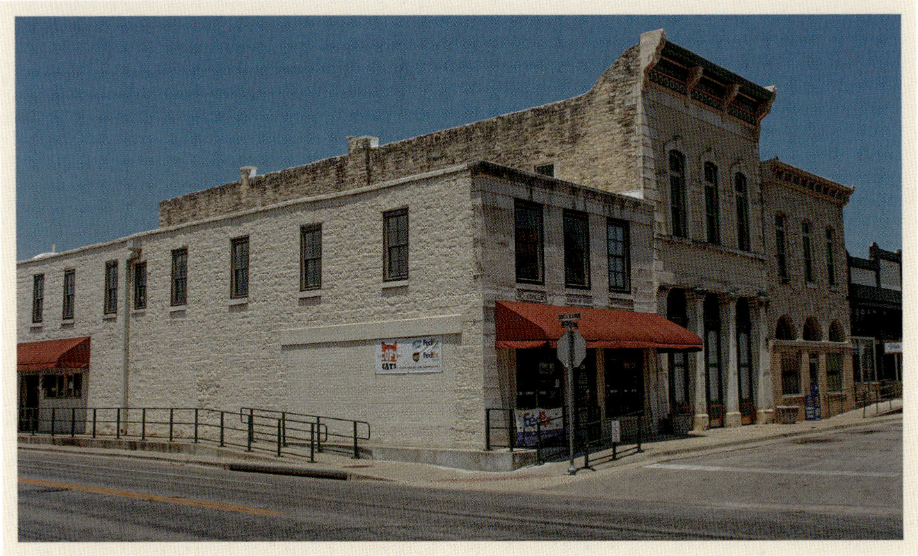

A September 1920 Lampasas *Leader* advertisement for the Lampasas Tire Hospital (below) features Firestone brand "high-test [tire] tubes" and lists the business's proprietors as the Word brothers. Located on the northwest corner of the square where Copy Cats is now, the Tire Hospital not only repaired and marketed tires but also sold Sinclair gasoline. The phone number was, simply, 147. The Tire Hospital, along with other local businesses, provided premiums and special prices to help promote Trades Day on the square. (Present, DP.)

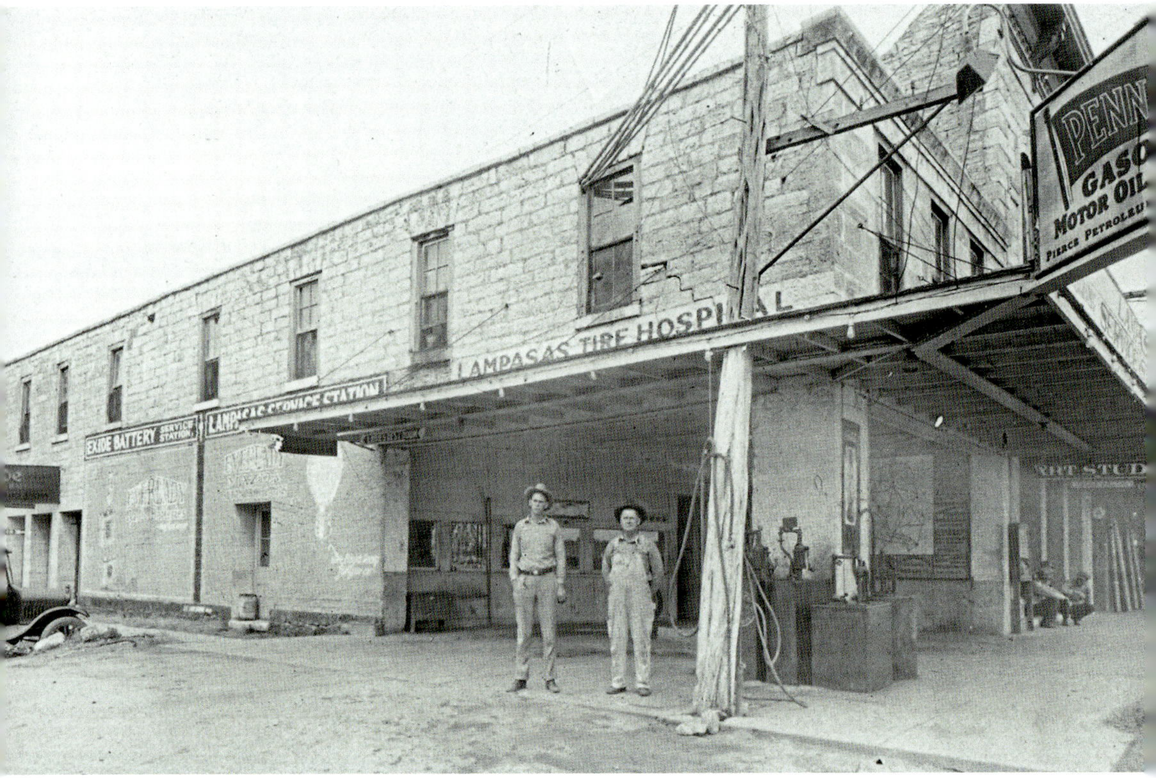

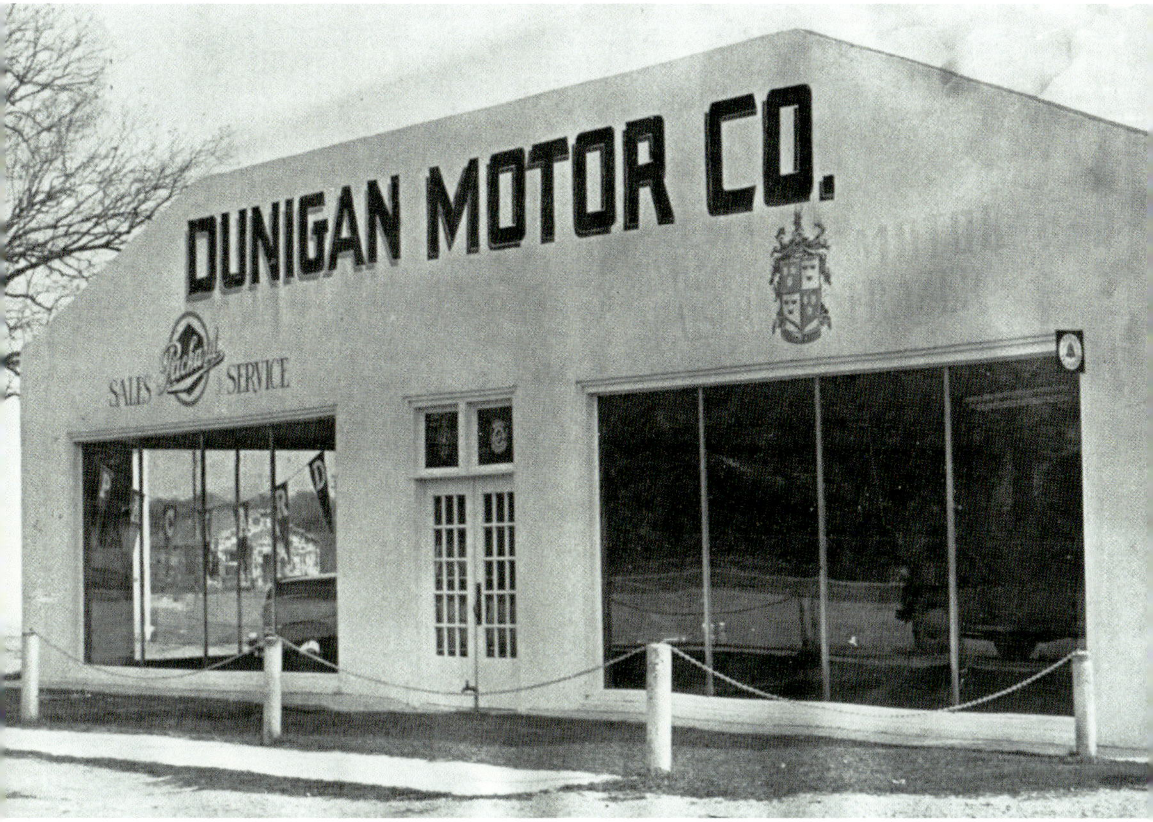

Ray S. Dunigan built the Dunigan Motor Company at 307 North Key Avenue, where the Country Kitchen is now. He sold and serviced Kaizer-Frazer, Packard, and Mercury automobiles. The dealership was built in 1948. A "giraffe" house, so called because of the patterned stone exterior, is visible through the corner windows. (Past, collection of Scott McLean, photograph by Frank Yates; present, DP.)

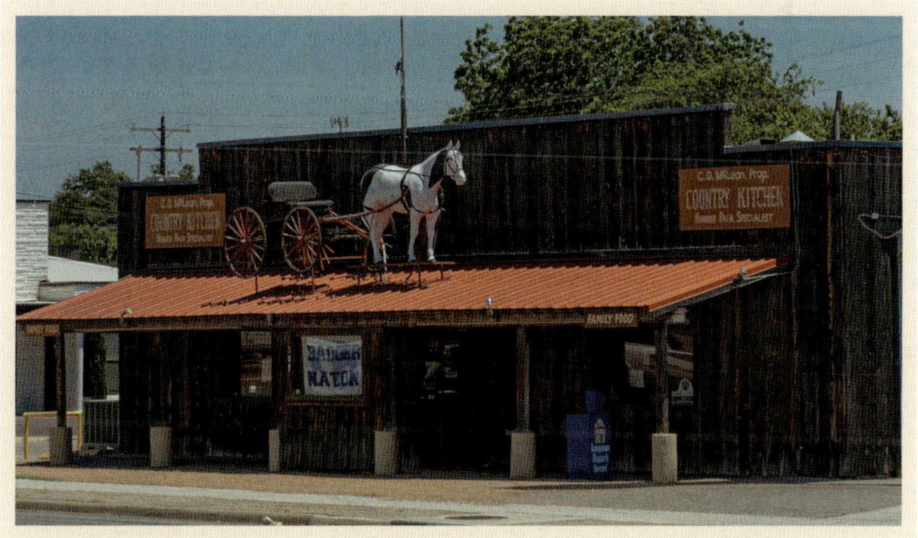

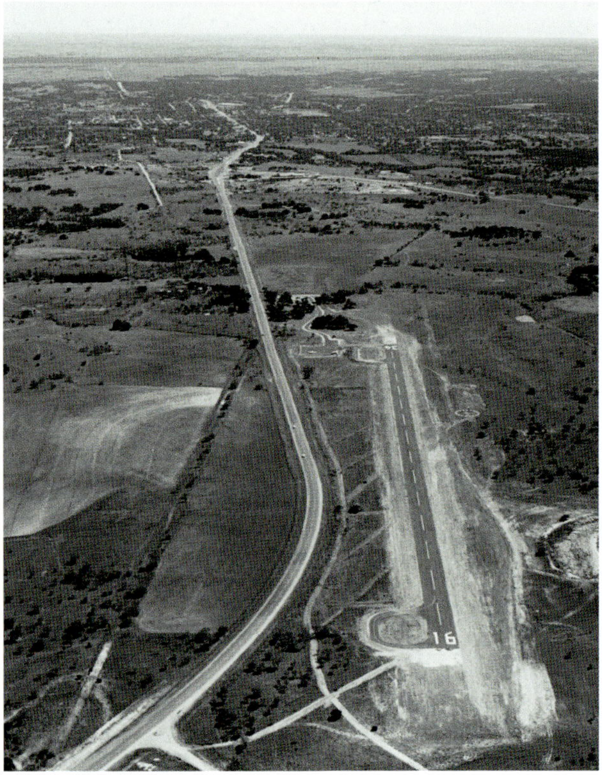

The first Lampasas County airport was built in 1944 near the intersection of County Roads 2010 and 2200. It was unpaved. In 1965, the property was sold and new property purchased by the city and county for a new airport three miles north of Lampasas on US Highway 281. It opened in 1966. The airport is still open at this location but has expanded with hangars and a longer runway. (Past, Gladden Corbin; present, JF.)

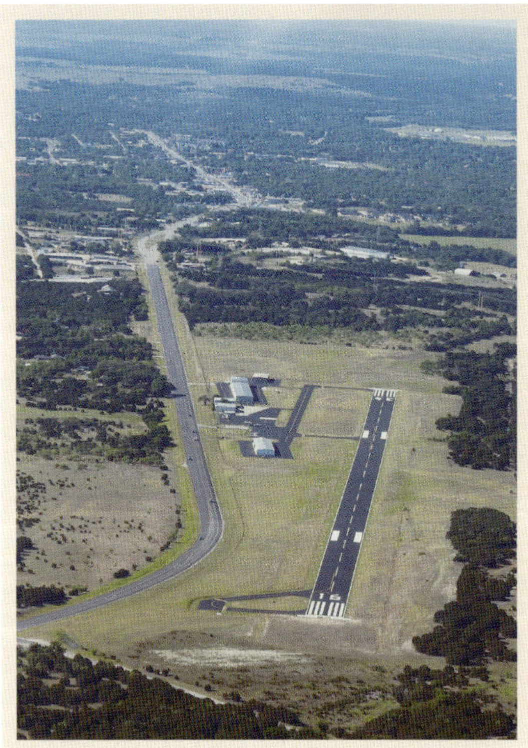

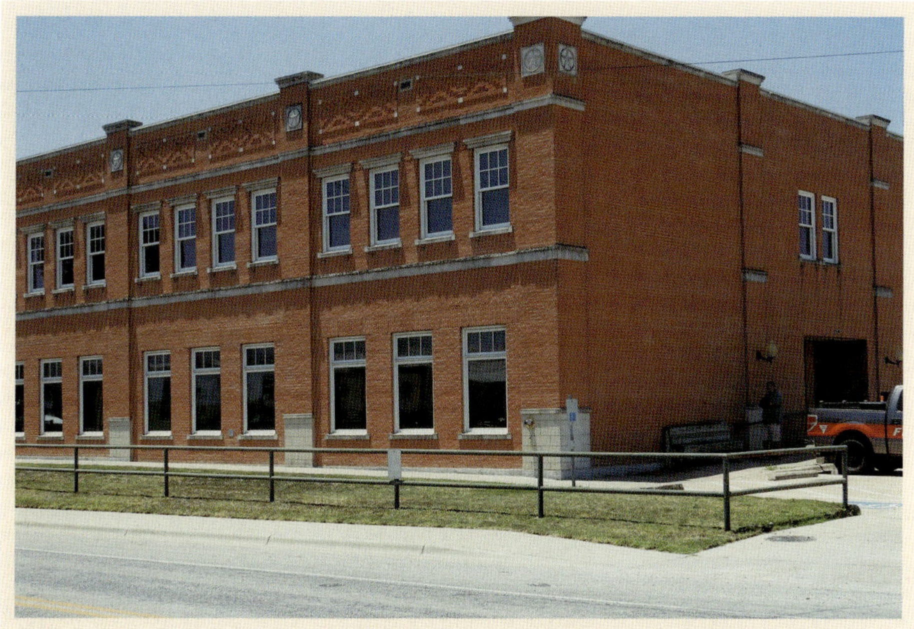

Claude Meeks opened this filling station on Fourth Street between Pecan and Elm Streets (below). Notice the sign advertising "visible gas." Visible gas was dispensed from gravity-fed pumps with clear gas cylinders at the top, as seen in this photograph. Corner filling stations such as this were prevalent in Lampasas as full-service stations. They often provided free air and water and offered tire and battery service as well. Today, the address is the side of the County Annex Building. (Present, AM.)

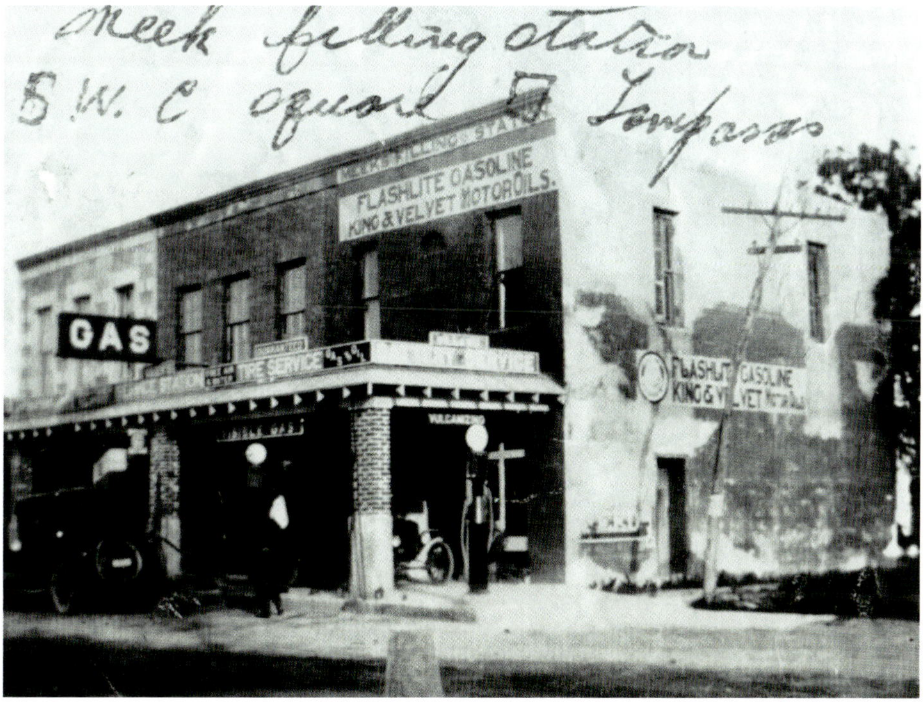

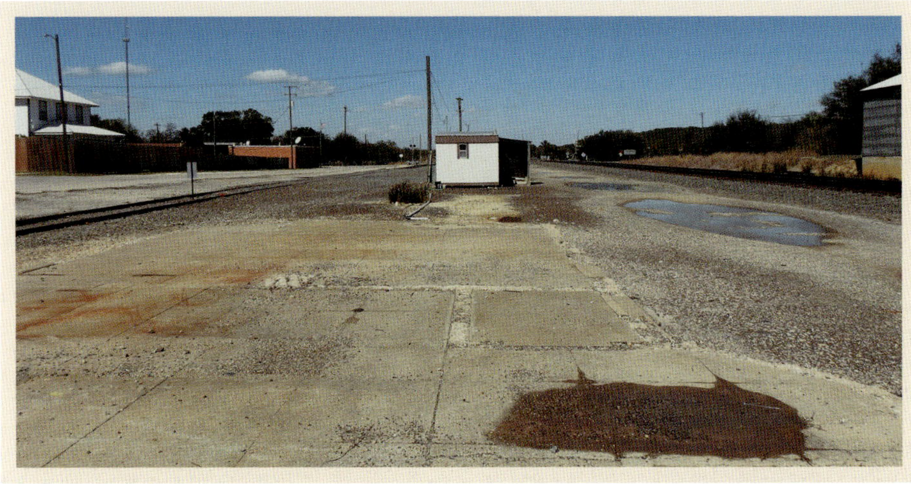

In 1885, the Gulf, Colorado & Santa Fe Railway built a small depot in what would become the city of Lometa. The line shipped local commodities to markets far and wide, while lumber, farming machinery, and household items were delivered to town. The second depot, pictured below in 1916, was built around 1912, during an era of prosperity for Lometa. Passenger trains, including those carrying World War I soldiers in 1917, stopped there. Today, freight trains bypass Lometa. (Present, AM.)

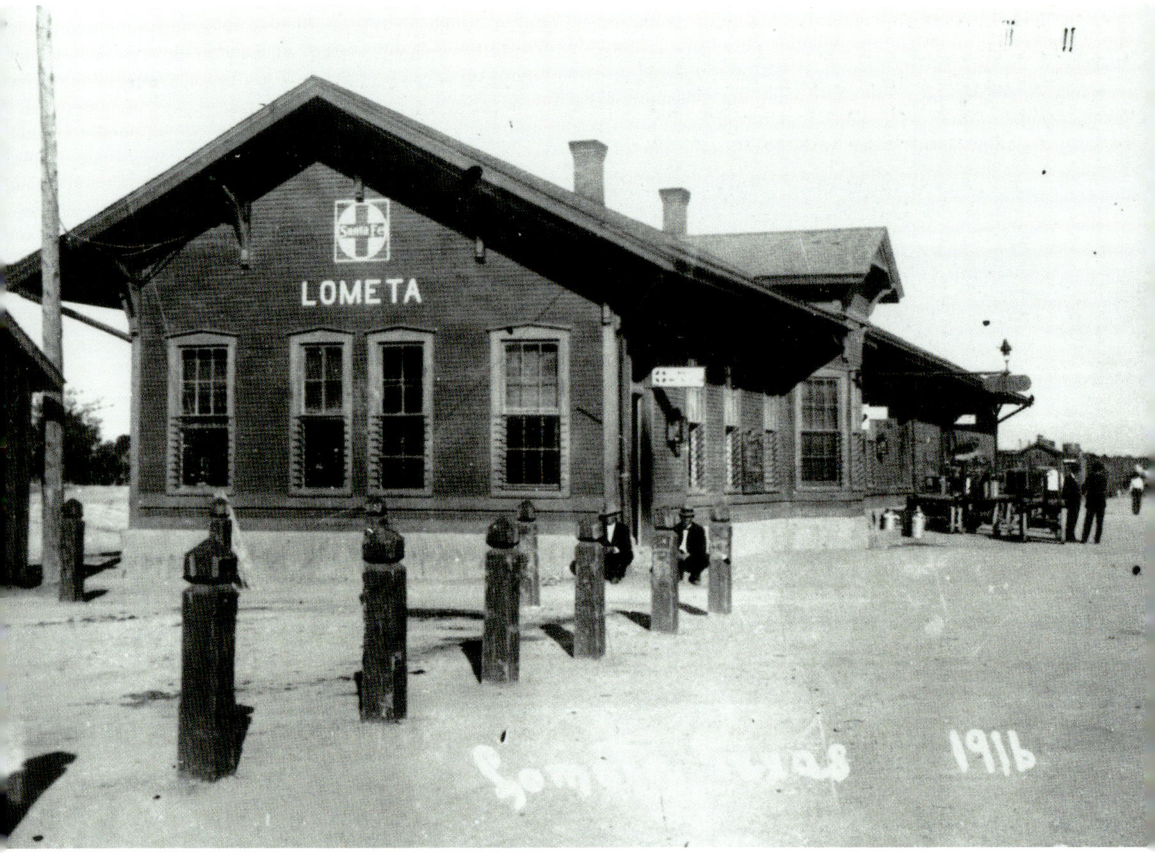

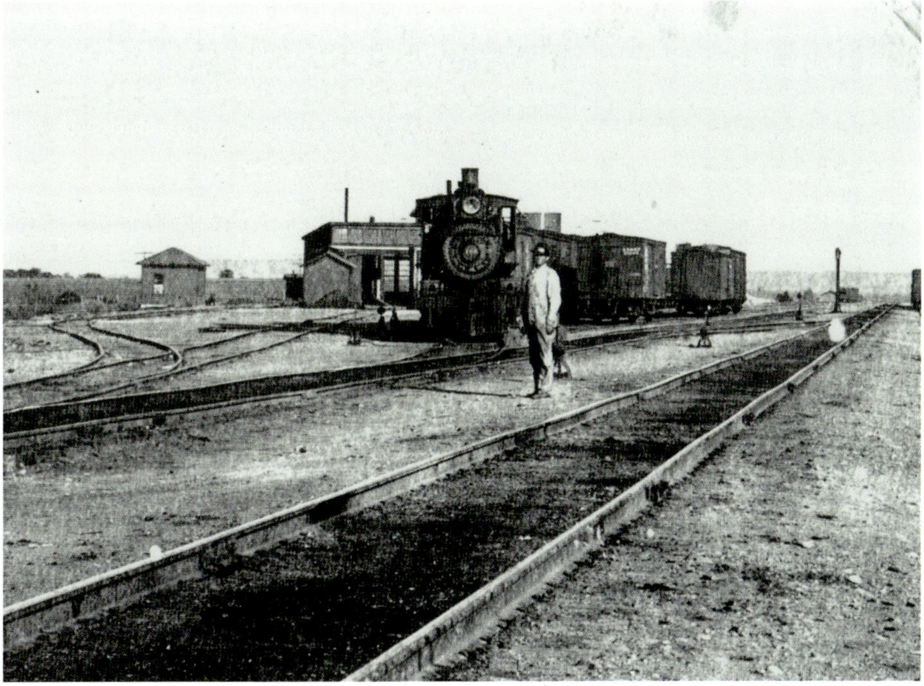

The Lometa Roundhouse was just north of Lometa and served as a locomotive repair shop for the Eden Branch of the Santa Fe from 1911 until the 1950s. In 1911, the Lampasas *Daily Leader* ran an advertisement for housing lots, exclaiming "Lometa is the center of Texas" and that "it is on the main line of the Santa Fe between Galveston and San Francisco, and where the Brady-Eden branch leaves the main line." (Present, AM.)

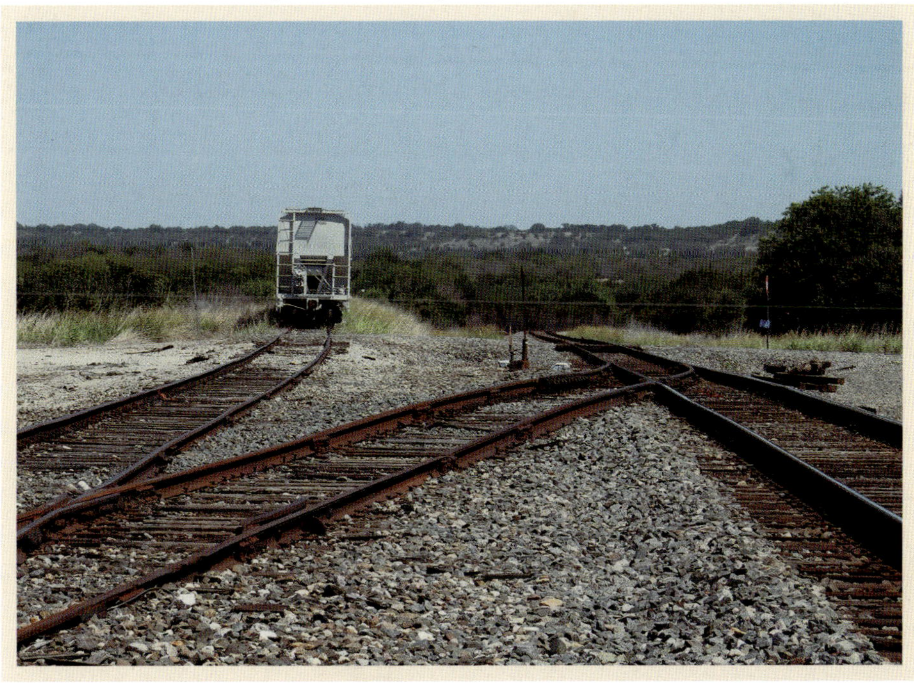

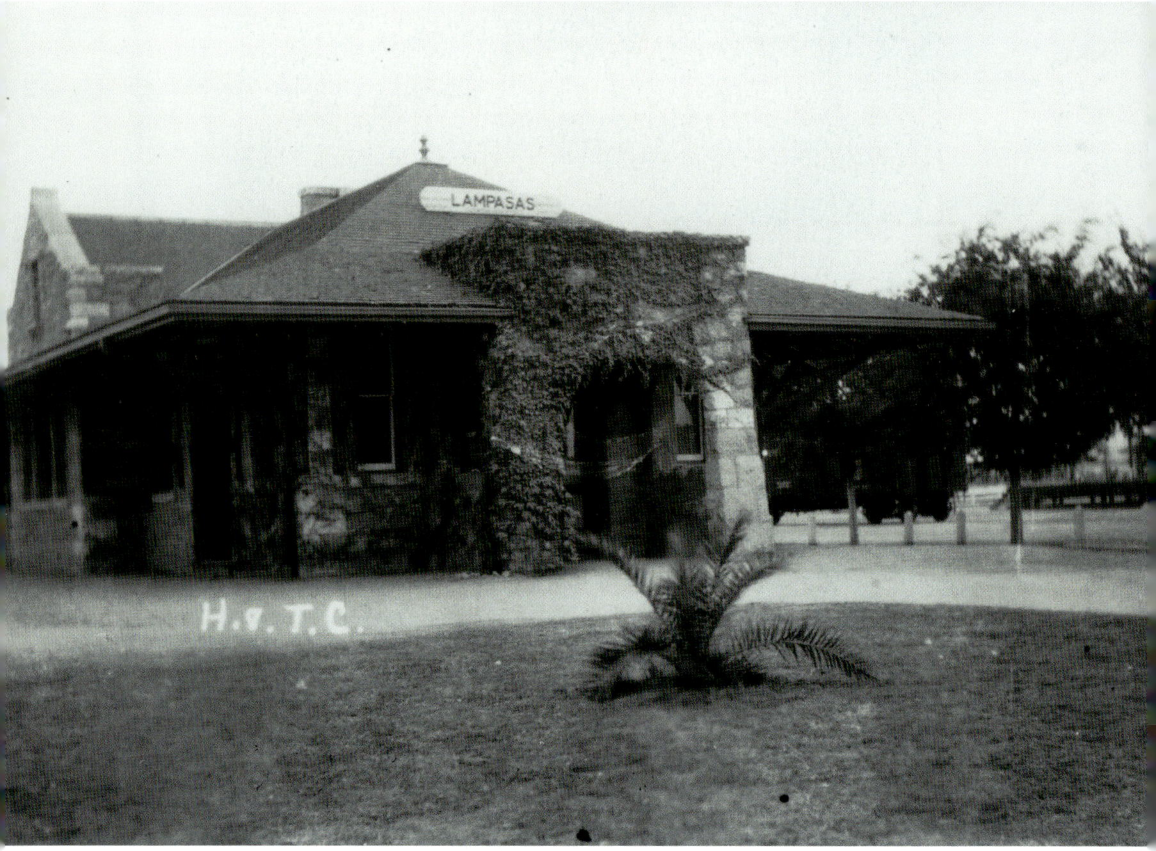

The Houston & Texas Central Railroad opened a stone passenger depot, pictured here at Fourth and Elm Streets, and a wood-frame freight depot on the southeast corner of the square. In November 1902, the Houston & Texas Central Railroad extended track from Burnet to Lampasas. The railroad became Southern Pacific and then the Texas & New Orleans Railroad, which closed the line in 1951. Today, the site is a storage lot behind Brown's Feed Store. (Present, DP.)

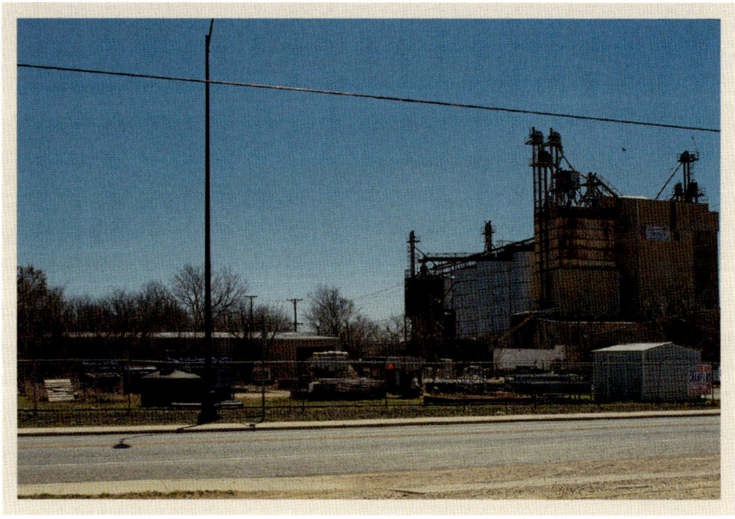

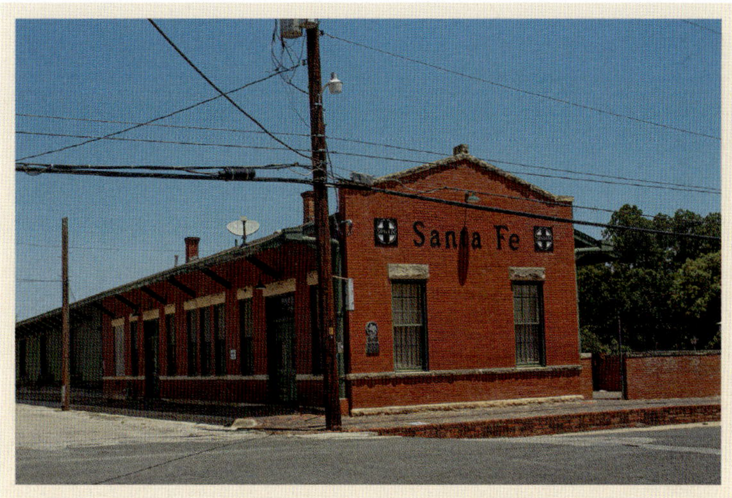

The 1904 Santa Fe train depot (below) on the corner of Second and Live Oak Streets was the second Santa Fe depot in Lampasas. The previous one was northeast of town. Construction of the new depot was begun in 1902, using timber from the earlier building. Charles D. Stokes received the contract for grading and masonry work related to the extension of the track to the new depot. The depot has been restored and is privately owned. (Present, DP.)

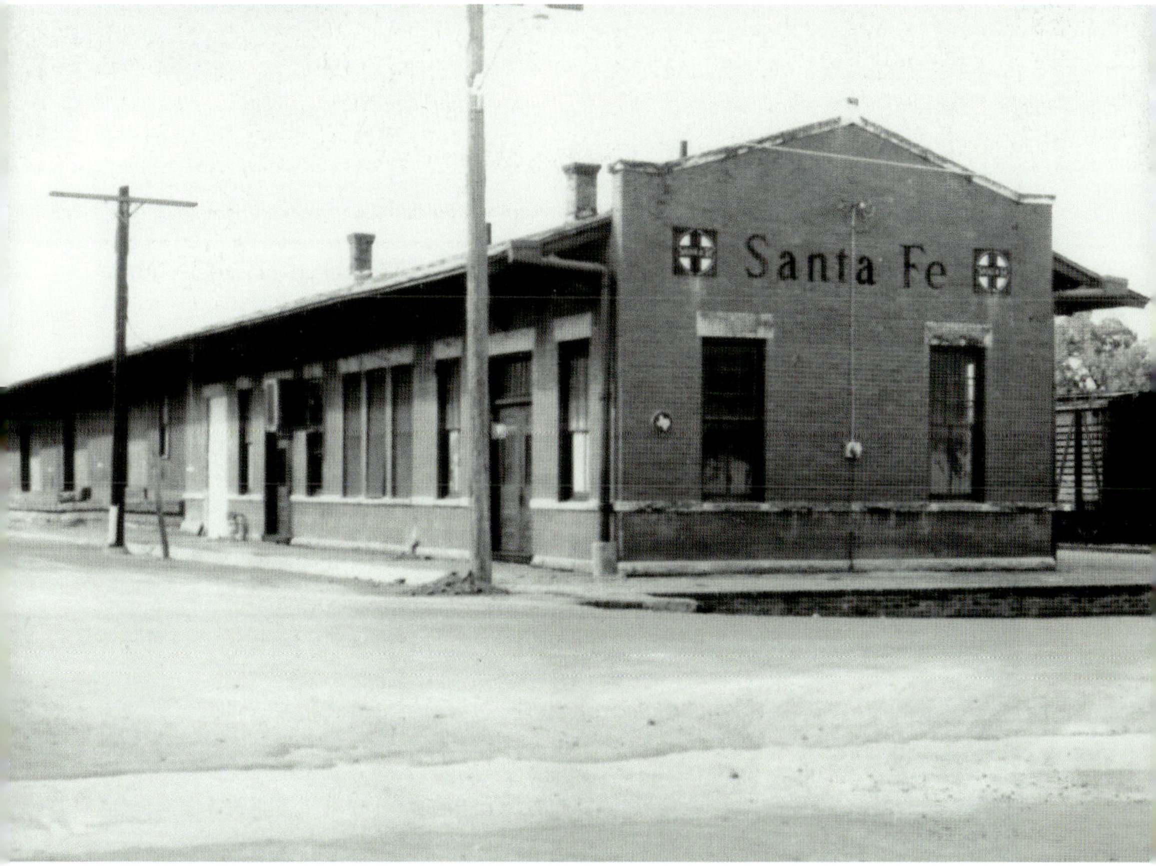

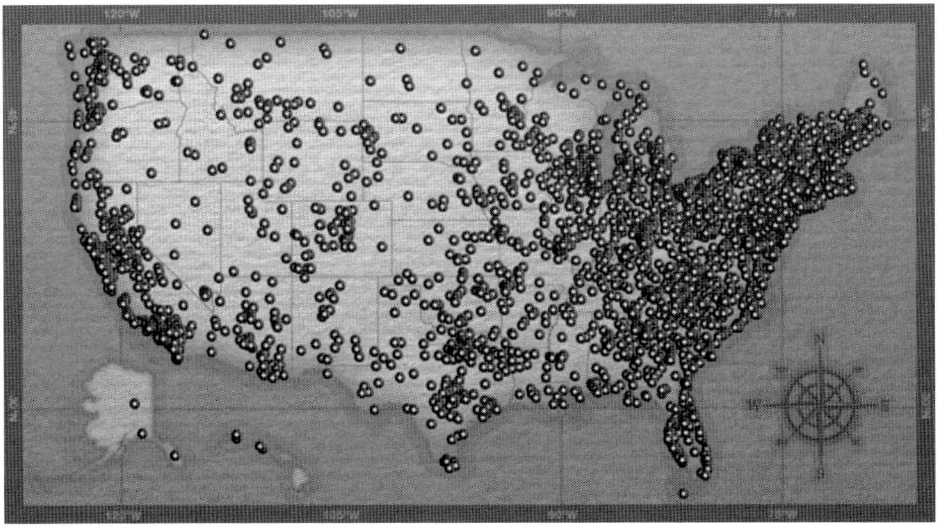